E-Mail Connections

Tragedy and Triumph of The TERMS

by Jacques Lasseigne

PublishAmerica
Baltimore

© 2009 by Jacques Lasseigne.
All rights reserved. No part of this book may be reproduced, stored in a retrieval system or transmitted in any form or by any means without the prior written permission of the publishers, except by a reviewer who may quote brief passages in a review to be printed in a newspaper, magazine or journal.

First printing

ISBN: 1-60672-619-6
PUBLISHED BY PUBLISHAMERICA, LLLP
www.publishamerica.com
Baltimore

Printed in the United States of America

Dedication

This book is dedicated to Brandon, Ben, Blake, Clyde, Scott, Greg, Wylie, Walter, Jay, and Angela. What a journey life has taken you on. Brandon, you are truly a miracle and an inspiration to us all.

Acknowledgments

There are so many people to thank for the completion of this project. I would like to thank PublishAmerica for the opportunity to tell this wonderful story. You provided me with superb assistance. A special thanks to Maple Jam Music Group, Dane Andreeff, Starr Andreeff, and Greg Ladanyi; thanks for your vision and your hard work and for allowing a group of young men from Louisiana to experience a life that most of us only dream of. Thanks to the multitude of friends, family, and acquaintances who helped make this book possible, from co-workers, fellow church members, medical professionals, media representatives, entertainment-industry people, and family. Thanks to many friends who encouraged me to take on this task in the first place. Thanks to the many physicians, nurses, and rehab specialists who kept Brandon alive and restored Brandon, Clyde, and Blake back to health. Thanks to Mark Adams for being so accessible and so willing to share. Thanks to Mark Jones and Brandon McGovern for their superb technical assistance. Thanks to my wonderful and supportive TERMS e-mail group list. Thanks to Ben, Clyde, Blake, Brandon, Scott, Greg, Wylie, and Walter. You have proven yourselves worthy of the title of friend. Thanks for your dedication, your great spirit, your vision, your hard work, and your never-say-never attitude. Thanks to Jay and Angela for the example you have set in this whole episode. Thanks to Anne, my dear wife, and to Christen and Scott, my two precious children, for allowing me to take time away from them in order to complete this project. And, Brandon, thanks for showing all of us what determination and drive can do for a person who is trying to overcome impossible odds. You are truly an inspiration.

Table of Contents

Chapter One: It All Started with a Phone Call 11
    E-mail Communication 13

Chapter Two: In the Beginning 16
    I Want a Set of Drums 16
    Early Band Practice 18
    Band Competitions 21

Chapter Three: A New Band Is Formed 25
    The Beginnings of the Band 25
    Early CD Recordings 30
    The Sidewalks Are Discovered 33
    Recording Contract Is Signed 37

Chapter Four: In the Big Leagues Now 41
    Recording Session—Capitol Records Studio 41
    Return to Baton Rouge and a New Name 44
    CD Release Party—April 2005 47
    New York Performances—Summer of 2005 51
    Shreveport Riverfront Performances 55
    New Bass Player 59

Chapter Five: Superb Recognition and Great Press 61
    Early Music Reviews 61
    The TERMS' 2006 Schedule 62

Rehearsals.com 67
The Viper Room 70
Dane's 40th Birthday Celebration 72
Centenary College—Gold Dome Performance 76
Opening Act for Pat Green 79
The Top 19 Independent Albums of 2005 81
More Music Reviews—Early 2006 86
The Best New Band of 2006 91
This Band Is Something New and Great 94
BillBoard Magazine 98

Chapter Six: The Travails of Touring 102
A Taste of Sushi 102
Highway Adventures 106

Chapter Seven: University Support 110
LSU Today 110

Chapter Eight: East Coast Summer Tour of 2006 114
The Storm 114
The Purple Moose Saloon 116
The Dancer 118
The Four Seasons Hotel 119

Chapter Nine: Mom Said You Would Have Days Like This ... 135
Welcome to the Now—Evo Devo 135
Early Fall Semester of 2006—Unwinding from the Summer Tour ... 149

Chapter Ten: That Fateful Day 155
September 30, 2006 155
Sunday, October 1, 2006—Holy Unction 167

Chapter Eleven: The America I Know 171
The America I Know 171

Chapter Twelve: Our Electronic Connection in Today's World 179
    The E-mail Connection 179
    The CD Promotion 187

Chapter Thirteen: The Accident's Aftermath—The Business Side 191
    The TERMS Are No More 191
    More TERMS Music 196

Chapter Fourteen: On the Lighter Side 199
    Amniocentesis Test 199

Chapter Fifteen: Almost There, but Not Quite 202
    The Megan Mullally Show and LSU Graduation 202

Chapter Sixteen: Favorable Media Coverage 207
    KTBS-Channel 3's Coverage of Brandon's Progress 207
    The Music Lives On 210
    Local Print Media Coverage 212

Chapter Seventeen: What Does It All Mean? 219
    A Journey Called Life 219
    What's Done Is Done 222
    Closure—Not There Yet 226

Chapter Eighteen: Emotional Healing Process Has Begun 230
    Weekend of December 28, 2007 230
    A Blip in the Road 236
    Unwavering, Heartfelt Support 238
    Coming to Terms 239

Bibliography 243

Chapter One
It All Started with a Phone Call

"Brandon's not breathing, Brandon's not breathing!" That was what my wife heard in her cell phone in the early evening of Saturday, September 30, 2006. Our son, Scott, was crying hysterically into his cell phone as he was relaying this news to his mother.

Eight hours later I sent this e-mail to my TERMS Group E-mail List:

October 1, 2006, 2 AM:

Dear Friends,

You have been so supportive of Scott and the band. When I've come to you asking for support for the band, you have come through with flying colors—whether it was to attend a performance or purchase a CD or to send an e-mail request to a radio station. Your support and gracious comments mean more to us than you will ever know.

This time I am again asking for something from you, but this time Scott, Anne, & I are asking for your prayers.

Anne and I had just voted late Saturday afternoon and were driving down the highway to get a bite to eat when Anne's cell phone rang. Thank God I was driving. Scott was crying hysterically into the phone to tell Anne that there had been a car accident & that Brandon was not breathing. Brandon is the band's bass player and has been a friend of Scott's for years. In fact, they were in the same band in high school. They practiced in our home many, many times.

JACQUES LASSEIGNE

The band had just finished a delicious meal prepared by Blake's father. They were driving in two vehicles, which is standard practice for them—to the place they were going to perform Saturday night in Monroe, Louisiana. Less than a mile from Blake's father's house, the Toyota 4Runner was hit by a car that ran a stop sign. That pushed the 4Runner, with Blake, Clyde, & Brandon in it, into a telephone pole, then it bounced back into the intersection and toppled over on its side. Ben and Scott were in the nineteen-foot box truck behind them. Ben and Scott caught a previous traffic light so they did not see the actual wreck. When they drove up they saw Clyde on the ground screaming in pain. Ben and a few other guys helped pull Blake out of the 4Runner. Scott was crying into the phone to Anne, "Brandon is not breathing. Brandon is not breathing!"

Anne & I returned home from the Monroe Hospital early this morning. This is what we know so far. Blake has a cracked vertebra in his neck and a deep gash near his right thumb. It seems that he will be okay. Clyde has a fractured pelvis and other cuts and bruises. It seems that he will be okay. Brandon is in serious condition. It seems that Brandon's head came in contact with the telephone pole at the scene of the accident. The neurosurgeon, who has an excellent reputation, stated that the next 72 hours are critical. If Brandon makes it, the doctors should know how much damage his brain sustained by day five. When the doctors talked with the family and the band members last night, he put it this way: On a scale from 3 to 15, with 3 being the most severe, he would rank this injury as a 4. Brandon also has a collapsed lung, cracked vertebrae in his neck, and is on a respirator.

Thank you for your prayers for all the boys, but especially for Brandon and his family. Thank God we could not find Brandon's parents' phone number so we had to drive to their house in order to break the news to Brandon's mother in person. Later at the hospital she told us that was a blessing, since she would not have wanted to hear that news alone.

Thank you for your prayers.

E-mail Communication

In the last few years, e-mail has become an extremely important tool of communication. Some praise it while others curse it. I remember entering the e-mail world in 2000. I had just been promoted to manager of the Louisiana Department of Labor Office in Shreveport, Louisiana. I was busy with what I considered "real work" when another manager called me to inquire if I had responded to the Secretary of Labor's e-mail request. I quickly opened up my e-mail and read his request for information. Oops, I was a full day late in responding to him. I contacted him to apologize, and he responded gracefully, "In the future it is a good idea to check your e-mail on a regular basis." I took his advice and entered the world of e-mail communication.

Many of us utilize this form of communication today in order to perform our jobs in an efficient and effective manner or to stay in contact with friends and family. In the last couple of years I had also used it to help promote the band my son was in. Now I was using it to get out word of this tragic accident to friends and family and to ask for their prayers and support. What a journey it has been. Let me share some of this journey with you.

Most parents think their children are the greatest and can do no wrong. They make sure to tell everyone their every accomplishment. I tried not to do that except for special accomplishments and then just with family and close friends concerning our two children, Christen and Scott. A good friend, Liz McCain, who is the vice-president of business development at the Northwest Louisiana Economic Development Foundation, sent me an e-mail during this time stating, "I just heard you have a daughter also; why don't you write about her?" I responded to Liz with up-to-date information on my daughter's life. But I also mentioned to her that I did not need to "promote" Christen and her chosen career as a registered nurse, since she would have no trouble locating suitable employment or to further her career, since the medical field is in desperate need of registered nurses. But I did need to promote the band my son was in so they would have a growing fan base, sell their CDs, have more people attend their performances, have people contact the radio stations to request their songs, etc. My daughter needed no such help to reach her career goals, but a new band trying to "make it" did. I tried in my own small way to make a difference.

JACQUES LASSEIGNE

TERMS Group E-mail—October 3, 2006: TERMS Update:

Dear Friends,

Thank you sooo much for your tremendous outpouring of support and prayers for the band members and their families. It is quite overwhelming. Quite an emotional time for everyone.

As the boys were leaving Blake's father's house in Monroe Saturday afternoon, it was Ben's turn to drive the big nineteen-foot box truck with all their equipment in it. Ben was walking toward that truck while everyone else went towards Blake's Toyota 4Runner. Ben called to them, "Well, isn't anyone going to ride with me?" Scott finally spoke up and said, "Sure, I will." And that is why Scott was not in the 4Runner with Blake, Clyde, and Brandon.

Blake is quite sore with his cracked vertebra in his neck, but he is at home now. He will have to be quiet for the next several weeks, but he will be okay. The deep gash in his hand/thumb area is stitched up and healing.

Clyde's fractured pelvis bone is in a non-weight-bearing location. He experienced a clean break so it should heal nicely. In the meantime it will be very painful. He will have to be still and get plenty of bed rest for the next seven weeks. He hopes to be out of the hospital by the end of this week. Clyde was thrown from the 4Runner on impact. When the vehicle bounced back from hitting the telephone pole it landed on its side right on top of Clyde. Thank God it landed on Clyde's hip and legs and not his chest and head. The two guys in the car that hit Blake's vehicle jumped out of their car to help lift Blake's Toyota 4Runner off Clyde.

As of 8 P.M. Sunday evening, Brandon, who experienced a collapsed lung, severe head trauma and has several broken bones in his neck, had a few encouraging signs also: no clotting (good news), no hemorrhaging (good news), brain swelling went down from 8 to a 6 (doctors use a scale of 0-14, with 0 being "good"), there is not as much bleeding in the brain as originally thought (good news), his body is responding to some outside stimuli (good news).

Update on Brandon as of 5 P.M. today (Monday):

No change in his condition since Sunday evening.

The 5th day after a severe head injury is crucial. The doctors will then be able to test his brain activity. That will tell a lot about Brandon's prognosis. He is still in a coma, and he is still on a respirator. In other words, he is still in critical condition, so please continue to keep him and his family in your prayers. His parents' names are Jay & Angela. Your prayers are definitely needed and very much appreciated. Thank you so much for your support. It means so much.

Chapter Two
In the Beginning

I Want a Set of Drums

The words parents do not want to hear from their children are many. Included in that list is the sentence, "I want a set of drums!" Our son, Scott, asked his mother and me if people sold used drums. We both told him, "NO!" After his research he discovered that his parents had given him false information; another way of saying that is, we lied to him! But parents are allowed to lie to their children in certain situations; this was one of those times. Alas, he would discover the truth soon.

At the age of 14 he began playing drums with the encouragement of Peter Fetterman, a church friend. His first drum set was a used set he purchased from a long-time friend, Paul Babineaux. They had started pre-kindergarten together. Anne and I did not know how long this phase of drum-playing would last, hence, the investment in a used set of drums. Scott taught himself how to play and would bang away for twenty minutes at a time in his room which was located in the back of our house. Anne wondered if he was bothering our next-door neighbor, who was in her late eighties, until one day our neighbor told Anne, "I sure do enjoy listening to Scott play the drums." Yes, many people experience hearing loss later in life and that fact seemed to have helped us keep a great relationship with our elderly neighbor, Mrs. Elaine Ross.

Scott was dedicated to practicing his craft. One day, as he was practicing on his drums, our handy-man extraordinaire, Jim O'Brock, happened to be at our home fixing something. Jim has a successful commercial and residential handyman fix-it business. We have used him on a regular basis over the years, since the word "handyman" is not associated with me. I have explained to my dear wife how much time and money we have actually saved over the years by using Jim. I did not have to invest $700-$1,000 in tools that I *might* use one day, and those tools would take up an awful lot of room in the garage. If I did have all those expensive tools and decided to take on various home-improvement projects, I would still have to call Jim to fix what I had broken or botched—and that may have cost us a lot more money. That same thought process is used when a wife tells her husband how much money she saved shopping that day since what she bought was on sale.

That day Jim quietly walked to the back of the house and peeked into Scott's room as he was beating on his drum set. After watching him for a while he walked back to the kitchen to tell Anne "He is very good." Before Jim started his business he was a drummer in a band that toured the country for seven years; therefore his observation carried some weight. When Anne told me what Jim had said, I did think that was interesting insight from someone who had been in those shoes before.

TERMS Group E-mail—October 4, 2006: Tuesday Update:

Dear Friends,

Adrenalin is an amazing thing. As Ben and Scott drove up to the horrific accident scene Saturday evening, they saw Clyde screaming in pain on the ground and Blake semi-standing up in the 4Runner that was lying on its side. Blake was bleeding from the deep gash on his hand/thumb area, and unknown to him, he had a cracked vertebra in his neck. He was pulled from the 4Runner by Ben and a couple of bystanders. Only after he had gotten out of the vehicle and sat down he said, "I can't move." His neck injury was finally overcoming his adrenalin rush.

Clyde, hopefully, will be home soon. He will need plenty of bed rest, but it will be nice to have him home.

Ben and Scott are back in Baton Rouge in school. They should both graduate in December. They are taking midterm tests this week.

As some of you know, in severe head trauma the doctors put the patient in a drug-induced coma. Reason: The doctors want the brain to "rest" and not think. That will help to reduce the swelling of the brain and to keep the rest of the body as relaxed as possible to help the healing process. Many different tests are run at various intervals, depending on the severity of the injury and other factors. Brandon is relying less and less on the respirator for his breathing. Good news.

He is also responding to outside stimuli. An example: yesterday the doctor pinched both his right and left chest area. Now, if someone pinches your left arm, your instinct is to have your right arm/hand go to that pinched area to rub it. Well, I'm happy to report that when the doctors pinched his chest, Brandon's arms went up to that spot—both arms responded. Of course, it is not as fast as you or I would do it, but you and I do not have as many drugs in us as Brandon has. That is good news.

The swelling in his brain continues to come down; other measurements are what they should be at this point, whatever that means, but it sounds good!

So many of you have e-mailed and called to inform us that you are praying for all the boys, but especially for Blake, Clyde, and Brandon. Well, I am praying for you also. Thank you so much for your support. These young men and their families really thank you for your tremendous outpouring of support and prayers in this situation.

Early Band Practice

Our daughter graduated from high school about the same time that Scott's high school baseball career came to an end. He had a great freshman baseball coach. That team was C.E. Byrd's best freshman baseball team in many years. They had a good thing going. But as sometimes happens in high school baseball, the coach can be the deciding factor on how good or bad a team performs. The varsity coach was not one of those stellar high-school coaches. The team did okay, and Scott had a decent year as outfielder and pitcher. His offensive output was also better than average, including a memorable three-run homer over the towering left-centerfield fence at Parkway High School one night. Upon his retirement from baseball he started a part-time job and put more time and energy into playing his drums.

His drum playing evolved into a band, as friends got together to practice various songs. As these things work out, band practice is normally held at the drummer's house due to all the bulky equipment, i.e., bass drum, snare drum, cymbals, and more. Band practice was held many, many times in our home—sometimes in the garage, but mostly in Scott's back bedroom. Anne and I encouraged Scott to wear ear plugs as much as possible so he would have some hearing later in life. We enjoyed having the guys over—at least we were getting to know his friends, and we knew where Scott was.

The guys named their band Dirty Sanchez. To this day Scott has not told us the full meaning of that name. Band members were Todd Pickering, lead vocals and rhythm guitar, James Ramsay, lead guitar, Nick Leuck, bass guitar, and Scott, drummer. Nick had moved out of state for awhile, so a good friend of Scott's took his place. His name was Brandon Young. They practiced Red Hot Chili Pepper songs and The Black Crowes' song "Hard to Handle." Our dear neighbors were very understanding during this time, except for one. He called the police one Saturday afternoon to complain about the noise coming from our garage. By the time the police arrived, the band had finished practicing and was long gone. Another neighbor, Mark Griffin, happened to be outside when the police car slowly drove around and he visited with the policeman for a short while, defusing the situation. No ticket, no siren, no panic, no citation, no problem. Thanks, Mark.

TERMS Group E-mail—October 6, 2006: Thursday Update:

Dear Friends,

Anne & I traveled to Monroe yesterday afternoon/evening for a hospital visit. Thursday was a good day.

We had a great visit with Brandon's mother, Angela, and his two sisters, Ashley and Angel, and with Blake and his father, Mac, and with many of their friends. Scott drove up from Baton Rouge with a long-time friend, Brandon McGovern, to visit. It was great to see Scott doing so much better.

Blake, upon being released from the hospital earlier this week, went to visit with Clyde in the hospital, then to the other Monroe hospital to visit with Brandon's family. Upon arriving back home he realized that he was overdoing it. Today he thought he would lay off those pain pills some—then around noon today he felt the worst pain he had ever experienced. As many of you know, a person needs to take the pain medication as instructed by the doctor—in this case EVERY four hours—in order to manage the pain. Of course, when the excruciating pain flooded over Blake, he immediately took his pain medicine, but it takes awhile for those magic pills to kick in. He stated tonight, "I WILL take my pain medicine on time from now on just as the doctor instructed!"

He is resting at home in bed with this tight neck brace on. He can only take it off to bathe. His neck injury is causing some tingling in one of his arms. He will have the doctor check that out just to make sure that is a normal side effect of his injury. But he seems to be in good spirits.

Brandon's mother said, "This was a good day." Brandon continues to improve his responses to outside stimuli, and his responses are getting quicker. He can be seen by family and friends every four and a half hours. Scott was able to go with the family to see Brandon at 5 P.M. today. He is still in a drug-induced coma, but his medications are not as strong as earlier in the week. When they are talking to Brandon and rubbing his arms and legs, he begins to move his arms and legs, and his blood pressure rises—which is good. In fact, they have to calm him down during some of these visits. He is trying to open his right eye (good news). Scott talks to Brandon about some of their private jokes.

Dr. Bernie McHugh, Jr., the neurosurgeon who is treating him, has changed his brain trauma score. Saturday night—the night of the accident—the neurosurgeon looked the family in the eye, then told Brandon's parents to look him in the eye as he was telling them, "This is a severe, severe head injury." Concerning head injuries, doctors rank the severity on a scale from 3 to 15, with 3 being the most severe. As you know, they ranked Brandon's brain injury a 4 the night of the accident. Well, I am happy to report that his score has been adjusted up to a 7!

The night nurses have a special bond with Brandon and the family. They fight for the right to have him as their patient. They are excited about caring for a "Rock Star"!

In an earlier update I mentioned that a big event will be the test for brain-wave activity. The doctors have put off that test until Monday.

Brandon's mother wanted to make sure I told you that she cannot emphasize enough how much all of your good thoughts and prayers mean to her and all the family. She really became emotional with Anne and me on that statement. Thank all of you sooooooooo much for your prayers. It is really making a difference.

Don't get me wrong, Brandon has a long way to go and there will be many hurdles along the way. For example, when he eventually comes off the respirator completely, one factor that comes into play is the possibility of pneumonia. But we all are celebrating with his family every small victory, every small step in the right direction concerning his recovery.

Thank you for being you. Thank you for your continued prayers for Brandon, Clyde, Blake, Ben and Scott and their families. As Brandon's mother stated tonight, "It is helping more than you will ever know."

Band Competitions

Dirty Sanchez band members began practicing much more frequently at our home. Yes, they wanted to get better, but they were also preparing for an upcoming talent competition at C.E. Byrd High School, called Buzz Fest. I guess the name of that competition had something to do with the school's mascot, a Yellow Jacket.

As many parents do today, we had our video camera ready to film the band's performance. Although we had heard many practice sessions in our home, we did not really know what to expect that evening. The curtain opened, the video camera was rolling, and the band exploded with sound as they performed "Hard to Handle" by the Black Crowes. The high school crowd absolutely loved it. Most were on their feet during that performance. I was so proud of Scott at that moment. Now I had witnessed many of my daughter's gymnastic meets. I was mostly nervous during those competitions due to the ghastly balance beam. What sadistic person came up with this type of sporting equipment and event? That event always made me nervous. But when the meet was over I would tell Christen how proud I was of her and her performance that day. At Buzz Fest I was not nervous since I knew it was difficult for Scott to fall off his drum seat, unlike his sister trying to balance herself on a 4-inch-wide balance beam.

The band performed very well that evening as was evident from the crowd's wildly-enthusiastic reaction. They did not win that competition. Another band won. That band's bass player was Scott's friend, Brandon Young. The band that Scott was in also entered another high-school competition later in the year, The Battle of the Bands at Magnet High School. They again performed well, but another band won that competition. The lead guitar in that band was a fellow church member and friend. His name was Clyde Hargrove.

Scott absolutely loved the band Blink 182. He was enjoying school and the band. Later that year, in the summer of his junior year (2001) he and a couple of his buddies ventured to Dallas to watch Blink 182 in concert. He was in heaven. During the concert it was mentioned that a tablet would be passed around for any band to sign up if they would like to be considered as a back-up band. Scott was ecstatic, until that tablet made it to him. There was page after page after page of bands listed. That burst his bubble about his future as a professional drummer in a band. With all those bands listed on that tablet, it brought home to Scott how hard it would be to make it as a band in the real world. He did venture to Dallas during the summer of 2002 to hear Blink 182 once again in concert. He was much more realistic about the chance to "make it" as a band by that time. He had graduated from high school, and it was time to change gears and head off to college and get serious about his future. He left his drums at home as he began his freshman year in Baton Rouge, Louisiana, at Louisiana State University (LSU).

E-MAIL CONNECTIONS

TERMS Group E-mail—October 10, 2006: Monday Update:

Dear Friends,

Anne & I visited with Clyde in a Shreveport hospital this past Friday afternoon. He is still in a lot of pain, but he did take his first shower in six days—with the help of two male hospital attendants. AND he took two steps that day with the help of a walker. He received a "buzz" haircut so he would not have to deal with hair much during his recovery. While we were there Billy Hargrove and Greg Chiartano brought Clyde some of his favorite food: Mexican Food with Hot Peppers! Then three seniors from Magnet High School brought Clyde a poster-size greeting card. It was signed by "The Front Row Girls." These young ladies were on the front row when The TERMS performed at the Centenary Gold Dome a few months ago.

Scott visited with Brandon and his family Thursday night and Friday morning and then again on Sunday evening. Brandon's family was upbeat Sunday evening since Brandon continues to make progress. Baby steps, but progress. Ben came up north to visit with everyone also. He is doing better this week also. The emotional toll is definitely having an effect on all of the band members. Yes, the accident has had a profound effect on all these young men.

Who knows why things happen, but they do. The band drove 4,000 miles this past summer during their LONG five-and-a-half week East Coast Tour. This accident happened in a residential neighborhood just a few blocks away from Blake's father's home.

The response by his neighbors was immediate. One couple we met at the hospital that fateful night was outside doing yard work when the accident happened. They immediately called 911. One neighbor who quickly responded to the injured was a medical doctor. Another neighbor, who worked on reviving Brandon—and did so—was a man who had medical trauma experience; in fact, one of his current jobs is CPR INSTRUCTOR! What a guy to have at the scene of a serious accident.

Brandon's family did not want to field all the calls from the media so they asked Scott to be the "spokesperson" for the family. Well, the local ABC Affiliate, KTBS Channel 3, has been talking with Scott. They have run some nice segments on the accident and The TERMS. Yesterday they called Scott as he was leaving town to travel to Monroe to visit with Brandon. He turned around and came home for the interview. The TV Station did an excellent job on the story. They gave an awful lot of air time to The TERMS and their recovery. Some people commented to me today after seeing that segment: "Jacques, your son represented the band quite well, and unlike you, he speaks ENGLISH!" Oh well, Anne says he is my son…

Monday morning, Brandon had an MRI performed. The family finally received the results of it Monday evening. The family is quite encouraged by the MRI. It shows that Brandon does NOT have to have surgery to repair the broken bones in his neck. It seems that they can heal properly without surgery. His spinal cord looks good! That is one less major ordeal that Brandon's body will have to be put through. If things keep on progressing, Brandon will stay at St. Francis Hospital in Monroe for five to six more weeks before being transferred to a rehabilitation hospital, which has a lot more experience in these kinds of injuries.

While there is still a long way to go, the positive results of the MRI are being celebrated by Brandon's family and friends this day.

Thank you for your prayers. You are appreciated.

Chapter Three
A New Band Is Formed

The Beginnings of the Band

When our daughter, Christen, went off to college, Anne was a basket case for a few days. She was upset, she was crying, she was lost—her baby girl was no longer home. Christen was not sitting in the La-Z-boy chair with her mother talking endlessly about things mothers and daughters talk about. When Scott went off to college two years later, Anne adjusted quite well. In fact, Scott was upset that his mother was not upset!

During his freshman year at LSU, Scott was asked by Clyde Hargrove through a friend, Greg Chiartano, to join the band they had formed. He declined. It was time to forge a new life, and a band was not in that picture. Later, Clyde asked Scott on two different occasions to join the band. He politely declined. Then Clyde saw Scott at a place called "Boogies" and asked him again, this time in person. This time Scott said yes. Anne and I first became aware of this when Scott was loading up his drum set in his truck to take back to Baton Rouge. We thought that was nice. Scott was pretty good with time management, so he should be able to attend school, work a part-time job, and practice in this band.

Blake Oliver literally dragged Ben Labat out of his apartment in order to join him and Clyde Hargrove in a new band Blake was putting together. Soon afterwards, Blake, Clyde, and Ben started performing as a trio named Mors Canvas. Clyde came up with that name. According to the website Wikipedia, Mors is the personification of death in Roman mythology. As Ben states, "Mors Canvas was the epitome of what a human being was. Weird, I know, but we were thinkers—ha!" This trio performed in various places in Baton Rouge playing cover songs.

When the original trio expanded to a "real band" they kept the name Mors Canvas for the first month or so while they practiced their new songs and their new style. But when they played together for their first gig at Chelsea's Café in Baton Rouge, Louisiana, they had changed the band's name. They left Roman mythology behind and made their official debut as The Sidewalks.

This new band consisted of Ben Labat, lead singer and guitar, Clyde Hargrove, lead guitar, Billy Hargrove, acoustic guitar, Greg Chiartano, bass guitar, Blake Oliver, percussionist, and Scott, drummer. Ben had an amazing singing voice, not to mention great stage presence. He could put together great lyrics in a heartbeat. Clyde was one of the best guitarists ever. He could tear up the strings on a guitar and make them scream. His head was filled with music just itching to get out. Billy was a calm presence in this beehive of activity. He kept things loose. Blake was a throwback to the '60s. Scott once stated that Blake was always happy. Blake actually started this whole band-thing. Greg played amazingly well for only having one year experience playing the bass guitar. He performed many times on stage without his shoes—he felt more comfortable that way. Scott loved composing music and performing with his band mates and friends. He played pretty well even though he had never had any formal drum lessons.

The band's practice location was a very small room on the second floor in a strip-mall shopping center. Clyde referred to that place as a closet. It was not much bigger than that. That is where the band practiced for the next few months.

The beginnings of the band were noted in an on-line article on www.skopemagazine.com after the release of their CD, *Small Town Computer Crash*. It stated: *For the five TERMS, life began in Louisiana. Three of them come from Shreveport, in the northwest. One, Blake Oliver, hails from Monroe, in the northeast. And Ben's home is Raceland, a crossroads town about an hour south of New Orleans, which is about as south as you can go.*

As undergrads, they all shared two key attributes: their willingness to party and a hazy view of the future, from which only music beckoned clearly. All five had played in bands back home; all also drew from different styles and tried to put what they'd found into a sound that was personal yet universal, uncompromised and also accessible.

It was inevitable that they'd meet, beginning with Blake and Ben, who shared a flat as sophomores. Blake soon noticed that his friend, in addition to being a thoughtful guy who enjoyed his philosophy classes as much as the courses required for his business major, was putting what he'd learned into songs. In fact, he'd been writing for a while; back in high school his fellow students chose a piece he'd composed over the usual sappy favorites for their graduation ceremony. But for some reason Ben seemed content to confine his performances to their flat.

So Blake did what any reasonable roommate would do: He more or less dragged Ben out into the world, where they hooked up with a freshman guitar whiz named Clyde Hargrove and started playing out as a trio. At their first gig they earned $300 and a case of beer. "I was like, 'This is awesome,'" Ben remembers. "Rock & Roll!"

Soon they'd landed a Tuesday residency at a club in Baton Rouge. "It was a blast, playing Johnny Cash and Lynyrd Skynyrd songs to these drunken people and having these sorority girls take care of us," Ben says. "I never had so much fun in my life. We did that for a while, though, and then I began thinking, 'I can write songs like this. We could probably even write songs that are a little better than these. So...let's write some songs.'"

As their repertoire shifted toward originals, their fans ate it up and asked for more. At the same time, their attitude changed. They started thinking about doing music together full-time once they were out of school. With that in mind, they added new members (Greg Chiartano, bass player, and Billy Hargrove, acoustic guitar, and Scott Lasseigne, drummer).

By now, they'd also settled into a serious practice schedule—so serious that they didn't even play their first show as a six-piece until they'd devoted four months to perfecting it. When they finally hit the stage, in February 2004, they were—no other way to put it—a smash.

I remember Scott calling home during this time and telling his mother, "We have a fan base—and it's growing."

Anne would comment, "That's nice; how cute."

They had a blast performing around Baton Rouge, Louisiana. Their hard work and practice were paying off. They were drawing larger and larger crowds at their performances. Word was spreading around town about this new band. What a life for young college students.

TERMS Group E-mail—October 13, 2006: Thursday Update:

Dear Friends,

Hope you are enjoying this change of weather—cool!

Clyde was released from the hospital Tuesday evening and is now at home. Pain is still there, of course, but he is taking more steps each day. He can't move his pelvis like Elvis yet, but he IS walking some.

Blake is recovering at home. Since he is in that stiff, plastic-and-metal neck brace, he did not want to have to mess with all his long hair sooooooooo he had it CUT OFF! Some of the lady fans groaned when they heard the news! But as Blake stated: "It'll grow back." Smart move.

The news story of the local ABC Affiliate, KTBS Channel 3's website that has the most "hits" is the article on The TERMS' accident; therefore, one of their reporters called Scott this past Sunday to receive an update on the band members' recovery. Scott had already left home Sunday afternoon to pick up a good friend, Brandon McGovern, when they called. They were going to travel east to the Monroe Hospital, but Scott returned home for the filmed interview. The TV station put together a nice video piece of the band, and the segment ran quite long for a news story. It came out very nice. Anyway, for those of you who live out of town or in town but missed it, you can go to their website: www.ktbs.com. Scroll down to the local news and click on "more local news," then click on "The TERMS Recovery" for the video and article.

Brandon's medication has been reduced so he has gone from a "drug-induced coma" to a "sedated state." Brandon has opened his right eye and is tracking movement now. He will follow his family around his room—good sign! The doctors are making some changes as they adjust to this new phase in Brandon's treatment. A couple of days ago when Brandon's sister was leaving the Intensive Care Unit, as her time with

E-MAIL CONNECTIONS

Brandon was up, she blew two kisses to him and said that she would see him later. She saw his look. That expression said, 'I want to desperately respond back to you, sis.' Being there every day, she has her ups and downs, but that was an "UP."

Friends and family of Brandon are getting together to help with the growing medical expenses and future rehabilitation expenses for Brandon. His recovery and rehab will be a long process—quite an expensive undertaking.

His sisters quickly put together a fund-raiser at El Chico's restaurant in Bossier City this past Tuesday evening. Scott did mention this to Channel 3, and they did mention it in their recent TV broadcast. The manager of that El Chico's stated that a group has to have at least 100 people come out to eat and tell the restaurant staff they are there for the person whom the fund raiser is for. He said normally they will generate between $3,000-$4,000 in sales on those fund-raising nights. If at least 100 come out for the fund-raiser, the restaurant will donate 10% of their net business that night to the cause. The fund-raiser was from 5 P.M.-10 P.M. that Tuesday evening.

By 5:30 P.M. Tuesday night, eighty people had already come in for Brandon. The manager stated: "We stopped counting at that time!" When Anne and I arrived there we saw many dear friends, along with Brandon's two sisters and Walter Schmidt, The TERMS good friend and tour manager. People came from all over to support Brandon that evening. Durwood and Annette drove 30 miles, one way, to be there that evening. Their good friends, Charlie and Murle, joined them; they drove 70 miles one way that evening to participate in this event. There were many, many fine folks who took time out of their busy schedule to do the same. The El Chico's manager could not believe the response. He told Anne the next day "It was 10 P.M. Tuesday night, and people were still coming in saying 'I'm here for Brandon.' I'm in a great mood today since this restored my faith in the goodness of people." I am happy to report that El Chico's business Tuesday night was a whopping $6,470! They will cut a check to Brandon's Medical Fund for $647!

Another dear friend, Ellen McGovern, helped to set up a bank account for Brandon. Anybody wishing to donate can write a check to "Brandon Young Donation Account" and mail to Capital One, 1927 North Market, Shreveport, La. 71107, or you can drop off a donation at ANY Capital One Bank. No account number is needed; just tell them you are donating to the Brandon Young Donation Account. These bank accounts need two signatures in order for a check to be written. Checks cannot be made out to an individual. They can only be made out to a hospital, rehab center, physical therapist, etc.

Brandon McGovern put together a website that has pictures of Brandon Young and the band along with information about the accident that you have already read from my e-mails. Brandon Young's mother said that he almost ALWAYS made some kind of "face" when his picture was being taken. You can view some of Brandon's various "faces" on that website. If you wish to check out that website just go to http://my.lsu.edu/bmcgov1.

You have done so much and we greatly appreciate it. If you wish to contribute to Brandon's medical-expense fund, then that is great. If you cannot, that is fine also. The main thing you can do is to continue your prayers for Brandon, his family, and for all the other young men—Clyde, Blake, Ben, and Scott.

Thank you so much. Words cannot express our appreciation.

Early CD Recordings

In the latter part of June of 2006, the comic strip "Hi & Lois," by Brian Walker, Greg Walker, and Chance Browne (Hi & Lois ©King Features Syndicate), ran a comic strip with this dialogue. The teenage son in the comic strip, Chip, is sitting outside on a porch with his friend. They are both strumming guitars as his friend says, "Listen! A mockingbird." He continues "I think it's cool how they can imitate so many other birds."

Chip responds: "I guess that's pretty cool. But it's like a cover band with no original material."

While the guys enjoyed playing a few cover songs, they worked diligently on their original material. Scott would patiently explain to us how the band would put together a song. That process just fascinated Anne and me. We would have loved to have been a fly on the wall just to watch them in action as their creative juices flowed. Of course, we would have to have been a fly on the wall in their original practice location since there was no room for anything or anybody else—it was *tiny,* and it was on the 2nd floor of this strip-mall shopping center! No elevators to get there, just outside stairs.

The guys decided to call themselves "The Sidewalks." They opened with this new name and their original music on February 11, 2004, at Chelsea's Café, 148 West State Street, Baton Rouge, Louisiana. From there they played many bars and clubs and even a couple of fraternity parties. They were trying out their new material, trying out their new style, making their way into the music scene, and building a good fan base along the way.

A few months later they contacted a good friend, Wylie Chris (W.C.) Whitesides, to record some of their music. Scott mentioned to us that he was driving to New Orleans to record his part. I asked him why the whole band wasn't going for this recording session. He explained to me that for many years now, the recording process is done individually. Once all members have their part recorded, those "tracks" are then put together. I had no idea this was how the recording process was accomplished, but then again the closest I have gotten to the music industry was my car radio. Scott came home one weekend from LSU and brought the CD Wiley had put together for the band. It had five songs on it. Scott went straight to the Bose radio in the living room to play their CD and to get our reaction. Of course a parent is partial to his son or daughter's accomplishments and their work product, but the music on that CD was good; really good. No wonder they were building a fan base—they actually have a great new sound.

Anne and I did not think much about the band's early success since Scott was doing well in school, working in his part-time job (a server at Serranos, an upscale Mexican Restaurant) and playing in this band called The Sidewalks. As long as his grades did not suffer there was no reason for concern.

A couple of months later, the band got with W. C. Whitesides again in order to record more of their songs. Again, Scott brought this CD home for us to listen to. Once again we were very impressed. The CD was put together well, the songs were well laid out, and their singer, Ben Labat, could belt out a tune like there was no tomorrow. What a voice. And what great guitar riffs from Clyde Hargrove. And I could definitely hear my son's drum part! I just told Scott, "Great job, great sound. Keep up the good work. Now, how is your school work coming along?"

TERMS Group E-mail—October 16, 2006: Sunday Update:

Greetings Dear Friends,

Sure hope you enjoyed the gorgeous weather we experienced in Shreveport this past Friday and Saturday—Cool and Sunny!

Progress continues to be made by our young men.

Ben and Scott continue working their part-time jobs and working on their college classes in order to graduate from LSU in December, although they both admit that it is hard to concentrate on their college class work with their friends hurting. Their record label, Maple Jam Records, did cancel their gigs for the months of October and November.

Blake continues to progress well in his recovery. He is probably moving a bit too much, but he has never been one to be still for too long.

Clyde continues to progress well in his recovery. He begins physical therapy this week and continues to walk some each day. His mother mentioned that his guitar teacher will visit him this week to begin working on that aspect of his recovery. Playing music again should be great therapy for Clyde. He has so much music in his head—it is truly amazing.

Scott was able to visit with Brandon and his family today in Monroe before heading back to Baton Rouge. Brandon's family was upbeat. Scott and the family will talk to Brandon a lot when they visit with him. Brandon's right eye is following them around the hospital room, including the new nurse that Brandon has......checking out those nurses—good sign!

On Friday the doctors performed a tracheotomy. That procedure went well. The respirator is not down Brandon's mouth and throat anymore. For the first time since the accident, Brandon's face was shaved, and his teeth were brushed. Scott said he looked a lot better! But seriously, his color was good, and he continues to have good movement with his arms and legs.

Anne and I hope to travel to Monroe Tuesday evening to visit with Brandon's family. We will extend to them your tremendous outpouring of support, thoughts and prayers. I know each one of you have many things going on in your life, but I thank you soooo much for taking the time to pray for Brandon and all the boys. It is really helping. And I will continue to pray for you.

Fund-raising activities continue: It seems there will be a Fund-Raiser at Flannigan's in Shreveport on Saturday, October 28th. I'll pass on more details as I receive them, but it seems that some bands will play that evening to help fund-raise for Brandon's medical expenses. That should include Ben Labat (Lead Singer for The TERMS) performing an acoustic show.

Thanks for being part of our extended family. Till later.

The Sidewalks Are Discovered

Scott and Christen have told Anne and me before that we are probably one of only three people in the whole city of Shreveport NOT to have caller ID on our home phone. Still do not have it. When our phone rings and we pick it up to answer—it is a SURPRISE! Just like Christmas morning with all those presents—you just don't know what will be inside that box, or in our case, who is on the other end of the phone line. What an adventurous life we live.

It was October of 2004. The Sidewalks had been playing together for eight months now, and our phone rings one evening. It was Scott—surprise! Two surprises: (1) That he called to talk with us. We normally had to call him; (2) No Caller ID on our phone, so what a pleasant surprise to find out it is our dear son calling his mother and father. Scott spoke in a serious tone to his mother. The gist of his phone call concerned this very successful Baton Rouge businessman who thinks The Sidewalks sound great. He wants them to go to his office this week to talk about signing them up with his record label. Whoa! Let's take a step back and be skeptical. The band members definitely were skeptical, so you can imagine how their parents felt. Anne called the Hargroves to find out what they knew about all this. More phone calls were made in trying to figure out just what in the world was going on.

Dane Andreeff, businessman and entrepreneur, was making plans to launch his own record label. In early October 2004 he ventured to a bar/club in Baton Rouge, Louisiana, called SoGo Live in order to listen to a band, called the Iguanas. He had been told to check them out. That night he happened to catch the opening act—The Sidewalks. As Alexandyr Kent wrote in *The TIMES Preview Friday Magazine* on April 29, 2005: *"When I first heard them,"* Andreeff said, *"I heard Ben's incredible voice and (saw) his rock-star status on the stage already. I also heard Clyde's guitar riffs, which were very unique."* Andreeff asked them to come by his business office the following week. *"This guy was coming at us with a real business proposal,"* Lasseigne recalled about their moment of discovery. *"It was surreal,"* agreed Oliver. *"We had been talking to him, but we didn't know (his) intentions. I was thrilled and nervous, too, because it was so big."*

After hearing the band perform that night at SoGo Live, Dane introduced himself and talked to them about the record label he was forming. Later Dane took a copy of The Sidewalks' CD and sent it to his sister, Starr. She was in the music business in California. She agreed that the band was a quality band and sent the CD to record producer, Greg Ladanyi. He agreed with Dane and Starr's impression of the band and agreed to fly to Baton Rouge to check out this band in person. He needed the answers to a couple of questions: (1) Did the band perform well "live"?; and (2) Would he be able to work with them? In the cramped quarters of The Sidewalks' practice room, Ladanyi made suggestions on how to change up a song, i.e., let's try this tempo, let's change a word or two, let's not hold that note as long, let's try this another way, etc. The guys obviously responded well, and he agreed that he could work with them.

The nervous parents quickly learned a little history about this Greg Ladanyi person. He was a record producer who had worked with bands and artists that we recognized—Fleetwood Mac, Jackson Browne, Don Henley, Toto, and more. The records he has worked on have sold 60 million copies. He had been nominated for sixteen Grammy Awards and had won a Grammy Award. His credentials were quite impressive. He obviously knew how to produce music and now was ready to work with another young band.

As Alexandyr Kent wrote in *The TIMES Preview* Friday Magazine section of April 29, 2005: *Singer Labat was happy with their progress, but he couldn't see the future. "We thought we were pretty good, and we knew we had the potential to write really good songs. We felt we could make this work, but we were in Baton Rouge. Who's going to hear us?" recalled Labat. "There's a one in 3 million chance that anyone with the economic muscle would come along and take on something like this. It just doesn't happen." Then Dane Andreeff walked into SoGo Live that night in time to catch their opening act. That changed everything.*

TERMS Group E-mail—October 19, 2006: Wednesday Update:

Dear Friends,

Anne & I traveled to Monroe Tuesday evening to visit with Brandon's family and Blake and his family. It was a good visit.

Blake is still wearing his hard-plastic-and-metal neck brace. He still has some tingling in his left arm, but the doctor said that is to be expected at this time. His hand/thumb is healing from the deep gash he had, so he will not be pounding on those bongos yet! His haircut is SHORT, which he does not mind at all since he only takes off his neck brace to shower. Short hair is easy to manage in that situation. We enjoyed visiting with Blake, his father, Mac, and his step-mom, Alise. We talked about frog-gigging, snake-killing and other assorted topics!

Brandon's father, Jay, had to return to work this week, but he calls his wife, Angela, many times during the day to check on Brandon. Brandon's sisters had to return to work also, but they visit the hospital a couple of times a week. Angela invited Anne and me into Brandon's

ICU room during our visit. There are pictures of the band all around the room along with their CD continuously playing in the background. Angela is staying at the Ronald McDonald House, which is about two blocks from the hospital. As you can imagine, she lives for those visits with Brandon every five hours.

Brandon looks good. He was looking at Anne and me with his open right eye as we talked with him. We told him how much we love him and that many, many people from all over the country are praying for him. The physical therapist really worked him hard on Tuesday. In fact, both the nurse and Angela were excited when Brandon moved his left arm quite high above his chest. His right side has progressed well, but his left side had been lagging behind, so this was a great new step in his recovery.

Angela did tell us that he looks so much better today since many tubes and wires are not connected to him now compared to a week ago. His color is good, and he is breathing on his own much of the time—with no assistance from the respirator! In fact, with all the work his body did on Tuesday the nurse was going to turn the respirator on so he could rest and get some sleep. About thirty seconds after we left his ICU room (we were talking with the nurse) we turned around and his eye had closed. He was getting some much-deserved rest.

Anne presented Angela with some forms and paperwork for Brandon's medical account and reported to her that $2,200 had already been donated to that account—and it has not been mentioned in the local paper or on TV yet…….working on that now. Thank you very much for your financial gifts—it will be a long road back for Brandon, and every little bit helps. Angela keeps saying: "I can't get over the goodness and generosity of people I don't even know."

Keep those prayers coming into St. Francis Hospital. It is really making a difference. Thank you so much.

Recording Contract Is Signed

Choices. We all have choices to make in our lives. The Sidewalks needed to make some choices. Things were happening fast with the band. Plans were being made, contract was being drafted, the future of school was being discussed, and of course, you had nervous parents. Billy Hargrove, acoustic guitar in the band, who had also written some of their music, had to decide if he wanted to sign the recording contract and take a chance that his studies might be interrupted. His major was architecture. It would be virtually impossible for him to miss a semester or two in that major, return to school, and pick up where he left off. He decided not to sign the recording contract. He would drop out of the band in order to continue his college career path.

What lawyer could the guys agree on to look at this recording contract? An entertainment lawyer was one option. A few names were bandied about. In the end the band members decided to seek the advice of a couple of local attorneys. These attorneys graciously donated their knowledge and time to this effort at no charge to these young band members. As Blake commented later, "We didn't really know what we were signing; we just wanted to write and play music!"

Dane Andreeff created the record label, Maple Jam Records. The contract was signed. Ben, lead singer, and Clyde, lead guitar, soon found themselves flying on the weekends to California to begin the process of cutting an album. The Fall Semester of 2004 was still in session. Alexandyr Kent captured the scene in *The Times* Preview Magazine of April 29, 2005: *During the next four weekends, Labat and Hargrove recorded the vocal and lead guitar tracks for a new album in the storied Capitol Record building. On Sunday nights, they flew back to Baton Rouge, Louisiana. Hargrove realized how quickly things were changing.* "It was exhausting, but it was so awesome," remembered Hargrove. "When you're on the airplane and going to see a Grammy-winning producer to record, it's nuts. I had always wanted to do something like that." *By mid-December, the whole band was in Los Angeles. But Ladanyi did not just shove them in a studio, hit a record button, and say, play.*

"As a young band, their playing techniques needed to be improved and worked on," Ladanyi said. He brought in seasoned musicians to teach them the ropes. "We learned a lot about dynamics," said Oliver. "Instead of playing full throttle all the time, I learned how to play my instruments in certain moments. We really learned how to create a more balanced sound." Chiartano feels grateful for Andreeff's and Ladanyi's willingness to make them better. "It's not every day that someone wants to shell out money to make you great at your instruments. Before the record deal, we were just a college band. Now we have a team of people working for us. In the studio we had to work out all the songs to make it perfect." The band spent six weeks in Los Angeles rehearsing, tweaking their music, and recording the album.

Ladanyi believes the band has great potential. "I just think this band drives emotional buttons. Music is a source of relief for all of us, and they clearly facilitate that," said Ladanyi. "That level of connection, the human aspect, is very big with this band." Each member seems eager to prove Ladanyi right during this summer's tour.

TERMS Group E-mail—October 23, 2006: Sunday Update:

Dear Friends,

Sure hope you were able to enjoy the gorgeous sunny and cool weather we experienced in Shreveport yesterday. It was so nice that Anne allowed me to cut the grass all by myself—what a good wife I have...

Anne & I had a great visit with Clyde and his mother on Saturday afternoon. Yes, he's still in pain, but his physical therapy is coming along fine. He is getting around really well with his new friend—a walker—and he enjoyed a good visit with his old guitar teacher last week. Yes, Clyde is back playing his guitar—great therapy. You can tell that he is feeling better. When we visited with him in the Shreveport hospital about a week and a half ago, he did NOT want to mess with any guitar. And he was very excited to see Texas beat Nebraska Saturday afternoon on the football field!

Come to find out, Clyde has four fractures in his pelvis, not three. Once his swelling went down, more X-rays were taken to confirm his breaks.

But he is progressing fine. His attitude is great, and he looks great.

In my last update, Brandon's news was pretty upbeat. Well, he had a set-back just a few hours after we left him last Tuesday evening. That evening his heart rate went up; his fever went up, and his respiratory function was quite irregular. His pulmonary doctor ordered a CT scan of his chest and legs and his neurologist ordered a CT scan of his brain. He had developed blood clots in both lungs. The good news from the CT scan of his brain was it showed quite a bit of healing from the first CT scan of his brain.

He underwent surgery, then was put on blood thinner to treat the blood clots, but the next day he had to be taken off the blood thinner due to internal bleeding (not in his brain, thank God). By Friday afternoon, his heart rate had come down some, his respiratory function was better and his temperature was better. He had to go back on the respirator/ventilator and back on sedation medicine. He has had a few rough days but yesterday (Sunday) was a better day. His sister told us that he seemed more alert yesterday.

Of course, the immediate goal is to get Brandon stabilized again and off the sedation medicine and respirator. Once he is off the respirator for 72 consecutive hours then he can be transferred to the rehabilitation center in New Orleans. Yes, it is an emotional roller coaster for Brandon's family and friends, but that is what you deal with in this type of situation.

Many of you have told me "Thanks for keeping me informed." Well, I thank you for your good thoughts and prayers.

Many of you have asked about the next fund-raiser. Once I get more details, I will pass them onto you, but I do know there will be a fund-raiser this Saturday, October 28th, at Flannigan's in Shreveport. Among other things, Ben Labat, lead singer for The TERMS, will perform an acoustic show that night. And Bruce Allen, Clyde's step-dad, has donated over 170 TERMS' CDs to be sold for Brandon's benefit. Once I confirm the details I will let you know. Yes, a person can skip the fund-raisers and just donate directly to the "Brandon Young Donation Account" at Capital One on North Market St. in Shreveport.

Thank you for your support and prayers for Brandon, Clyde, Blake, Ben, and Scott. They are needed and welcomed. Appreciate you very much.

Chapter Four
In the Big Leagues Now

Recording Session—Capitol Records Studio

What an experience. What an education. What an opportunity. What an introduction to the music industry. The band spent five and a half weeks in Los Angeles working on their first album, *Small Town Computer Crash*. It was an intense experience. Scott was self-taught on the drums. He had never had a drum lesson in his life, and now he needed to step up to the plate to record very good music at Capitol Records Studio in Hollywood. That was quite intimidating. Scott said of the whole experience: "That was the hardest thing I've ever had to do."

Only a month before the recording session Scott purchased a metronome. Wikipedia, the free encyclopedia, describes a metronome as "a device that produces a regulated pulse, usually to establish a tempo, measured in beats-per-minute for the performance of musical compositions. It is an invaluable practice tool for musicians that goes back hundreds of years." He was very new to that technology during the recording session process, which made it, as Scott recalls, "a tad bit harder."

Scott was very fortunate to have a superb drum technician work with him during those weeks in Los Angeles. Mike Harrison was a God-send for Scott. He was not only very good and very professional, but very patient. During one tough recording session for Scott which lasted over three hours, he was having a difficult time getting a part right. Mike Harrison spoke into the microphone from behind the glass wall saying, "Scott, you can do this." That soft-spoken encouragement helped Scott through those difficult times of self-doubt. Some songs Scott did quite well and finished the recording session in less than an hour, while other songs took many hours to complete. On the website www.mishmashmagazine.com Scott stated: "It was intense and amazing because I got to record in Capitol Records Studio just a few weeks after Green Day finished with *American Idiot*."

There was Scott in this large recording room with eleven microphones recording his effort. The Beatles had recorded some of their music there. Ben recorded his vocal tracks on a microphone once used by Frank Sinatra. The storied history of this place and the immense pressure of this place weighed heavily upon these young men. When Scott returned home from Los Angeles our family was all around him pelting him with questions. In the midst of this exchange I stated to Scott, "No matter what you tell us we just will not fully understand and appreciate what you experienced there."

He responded, "That is very true."

Ladanyi was very smart in not throwing these young men into a recording situation right off the bat. Music technicians worked with them to tweak their skills, Ladanyi worked with them tweaking the songs, "cleaning them up," as Clyde would say, and there was practice, practice, and more practice. Ben stated when he returned from Los Angeles, "I need a break; I am just tired of singing." A normal day in Los Angeles would begin around 11 A.M. and finish around 1 A.M. the next morning.

The band rehearsed in a place called "The Alley," a studio complex. As the website www.skopemagazine.com notes, "They were in the room where the Black Crowes had conceived *Shake Your Money Maker*." And right next door, the Red Hot Chili Peppers were practicing. Scott stated in one phone call home, "Mom, we took a break and walked outside, and there were the Red Hot Chili Peppers taking a smoke break. It was awesome!" Scott had a picture taken of him sitting at the piano that John Lennon used to compose one of The Beatles' songs (he thinks it was the song "Imagine").

In the band's first album, *Small Town Computer Crash*, it included a DVD that captured some of their experience recording the album. From sixty hours of video that was shot, twenty-three minutes were placed on this DVD. It has a brief history of the band, it introduces each band member, along with Dane and Greg, and it gives some insight into the process of recording music, not to mention some shots of The Alley and Capitol Records Studio. It also shows the band members letting off some steam—obviously they had indulged in some adult beverages that evening. Scott stated they were just trying to unwind from a tough few weeks.

E-MAIL CONNECTIONS

TERMS Group E-mail—October 27, 2006: Friday Update:

Dear Friends,

Anne and I ventured to Monroe last night to visit with Brandon's parents, Jay and Angela. They were in good spirits, but anxious to get Brandon to the rehab center in New Orleans. The Monroe ICU unit is taking very good care of Brandon, but he needs specialized rehab to truly begin his comeback.

Brandon is recovering from his bout with the blood clots. The doctors want him weaned off the ventilator—that has been occurring this past week. His right eye is still open, and when the doctor checked his left eye this week he noticed "decent activity." The doctor stated that his left eye will—as he put it—"awaken" soon.

The physical therapist continues to work with Brandon each day, including putting him sitting up in a chair again—that practice was stopped last Wednesday with the blood-clot situation. The doctor stated that they really cannot do much more for Brandon at their Monroe hospital. He needs to get to the New Orleans' rehabilitation center, Touro. To do that, Brandon must be off of the ventilator for 72 consecutive hours. When he gets off the ventilator his respiratory rate and his heart rate increases since his body is working harder. This information comes from Angela. She is constantly checking out the gauges on his monitor, as any good mother would do.

Angela just informed me that at 11 A.M. this morning (Friday) they took Brandon off the ventilator. Please keep him in your prayers so he will have the strength to sustain himself in this process. His family is very anxious to get Brandon to the rehab center so he can begin his recovery. Angela and Jay would like to express to you again how much they appreciate all your support and prayers. She said your support is just overwhelming.

As of noon this past Wednesday, the account for Brandon at Capital One was $4,000, and that was not counting the $647 check coming from El Chico's. And Saturday night, October 28th, at Flannigan's in Shreveport, a fund-raiser will be held for Brandon's medical expenses. For those of you in Shreveport, the details were in the paper today—in the Entertainment Insert. Lead singers from five bands, including Ben Labat, lead singer for The TERMS, will perform an acoustic show beginning at 9 P.M. Cover charge is $10, with all proceeds from the cover charge going to Brandon's medical account. We thank all the musicians and Flannigan's for this great gesture of support. Thank you for your thoughts and prayers.

Return to Baton Rouge and a New Name

It was back to LSU in Baton Rouge for the beginning of the spring semester of 2005. After a memorable few weeks in Hollywood it was back to books and studying and practicing. Soon the band was moved from their "closet," where they had been practicing to a very spacious studio with four and a half rooms. Dane Andreeff made a huge financial commitment to kick off his record label, Maple Jam Records, by sending these young men to California for six intense weeks. The cost of the studios, the cost of the musicians, the cost of recording, the cost of the condo for the guys to stay in, the cost of the airline flights, and now this major upgrade in a rehearsal/practice facility. He was doing things first class. As Mrs. Resweber, one of my high school teachers, used to tell her students, "It only takes five cents more to go first class." That may have been true in the early 1970s, but with inflation, that amount has gone up quite a bit. Dane realized that and was not deterred. He was immersing his newly-discovered and very talented first-rate band in a first-class environment, including hiring Clayton Harris as their road and booking manager. The band needed to concentrate on their music and performance and not be distracted by the details on the business side of their gigs.

There is a law in California that states musicians must receive up-front royalties. The band members were pleasantly surprised to learn about this. But they took Dane's financial commitment as an example as to what they should do with much of that financial windfall. For the recording session, all-new musical instruments were used. The guys decided to purchase these musical instruments along with the very nice and practical carrying cases that had wheels on them! That would make setting up and taking down and loading up the truck a lot easier. Scott received a brand-new drum set, and we did not have to purchase it. What a country!

But soon there would be no more Sidewalks. As Greg Ladanyi, Niko Bolas, and Mike Harrison were putting the recently recorded tracks together and deciding another very important aspect of an album—the order of the songs—the record label was registering The Sidewalks in the national database. "Houston, we have a problem." It seems that another music organization already had the name, "The Sidewalks." It was not a band, but a business organization in the music industry. The decision was made to change the name of the band.

Many, many names were bandied about in a two-week period. Ben and Scott describe the night a decision was made. The band members were sitting at a table in the outside patio section of the restaurant Serranos, where Scott worked as a server. Scott was working that night but joined the group in between his table responsibilities. They all had notepads with literally hundreds of names written down. That evening they kept eliminating potential names. Some of the names suggested were The Rooze, The Turns, The Banquettes (that is French for "sidewalks") and The Terms. At some time during that marathon session, The Pigeons were bandied about to lighten the mood. Scott remembered Ben commenting, "If we can succeed with a name like THAT, then you know we are good!"

Ben responded to that recollection of Scott's, "It is quite possible I said that. We were having margaritas that evening!"

Ladanyi was not at the brain-storming session at Serranos. Later he was presented with the few winning names. Ladanyi stated they were a serious band and they needed a serious name. Ladanyi, Starr, and Dane all liked the name The TERMS and strongly encouraged that choice. That is how the band's new name came about. The decision was made; they would be called "The TERMS." We should have had a ceremony to bury the name, The Sidewalks; after all, the band and the fans LOVED that name and identity. Alas, time did not permit stopping for anything, not even to acknowledge the death of a beloved part of your past.

After a week or two off to get into the new semester at school and to take a break from the previous intense six weeks in California, it was time to get the band together and practice. When I asked Scott how was their first practice session since returning from California, he smiled and said, "We were awful!" For the past six weeks they had been learning their parts individually and recording them individually. No wonder they were not in sync! For the next three and a half months their job was to practice, learn all the songs very well, and then practice some more.

TERMS Group E-mail—October 31, 2006: Monday Update:

Dear Friends,

And a good Monday to you.

Brandon did very well off the ventilator this weekend. He finished his 72 consecutive hours off the ventilator at noon today (Monday). In fact, the ventilator has been moved OUT of his ICU room! He does have pneumonia, but the doctors do not seem concerned with that condition. He does have fever from an infection that could not be easily diagnosed, so a specialist was brought in who diagnosed a bacterial infection in his lungs—that can be treated. Brandon was put on a new antibiotic yesterday to treat that infection. They will see how he responds to that treatment before giving him the okay to travel to Touro, the New Orleans' Rehabilitation Center. The whole family is anxious to get Brandon there so he can move on to the next phase of his recovery.

People ask me, "Will Brandon ever be the same as before?" That answer is unknown at this time. Doctors have stated that in some head injury cases, it takes six months to determine how much a person will be able to recover. Of course, we are praying for a full recovery, but we are still celebrating each small victory.

Thanks to Flannigan's, the musicians from four other bands, Ben Labat, lead singer of The TERMS, fans, friends, and family who supported the fund raiser for Brandon this past Saturday night in Shreveport. There was a decent crowd, a good raffle, and great conversation. Ben sang five songs that night, including four BRAND-NEW SONGS! He is so good. It was great seeing him perform again. He did an outstanding job. His part was worth the price of admission, PLUS we were able to turn the clock BACK an hour when we returned home due to the end of Daylight Savings Time! Sleep is good for this old man...

And thank you, Mary Helwig and Seth Busby. They joined us that night at Flannigan's. Mary purchased many raffle tickets and four CDs (to give away as Christmas gifts). She even won a couple of the raffle prizes! Thanks for being there.

I should have figures soon on how much was brought in that evening. And thanks to the generosity of Bruce Allen, Clyde's step-father. He donated over 170 TERMS' CDs to be sold, with all proceeds going to Brandon's medical account. If you don't have one of those CDs and would like one, let me know. I bought a few extra and I'm sure I can get my hands on more before they sell out. They are going for $5/CD.

People's generosity is humbling to me. Just yesterday, Anne and I received two checks in the mail totaling $300 for Brandon's medical account. Thank you for your support. It means so much. Thanks for keeping those young men in your prayers—they all need your prayers. Thank you so much.

CD Release Party—April 2005

A new world greeted the band that Spring Semester of 2005. They went to school (Clyde and Blake would graduate in May of 2005), practiced, had meetings with Dane, had conference calls with Starr in California, had intense days when Greg Ladanyi was in town, and they "worked the band" on the Internet: network, network, and network. Promoting bands on websites like MySpace.com had become very prevalent. Working those websites in order to build their fan base was one of the major tasks of the band members.

My job with the Louisiana Department of Labor took me to our administrative office in Baton Rouge on a regular basis that year. During one of those weeks the band was scheduled to perform outside in an amphitheater setting on the LSU campus. That night I met Greg Ladanyi and Dane Andreeff for the first time. The weather was great that evening. An enthusiastic crowd of The Sidewalk's fans greeted the band that night. This was the first public performance of the band since returning from their California recording session. The performance was quite good, including a new song they introduced that evening, "Cupid's Machine Gun," a very fast-paced song. I liked that song for two reasons. It was new, and it emphasized Scott's drum part. That could be expected in any song that had the words "machine gun" in the title.

Finally, the CD was ready. The CD Release Party date was set for early April, then changed to late April 2005. It was debut time—Friday night, back at SoGo Live where Dane had discovered the band a short six months before. Anne and I drove down to Baton Rouge with Debbie Chiartano, Greg Chiartano's mother, that Friday. The plan was for the parents of the band members to meet at a popular po-boy restaurant called Past Times before the show for a meal and to meet one another. As we drove into Baton Rouge we were listening to 104.9 the X on the FM dial. That radio station had been playing The TERMS' song, "Ugly." The DJ, Fish, had been giving this song regular playing time on this station, and we were hoping to hear it. What we did hear was a polished commercial advertising the band's CD Release Party for that evening. We were all excited. In the commercial's background The TERMS' music was playing. What would any mother do at this point, but get teary-eyed? That's just what Anne did. She was so proud.

The evening was a success. There were literally hundreds of people at SoGo Live that evening. Andy, one of my brothers, even made it to the performance despite having to get up early the next morning for a mandatory test his job required. People were there from Baton Rouge, Raceland, Monroe, Shreveport, and many other cities. On the various television monitors throughout the establishment, the DVD of The TERMS was playing. There was much activity before the band's performance that evening. People were watching that video, Starr was in the back of SoGo Live selling CDs, T-Shirts, Bumper Stickers, the band members were signing autographs for their friends and new fans; it was quite a festive occasion. For these performances, the decibel level was sometimes turned up quite high. It sure was that evening. We all left SoGo Live that evening with a ringing in our ears and a few songs in our hearts.

My fellow regional manager from Monroe, Louisiana, Truman Miers, worked in Baton Rouge the following week. He ventured to SoGo Live early

E-MAIL CONNECTIONS

one evening and struck up a conversation with the manager. He asked him if a band called The TERMS had played there last week. The manager replied: "Yes, they sure did. I'll have to put on more wait staff and bartenders next time they play. They sure did bring in a huge crowd." And the band with a new name was launched.

Around the time of the CD release party in the spring of 2005, I began an e-mail campaign to spread the word of The TERMS to a few friends and family. It was time to sell a few CDs, get people to their gigs in Louisiana, Texas, Arkansas, Florida, New York, or wherever they were performing, do anything I could on my part to help build their fan base. People were very supportive and excited to hear the latest news on the band. Mark Porter, CEO of Porter's Cleaners and a friend from way back, confessed to me his early feelings concerning my "promotional e-mails" at an event at the Bossier Civic Center. He stated, "When you put me on your e-mail list I was dreading receiving these e-mails from you, but once I began reading them I really looked forward to them. Reading about the band and Scott's journey was more enjoyable than I imagined. I read every word. I couldn't wait for the next one!" Mark bought three CDs! One by one, that is how the TERMS' group e-mail list grew.

The spring semester at LSU was now over, and it was time to tour, build a larger fan base, and sell those CDs. That was just what they did. The next weekend the band performed at the Film Fantasy Fandango Gala and Fund-Raiser for The Robinson Film Center in Shreveport, Louisiana. Tickets were $100 each. I had never before attended such an event like this, but I did this time. The next night they played at Squintfest 2005: A Benefit Concert for the National Parkinson's Foundation in downtown Shreveport. That summer the band's schedule took them to perform in many places in Louisiana, Texas, and Georgia.

Many questions arose that summer. Would this pace keep up in the fall? Would the guys who were still in college (Ben, Greg, and Scott) have to drop out? What direction would be taken? Greg Ladanyi was a proven record producer, and Dane Andreeff was a proven businessman, but neither had run a record label before. Starr Andreeff had great energy, but this was new to her also. As for these young men in the band, this was definitely new territory. Two had their college degrees, but all five were receiving quite an education in life—and in the business side of the music industry.

JACQUES LASSEIGNE

TERMS Group E-mail—November 3, 2006: Brandon Update:

Dear Friends,

With Anne at church Wednesday night for a special service and choir practice, I was home getting things checked off my list. One item was "iron shirts." My normal routine is to bring the Bose radio into the utility room, put in a CD and get to the task at hand—ironing. As I flipped open my CD bag, it opened to a CD I had not heard in a long time. It was labeled, "The Sidewalks….August 2004." That was a CD the band put together a mere three months before they were "discovered." I heard raw talent and energy on that CD….brought back many memories.

Speaking of memories, we are praying for new good memories, although it has been another one of those up and down weeks. The New Orleans Rehabilitation Facility declined to admit Brandon this week even though he stayed off the ventilator for 72 consecutive hours as the Rehab Center had requested. It seems that Brandon is still weak from the episode with the blood clots, the pneumonia, and the bacterial infection. This was tough news for Brandon's family since he had already been accepted by Touro, the New Orleans Rehabilitation Facility, before the episode with the blood clots.

Touro will re-assess Brandon's condition this Monday, November 6th. Please continue your prayers that his condition will improve to the point where he will be accepted. If not, we are looking at Plan B and maybe Plan C.

And thanks to many of you for helping with the CD sales. Bruce Allen graciously donated 170 TERMS' CDs for sale, with all proceeds going to Brandon's medical account. They are going for $5 each. People have purchased a few for Christmas gifts, stocking stuffers, etc. We now have 100 left.

Thank you for your continued wonderful prayers for Brandon and his family and for the rest of the band—Clyde, Blake, Ben, and Scott. They are greatly appreciated, not to mention, greatly needed. May you be blessed in your life.

E-MAIL CONNECTIONS

New York Performances—Summer of 2005

There was much discussion in the summer of 2005 concerning what direction the band would be headed. Would they continue on the road touring and building up their fan base or would they return to LSU in order for Ben, Greg and Scott to finish their college degree or another direction or a combination of all of the above? Finally it was decided by the record label that The TERMS would be a "college band" for now. That meant college course work for Ben, Greg, and Scott as well as basically performing as a full-time band. That translates into classes missed. If one takes college work seriously it is hard enough dealing with the studying, the papers, the projects, class time, and the academic *stress* that goes with it, but to throw in time away from that world in order to meet the demands of a band with a new CD, a new recording contract, and a touring schedule that puts you on the road—that is tough.

Ben, Greg, and Scott met with their college professors late that summer and explained the situation to them. They were all in the College of Business. Ben and Scott were seniors and had a good school track record. Their professors were very understanding of the situation. They were pleased with Ben and Scott's college course work and stated they could work with them whenever they had to be out of town for their performances. Greg had a good track record also, but he was a sophomore. A couple of his professors were not as accommodating concerning this situation. All three guys stayed in contact with their professors via e-mail concerning any changes in their tour schedule.

Summer was over, and it was time to return to class for the fall semester of 2005. But The TERMS were in New York for a two-week period. It was time to make their debut in the Northeast. School would have to wait.

They were scheduled to play five or six times in that two-week period. The two most pressure-packed performances were in front of 150 Executives with Trans World Entertainment and with Richie Cannata and Gerado Velez at The Cutting Room in New York. Trans World Entertainment was having their national conference in New York. Their organization includes music stores such as FYE, Sam Goody's, Wherehouse Music, and Planet Music, The Music Superstore. At this conference very few bands get to perform live in front of all these executives, especially new and upcoming bands, but the record label was able to pull that off. I guess having a Grammy-Award Winning Producer helps open doors.

Live performances are just that—live. Anything can happen, especially in a pressure-packed environment where you have to play your absolute best to make a good impression. The band performed a few songs in front of these executives. Simply stated, they were a hit. Many of these executives came up to the band members immediately after their performance to sing their praises of what they had just witnessed. Scott told me later that some of these executives said to him, "We thought you were a 'boy band,' but your band is really good." I asked Scott what that meant. He explained that the term "boy band" referred to a band of good-looking guys who were not really true musicians, could not really play musical instruments, could not write their own music, and were not a real live, performing band—but they looked and sounded good! They were so pleased with what they heard that Trans World Entertainment agreed to put The TERMS' new CD in all of their stores nationwide. They passed that test! What a giant step forward for this new band and for this new record label.

More performances were on the schedule in New York, including their upcoming gig at The Cutting Room. It was at that time when our phone rang late one night. It is almost never good receiving a phone call late at night, even if it is just a wrong number. Anne answered the phone and I began listening intently to Anne's conversation. Scott was calling from New York and telling her some upsetting news. Greg Chiartano had made a decision to quit the band. He would be catching a plane back to Louisiana as soon as possible in order not to miss any more classes at LSU. It seemed that one of his professors was not giving him any leeway concerning missing class, and he would penalize Greg for it grade-wise. That was weighing on Greg's mind as he was away in New York, and the fall semester had begun. Two weeks of college classes were a lot to miss, especially if a professor was not being cooperative. Many phone calls were made in those early morning hours. Greg's mother tried to calm him down and asked him not to leave the band during this trip. Anne and I were very grateful that Starr was with the band on this trip to New York. Starr did catch Greg at the airport and was able to convince him not to leave that day. Greg agreed to finish out the New York trip with the band, and he also agreed to stay with the band that semester until they found a replacement, but he would still leave the band.

The intensity of their schedule, the effects of touring, and the regular, and sometimes stressful, interactions of a new band with a new record label weighed heavily on Greg Chiartano. Night after night of performing in different places can get to anyone. Greg vividly remembers playing a show in South Louisiana in front of a whopping crowd of 15 people. For that gig they were playing for door money. That translates into 15 people times $5 cover charge. That would definitely not cover their gasoline expense, much less heal their wounded pride that evening. The bar they played at that evening was part of a strip of bars where other bands were performing. A gentleman in his late 40s came up to the band after their sound check. He had a white ponytail, and his countenance was that of a person who had aged prematurely due to a lifetime of touring. He gave the band a copy of his CD and told them "We're about to get huge!" That was Greg's epiphany. He did not want to be that man with a long mullet-ponytail who was aged well beyond his years holding onto the "We're going to be huge" hope. That scared him to death. That mental picture and the critical college classes he was missing at LSU sealed his decision.

Greg left the band later that fall semester of 2005 and went on to concentrate on his studies. He finished his undergraduate work at LSU with an excellent grade-point average. His course work and activities enabled him to enter Loyola Law School in New Orleans, Louisiana, in the fall of 2007.

The TERMS had one more major performance in New York—The Cutting Room. The place was packed. The band put on an exceptional performance. Scott gave me a couple of recordings from that night's performance, including their final song of their set—which brought on a loud chorus of "ENCORE! ENCORE!" from the audience—to which the band complied. One song the band played was The Rolling Stones' "Sympathy for the Devil." Richie Cannata, Billy Joel's saxophone player, and Gerado Velez, percussionist for Jimi Hendrix, accompanied them in that song. That recording is ten minutes of great rock and roll music. In fact, on the recording you can hear Greg Chiartano a couple of times agreeing. At the end of the song he exclaims, "Oh my God! That was the most awesome thing ever!" And it was.

When Anne heard that recording she turned to Scott and remarked, "That must have been fun!"

He smiled and said, "It was."

On these trips the band drove two vehicles. One was the nineteen-foot box van with all of their equipment, and the other was a suburban. In the box van one person drove and one rode shotgun. The rest of the crew rode in the suburban. The band took two days to drive up to New York on this trip, but drove straight through to return to Baton Rouge in order to make class that Monday morning. That is the price you pay when you have two full-time commitments—college and a music career. That was a very long trip for the guys. The kind of trip that makes parents worry; after all, that is a lot of highway to cover between New York and Louisiana. The band pulled into Baton Rouge around 5:30 that Monday morning. Yes, they were dead tired from their two-week experience and from their all-night ride back to southern Louisiana, but at least Greg and Ben and Scott could make class that morning. Blake and Clyde had graduated a few months before. They could go to sleep, and that's just what they did.

TERMS Group E-mail—November 7, 2006: Brandon Update:

Dear Friends,

Sure hope your holiday (for those who are non-state workers, we had Election Day off yesterday) was a good break from the regular routine. I was hoping to bring you an update today with the headline, "Brandon is moved to a Rehab Facility!" Well, that will have to wait a bit since the up-and-down-emotional-roller-coaster ride continues.

Brandon developed a large blood clot Sunday which extends from his shoulder to his elbow. The doctors ordered a CT-scan to make sure there was no bleeding in his brain. There was none; therefore, he was put on a blood thinner. That clot is very dangerous, as most of you know.

With all this going on, Touro, the New Orleans Rehabilitation Facility, after their evaluation today, declined to admit him—again. When they turned Brandon down last Monday, many of us began to look at Plan B and Plan C. Angela sent out an e-mail to all of her friends explaining this situation. Three of her high school classmates remembered that one of their high school classmates was now the CEO of Methodist Rehabilitation Center in Jackson, Mississippi. Unknown to Brandon's parents, one of these friends called their classmate, Mark Adams, and explained the situation to him. He immediately sent a representative to St. Francis Hospital in Monroe to visit with Brandon and his doctors and nurses. They accepted him that same afternoon.

The family was extremely relieved and very, very grateful, but wanted to wait until today to see what Touro's decision was. Even though Touro declined to admit Brandon today, the Jackson Rehabilitation Facility again stated that they would take Brandon. That is great news.

Once Brandon gets through this latest tough episode, it looks like he will be traveling east! Even with all these setbacks, his doctors firmly believe that once Brandon gets into the specialized rehabilitation setting he will make good progress. That is indeed encouraging.

Thank you soooooo much for your good thoughts and prayers for Brandon and his family. They especially need it at this difficult time. Anne and I plan to travel over to Monroe tonight to visit with Angela and to visit with Blake. The outpouring of support and prayers is humbling to witness—and it is sustaining Brandon and his family at this time. Thank you for your prayers for Brandon, Clyde, Blake, Ben, and Scott and their families.

And the financial support continues to pour in. Just today I made another deposit to Brandon's Donation Account at Capital One Bank for over $220. Thanks to Emmy, a co-worker and friend of mine, who brought me two boxes of TERMS' CDs that she picked up from Scott when she was in Baton Rouge last Friday, we have more CDs to sell for Brandon's medical account. Thanks to your generosity, I only have one box left. You have many things going on in your own lives, but you have taken the time to pray for and support these young men in their time of need. I can't thank you enough.

I will continue to keep you in my prayers. Thanks again.

Shreveport Riverfront Performances

The TERMS performed twice on Shreveport's new Riverfront stage in the second half of 2005. The first time was for the July 4th celebration on Shreveport's Riverfront. That is always a huge celebration, and it tends to get bigger each year. Dane, the owner of Maple Jam Records, wanted to make this trip to Shreveport special—and he did. He arranged to have the band arrive in a new Motor Home Coach—yes, the size of a Greyhound Bus! There were plenty of beds to sleep in. Each bed had its own flat-screen plasma television. This was a huge step up from the band's normal driving accommodations. In this vehicle they could play video games, watch television, sleep, compose music and leave the driving to someone else! That is just what they did when they left town to return to Baton Rouge at 1:30 the next morning.

One of the local television stations, CBS affiliate KSLA Channel 12, co-sponsors the July 4th Celebration. They produced a great segment on The TERMS' story and their performance that evening. They gave the band a lot of air time that night, which is unusual for a 30-minute news program. The opening television shot was of the band exiting the motor-home coach. What a progression from recording their album a few months ago in California to releasing it in late April of 2005 to a grand celebration on the new Riverfront stage in Shreveport, Louisiana, in front of a couple of thousand people. What a journey it had been. Just the day before their producer informed the band that they would be heading up the East Coast for performances in New York City in a few weeks. A new world was opening up to these country boys from Louisiana.

I sent information about the July 4th performance and of the upcoming New York trip to my TERMS' e-mail group the next day and signed it "Groupie Manager."

Rhonda Sellers, Human Resource Manager in our Baton Rouge Administrative Office, replied back to my e-mail: "Wow! This is so exciting. How many young artists get this lucky? Just goes to show you that good talent never goes unnoticed. I am so happy for them and their Groupie Manager."

I replied back with a bit more information that I did not share with the whole e-mail group. E-mail of July 5, 2005, to Rhonda: "Last night, after the performance, the band members were under their merchandise tent signing autographs on their CDs, T-Shirts, and Posters. Then my dear wife asked me: 'Do you know what your son is doing?' I replied: 'Yes, he is signing autographs and talking with his fans.' She responded: 'Yes, he is signing autographs for those three young ladies over there, but do you see what he is signing?' It seems they wanted him to sign a part of their anatomy, which he graciously agreed to. It was in their front, upper section of their body, if you know what I mean. In biology class that part of a woman's anatomy is said to have a lot of adipose tissue. I wanted to ask my son if he needed any help, but I'm sure my dear, sweet wife would NOT have appreciated that feeble attempt at humor from me! She is just not allowing me to perform my Groupie Manager duties."

Rhonda responded: "Can't stop laughing! Have to agree with the wife—leave that sort of thing for your son to enjoy. I guess that is one of the perks of being a rock star!"

That was a special night for the band. Great music, great reception from the fans, merchandise sales went very well, the weather cooperated, and first-class motor-coach accommodations to rest up in. A small taste of what the future could hold for them.

Just three months later The TERMS returned to the Shreveport Riverfront, performing on the first night of a huge arts and crafts festival called Red River Revel. This time the stage was even larger than it was for the July 4th performance. The crowd was much bigger—the largest crowd that the band had played in front of to date. Many friends were in attendance to lend their support. Since so many of their high-school and college friends swarmed near the stage, the police had to set up barriers in order to keep some kind of crowd control. Performance went very well, as well as merchandise sales. They sold a ton of CDs; in fact, they sold out their T-Shirts and Bumper Stickers. Their fan base in the Shreveport area was solid and growing. With three band members from Shreveport you would hope that would be the case, and it was.

I would send Starr Andreef, Vice-President of Maple Jam Records, short e-mail updates sometimes of these performances since she was in California. On October 3, 2005, I e-mailed her an account of the band's Red River Revel performance. Her e-mail reply on October 4, 2005, "I love getting the rundown. Glad your friends liked their new music. Since they performed for an hour and a half they had to play some of their new material."

On October 7, 2005, I sent Starr this e-mail: "My wife shopped at Bed, Bath & Beyond yesterday afternoon. The woman at the register, checking out in front of her, walked outside to her Lexus SUV. It was parked next to my wife's Honda Pilot. She started to back out, then drove back in her parking space and motioned to my wife to roll down her window. She yelled to my wife: 'I LOVE THE TERMS!' She had noticed The TERMS' bumper sticker on the back window of our Honda Pilot. 'We went to their performance at the Revel last Saturday—they are GREAT!' My wife responded: 'I'm glad you like them. By the way, I'm the mother of the drummer.' The lady responded, 'My friend

LOVES your son. He was soooo cute in his shirt and tie.' This woman was probably in her 40s. The fan base is growing!"

Starr responded, "Oh my God. Fantastic! Going to pass this on to Greg and Dane."

One more e-mail concerning the growing fan base. This one is from my first cousin, Nena Leake, who lives in Houston, Texas. She wrote on July 17, 2005, "We have been enjoying The TERMS' CD. I am sure they are going to be famous when one morning Jonathan (their teenage son) came down the stairs singing the chorus to the song 'Ugly.'"

TERMS Group E-mail—November 10, 2006: Brandon Update:

Good Friday Morning to all my Dear Friends,

Anne and I visited with Brandon's mother Tuesday evening in Monroe. Brandon had been too quiet the previous four days, but Tuesday was a good day. He began moving his right leg a lot! I call it the "Elvis Leg-Movement Therapy." In fact, every time a new person would walk in his ICU room, he would move his right leg quite a bit as if he was saying, "Hey, look what I can do!" or "I'm alive and well in here!"

AND he began moving his lips a lot. The nurses watched him and stated to Brandon's mother: "He's trying to talk to you." Since he still has an endo-tracheal tube, he cannot make any sound, but that was a great sign.

His arm was quite swollen from the blood clot on Tuesday. The doctors are watching that closely. And yesterday he came down with another @#%! infection. If Brandon responds well to the new medicine and there are no more surprises over the weekend, we hope that he will be on his way to the Methodist Rehab Center in Jackson, Mississippi, by Monday or Tuesday.

The TERMS' gigs had already been cancelled for the months of October and November. Their performances in December have just been cancelled also. In fact, tomorrow (Saturday) they were scheduled to perform at a University-sponsored Tailgating Party before the LSU-

Alabama football game. It brings a smile to my face when I picture them performing. The last time Anne and I saw the band performing was at Rabb's in Ruston, Louisiana, just a couple of weeks before the fateful accident in Monroe. They had great chemistry that evening. And as their first set was coming to a close, Ben stated on the microphone: "We'll take a short break," but the rest of the band kept on playing. Ben then said, "Then again, maybe not," as he changed places with Brandon on stage. Then Brandon began singing his rap song. He has worked on this song since his high-school days. It was GREAT! Brandon's parents were there that night to see this. It was great fun. It was a special moment. Looking back, I am so happy that Brandon's parents and Anne and I were there that night to witness all this. What a splendid time we experienced that evening.

Thanks again for all your support and prayers for Brandon, Clyde, Blake, Ben and Scott. It is needed and very much appreciated—and, at times, overwhelming.

New Bass Player

The fall of 2005 consisted of band practice, band meetings, conference calls, numerous media interviews, many performances, touring, college classes, and finding a replacement for Greg, the bass player for The TERMS. The first person Scott thought of and the first person Scott contacted to replace Greg was his good friend from high school, Brandon Young. Brandon could play quite well and was also a pretty good back-up singer. Scott fought hard for Brandon to join the group. The other band members got along great with Brandon; he had their vote also. Greg Ladanyi, from the record label side, wanted another bass player. This person could play the organ in addition to the bass guitar. In any organization where people are passionate about their profession there are differences. It was no different with The TERMS and Maple Jam Records. It's called "artistic differences." It's also called *tension!* This back and forth went on for weeks that fall.

Brandon would get a call that Greg Ladanyi would be in Baton Rouge; therefore, he needed to drive down to audition. Brandon would pack up his gear, make the four-hour drive to Baton Rouge, and hang out with the guys at their studio. A couple of times, Greg's plans either changed or he just could not fit an audition into his schedule. These were not wasted trips, since Brandon had a chance to visit with all the band members, practice with them in their jam sessions, and build that bond. It was an anxious time for Brandon. He was attending college that semester in Shreveport, but due to the many trips to and from Baton Rouge, his grades started to suffer; therefore, he dropped his classes so his grade-point average would not be adversely affected. Finally, auditions were held with Ladanyi. Brandon had memorized The TERMS' songs and performed quite well. He was allowed to join the band in December of 2005, but was put on a 3-month probationary period. After two months, the record label decided to take him off of probation. He was now, officially, one of The TERMS.

TERMS Group E-mail—November 15, 2006: Brandon Update:

Good Wednesday Morning!

Brandon had a BREAKTHROUGH early Saturday morning. His nurse called Angela, Brandon's mother, at 4 A.M. Saturday morning to tell her that Brandon was moving to command on his right side. That is HUGE news!

And more good news: Brandon left for Methodist Rehabilitation Center in Jackson, Mississippi, yesterday morning! FINALLY!

He was still battling an infection, but the doctors gave the okay anyway. Now Brandon can get the intense and specialized rehabilitation that he needs. We thank the staff at the Monroe St. Francis Hospital for everything they did—they literally kept Brandon alive and helped to bring him back. What more can you ask for?

Thank you again for your continued support and prayers for Brandon, Clyde, Blake, Ben, and Scott. They are needed and most welcomed. Your prayers have brought these young men to a brighter day today. I thank you.

Chapter Five
Superb Recognition and Great Press

Early Music Reviews

2006 was shaping up as another busy year for the band. The guys were working hard to improve, to write new music, to perform better, and they were really beginning to get noticed. A few reviews from critics in 2005: *All you need is ears to notice...they are the band most likely to succeed. It's obvious in the band's beautifully written and arranged songs, and Ben Labat's southern toned vocals.* (John Wirt on June 10, 2005, *The Advocate* [Baton Rouge, La., newspaper])

The band's music does everything...It cannot be ignored...Labat delivers catchy lyrics with a rich and memorable baritone voice. Hargrove's guitar work is bright, tight and imaginative. (The TIMES [Shreveport, La., newspaper])

...beneath the heartland charisma lays something more...The TERMS are extremely serious about music and their approach to it...which contributes to their ability to write universal music. (The MUSIC EDGE)

Another review came out on October 14, 2005, from Robert Velasquez on upbeetmusic.com website. He gave the album four and a half stars out of five: *The comforts of the South have never sounded this good... Everything seems to have molded into one...it's easy to point out how exceptionally these components have managed to work together.*

The TERMS' 2006 Schedule:

1-13-06 WICHITA FALLS, TX., IRON HORSE PUB
1-14-06 HAMMOND, LA., CAFÉ STREET BAR
1-20-06 MONROE, LA., 6TH STREET BAR
1-21-06 BATON ROUGE, LA., FRED'S BAR
1-24-06 LOS ANGELES, CALIF., VIPER ROOM
1-26-06 LOS ANGELES, CALIF., PRIVATE SHOW (REHEARSALS.COM PRODUCTION)
1-27-06 LOS ANGELES, CALIF., THE MINT
2-10-06 GAINESVILLE, FLA., COMMON GROUNDS WHHZ—THEBUZZ RADIO EVENT
2-11-06 BATON ROUGE, LA., MUSCULAR DYSTROPHY BENEFIT—REGGIE'S
2-18-06 NASHVILLE, TENN., WBUZ—THE BUZZ RADIO EVENT
2-23-06 BATON ROUGE, LA., VARSITY THEATRE—OPEN ACT FOR BLUES TRAVELER
3-4-06 BATON ROUGE, LA., FRED'S BAR
3-10-06 HOUSTON, TX., CONTINENTAL CLUB
3-11-06 BATON ROUGE, LA., PRIVATE PARTY
3-17-06 WICHITA, KS., PORT OF WICHITA
3-18-06 DALLAS, TX., POOR DAVID'S PUB
4-1-06 HATTIESBURG, MS., MISSISSIPPI MUSIC FESTIVAL
4-3-06 MONROE, LA., ULM SHOW
4-4-06 BATON ROUGE, LA., VARSITY THEATRE
4-7-06 BATON ROUGE, LA., SPANISH MOON
4-8-06 SHREVEPORT, LA., ROBINSON FILM FESTIVAL GROUND-BREAKING PARTY
4-19-06 RUSTON, LA., RABB'S STEAKHOUSE—OPEN FOR PAT GREEN
4-20-06 NEW ORLEANS, LA., HOUSE OF BLUES—OPEN FOR PAT GREEN
4-21-06 SHREVEPORT, LA., CENTENARY COLLEGE—OPEN FOR BETTER THAN EZRA
4-22-06 HAMMOND, LA., CAFÉ STREET PUB
4-25-06 BATON ROUGE, LA., VARSITY THEATRE—CD RELEASE PARTY

E-MAIL CONNECTIONS

4-27-06 BATON ROUGE, LA., EPISCOPAL HIGH SCHOOL—ALL DAY
4-27-06 NEW ORLEANS, LA., RED-EYE GRILL
4-28-06 MONROE, LA., 6TH STREET BAR
4-29-06 BOSSIER CITY, LA., WAL-MART—1 P.M. ACOUSTIC SHOW
4-29-06 SHREVEPORT, LA., FLANNIGAN'S
5-5-06 BOSSIER CITY, LA., BAFB
5-6-06 LINDEN, TX., MUSIC CITY TEXAS THEATRE
5-12-06 LEESVILLE, LA., FORT POLK—DAYTIME SHOW
5-19-06 WICHITA FALLS, TX., IRON HORSE PUB
5-20-06 WICHITA FALLS, TX., SHEPPARD'S AIR FORCE BASE
5-22-06 SHREVEPORT, LA., PRIVATE PARTY
5-27-06 NEW ORLEANS, LA., SPICEY ROCK FEST—HOWLIN' WOLF
6-2-06 LITTLE ROCK, ARK., STICKY FINGERZ
6-3-06 LITTLE ROCK, ARK., LITTLE ROCK AIR FORCE BASE
6-3-06 TEXARKANA, ARK., ASHDOWN
6-8-06 HOT SPRINGS, ARK., THE ATTIC
6-9-06 EL DORADO, ARK., EINSTEIN'S
6-10-06 JACKSON, MISS., W.C. DONS
6-12-06 VIRGINIA BEACH, VA., PEPPERMINT BEACH CLUB
6-14-06 WORCESTER, MA., LUCKY DOG
6-16-06 NEW YORK, NY., KNITTING FACTORY
6-17-06 NEW YORK, NY., HUDSON BEACH CAFÉ—LSU FUNDRAISER—5 P.M.
6-21-06 NEW YORK, NY., THE BITTER END
6-22-06 ASHBURY PARK, NJ., THE SAINT
6-23-06 NEW YORK, NY., THE CUTTING ROOM-MIX/REMIX MAGAZINE EVENT
6-24-06 SHREVEPORT, LA., PRIVATE PARTY
6-26-06 NEW YORK, NY., CONTINENTAL
6-27-06 BROOKLYN, NY., TRASH BAR
6-29-06 NEWTON CENTRE, MA., THE ATTIC
6-30-06 HAMPTON, VA., LANGLEY AIR FORCE BASE
7-1-06 FORT BELVOIR, VA., FORT BELVOIR

7-2-06 ITHACA, NY., MAXIS OYSTER BAR
7-4-06 WASHINGTON, D.C., BOLLING AIR FORCE BASE
7-6-06 PHILADELPHIA, PA., THE FIRE
7-7-06 OCEAN CITY, MD., THE PURPLE MOOSE SALOON
7-8-06 OCEAN CITY, MD., THE PURPLE MOOSE SALOON
7-9-06 OCEAN CITY, MD., THE PURPLE MOOSE SALOON
7-10-06 VIRGINIA BEACH, VA., HALF SHELL
7-11-06 WASHINGTON, D.C., GROG & TANKARD
7-12-06 FAYETTEVILLE, NC., FORT BRAGG
7-13-06 MORRISTOWN, TENN., THE DOWNTOWN
7-14-06 MEMPHIS, TENN., BROOKHAVEN PUB & GRILL
7-21-06 BATON ROUGE, LA., THE VARSITY—STUDIO LIVE
7-28-06 GONZALES, LA., BINX BAR
7-29-06 BATON ROUGE, LA., BLUE BAYOU WATER PARK
8-2-06 RUSTON, LA., RABB'S STEAKHOUSE
8-3-06 BIRMINGHAM, ALA., THE NICK
8-4-06 HOUMA, LA., THE HEIGHTS
8-5-06 HAMMOND, LA., CAFÉ STREET PUB
8-12-06 HOUSTON, TX., CONTINENTAL CLUB
8-15-06 AUSTIN, TX., RED EYED FLY
8-18-06 SHREVEPORT, LA., FLANNIGAN'S
8-19-06 DALLAS, TX., FIREWATER BAR & GRILL
8-21-06 DALLAS, TX., GYPSY TEA ROOM
8-25-06 LOS ANGELES, CA., THE MEGAN MULLALLY TV SHOW
8-25-06 LOS ANGELES, CA., THE JOINT
8-30-06 BATON ROUGE, LA., FRESH-FEST—LSU ALUMNI CENTER
8-31-06 LAFAYETTE, LA., BLUE MOON SALOON
9-1-06 BIRMINGHAM, ALA., WORKPLAY
9-8-06 BATON ROUGE, LA., THE CATERIE—ALL AGES 7 P.M.
9-8-06 BATON ROUGE, LA., THE CATERIE—10 P.M.
9-14-06 RUSTON, LA., RABB'S STEAKHOUSE
9-16-06 SAN ANTONIO, TX., SAM'S BURGER JOINT
9-22-06 HAMMOND, LA., CAFÉ STREET PUB
9-30-06 MONROE, LA., 6^(TH) STREET BAR
10-6-06 WITCHITA FALLS, TX., IRON HORSE PUB

E-MAIL CONNECTIONS

10-7-06 EL DORADO, ARK., MUSIC CITY TEXAS THEATRE
10-13-06 EL DORADO, ARK., EINSTEIN'S
10-14-06 HOUSTON, TX., WAREHOUSE LIVE
10-20-06, KNOXVILLE, TN., CORNER LOUNGE
10-21-06 MOBILE, ALA., SOUL KITCHEN—OPEN FOR THE BENJY DAVIS PROJECT
10-27-06 BATON ROUGE, LA., BATON ROUGE STATE FAIR
10-29-06 BATON ROUGE, LA., PRIVATE EVENT
11-3-06 AUSTIN, TX., MOMO'S
11-10-06 BATON ROUGE, LA., THE CATERIE
11-11-06 BATON ROUGE, LA., LSU TAILGATE PARTY—ALABAMA GAME
11-24-06 NEW ORLEANS, LA., THE REPUBLIC
11-25-06 HOUMA, LA., THE HEIGHTS
12-8-06 BATON ROUGE, LA., THE CATERIE—ALL AGES-7 P.M.
12-8-06 BATON ROUGE, LA., THE CATERIE—10 P.M.
12-12-06 LOS ANGELES, CALIF., THE MEGAN MULLALLY SHOW

Performances from coast to coast were scheduled and made. The band played at The Viper Room, a famous establishment in Los Angeles that had recently been owned by Johnny Depp, the Continental Club in Houston, a return engagement to The Cutting Room in New York where they had a fabulous show with Richie Cannata back on September 12, 2005, the House of Blues in New Orleans, the Hudson Beach Café in New York, and the Purple Moose Saloon in Ocean City, Maryland. They played in front of many music executives in California during the filming of their production work on Rehearsals.com, performing for The Megan Mullally Show in August of 2006—doing so well they were invited back for two more shows—and many places in between. They were the warm-up act for Blues Traveler, Pat Green, and Better Than Ezra. What a year it was.

Most of these commitments on their 2006 schedule were fulfilled. Exceptions included a couple of shows cancelled due to engine breakdown (ah, the joys of traveling on the road) and re-arranging of the schedule at that last minute due to conflicting commitments. Of course, all performances after September 30, 2006, were cancelled.

JACQUES LASSEIGNE

TERMS Group E-mail—November 20, 2006: Brandon Update:

Dear Friends,

Sure hope you enjoyed this Beautiful, Sunny Weekend!

Brandon was transferred to the Methodist Rehabilitation Center in Jackson, Mississippi, on Tuesday. He was evaluated with a series of tests on Wednesday. On Thursday Brandon must have been exhausted, because he did not do much at all that day; then we have today (Friday).

He had the full range of work today: physical therapy, speech therapy, and occupational therapy. He is doing something all day long. They have started capping off the trachea periodically. If things go well, that will be capped off permanently soon.

Angela was attempting to brush Brandon's teeth today. Well, Brandon kept swatting at his mother's arm. So Angel, Brandon's sister, said: "Let him brush his own teeth." And that is exactly what Brandon wanted! After a couple of attempts and a couple of drops of the toothbrush, he was brushing his own teeth!

He also helped dress himself today. He picked up his arm to help, and he grabbed hold onto the rail to move his body in the right position.

Speech Therapy Session: "Brandon, point to the blue ball on this page." He did just that. "Brandon, point to the red ball." He did that. In fact, he pointed to all his colors correctly! He swallowed on command. He grabbed and pulled the appropriate items out of a basket each time a different item was named, i.e., a toy truck, car keys, and a penny. He pointed to the word "yes" when asked, "Is your name Brandon?" and pointed to the word "no" when asked, "Is your name Mark?" He grabbed the appropriate-color bean bag when asked to do so—he was choosing from five bean bags. An outstanding day in speech therapy…hell, an OUTSTANDING DAY, PERIOD!

When put in a big harness that placed him in a "standing position," he was really looking around and checking everything out. That was the first time he was in an upright, standing position since the accident. One can only imagine what was going through Brandon's mind.

One change from the ICU in Monroe to this rehabilitation facility is that Brandon's mother stays in the same room with him and is very involved in his rehab. That is both good and bad. Good in that she can see his daily progress; bad in that it is both physically and mentally exhausting for her. She is literally with him twenty-four hours a day.

Brandon made a lot of progress for one day, but everything is a time-consuming activity. Yes, we are still looking at a long road to recovery, but at least now, the long road back has begun.

Thank you for your wonderful support and prayers for Brandon, Clyde, Blake, Ben, and Scott and their families. We can't thank you enough.

Rehearsals.com

Spring semester of 2006 started. It was time for classes to begin. That, of course, meant it was time for another long trip to the coast. In the previous fall semester it was the East Coast. This time it was the West Coast. California, here we come. On their 2006 schedule it is listed as "Private Show in Los Angeles—January 26, 2006." In the summer of 2008, one could still check out some of that private show on the website www.rehearsals.com. On The TERMS' page on the website, Doug Miller titles his piece, "The TERMS Emerge from the Bayou." He writes: *At the world-famous CenterStaging rehearsal space in Burbank, California, where The TERMS were recorded in high definition for the exclusive content on the complex's state-of-the-art web site, rehearsals.com, The TERMS got a chance to practice in one of the most revered spots in the music industry while offering their burgeoning group of fans the opportunity to get a behind-the-scenes look at what it takes to get their live show where they want it to be. There's no doubt that the band has already been helped out by both their fresh rock sound and Ladanyi, who has a watchful eye and powerful connections.*

JACQUES LASSEIGNE

The website features three songs from The TERMS: the rehearsal of the song "Isthmus," the performance of "Big City Concrete Wildflowers" (web site states: "chiming guitars"), and the performance of "Welcome to the Now" (web site states: "unleashing an anthem"). The TERMS performed quite a few songs in front of music and television executives—what an opportunity. A couple of executives told the band, "You are very good. All you need to do is get on the radio more, and we can have you on our show." What great exposure to powerful connections in the entertainment business. Yes, a couple of the band members were missing a few days of classes, but what an education they were receiving in the game of life.

More from Doug Miller on the rehearsals.com web site: *Veteran rock producer Greg Ladanyi has been associated with some of the biggest albums in rock history. He has a Grammy under his belt, and he's worked with megastars like Don Henley and Fleetwood Mac. That's why it's hard for anyone not to share his enthusiasm when he speaks endearingly about his latest project, the up-and-coming alternative rock quintet from Louisiana State University known as The TERMS.*

"Greg really helped us to figure out how to layer things and make each part of the song more significant," said Ben Labat, The TERMS lead singer. "Greg's extremely professional. He's given us everything. What he's contributed musically, besides his genius ear—when he's in the production process and mastering stuff—is the structure of a song. We were not inexperienced, but we were raw. We knew we wanted to write music, and we knew that we could write music, but we didn't exactly know how to make it fit each others' instruments, to fit exactly like a puzzle."

So far, it seems, the pieces are fitting quite snugly. The TERMS' song "Ransom Groove" was chosen to be the end title song for an upcoming Kevin Spacey-produced film, Mini's First Time, which is premiering in May at the Tribeca Film Festival. LSU chose The TERMS to write an original song for its 2006 national image campaign. "Welcome to the Now" features the LSU marching band and choir. The TERMS recently performed a sold-out show at New York City's The Cutting Room, where they encored with the Rolling Stones' "Sympathy for the Devil" and were joined by Richie Cannata (sax player from Billy Joel's band) and Gerado Velez (percussionist for Jimi Hendrix). "Those things are really gratifying because the music is making it work," Ladanyi said. "The music has to take you there. And it's doing it."

E-MAIL CONNECTIONS

TERMS Group E-mail—November 22, 2006: Brandon Update:

Good Wednesday Morning to you!

Yesterday, Brandon—with his right hand—WROTE HIS COMPLETE NAME!

They are still working on his left side, which is not as responsive as his right side—so far.

One of Brandon's sisters, Angel, took her seven-year-old daughter to see Brandon for the first time since the accident. As her daughter was sitting next to Brandon talking to him, Brandon grabbed her hand and brought it up to his mouth and he kissed her hand. Then he kissed her on the top of her head.

Thank you for all your prayers and support for Brandon, his family, and all our other young men, Clyde, Blake, Ben and Scott.

If you would like to send a note to Brandon, his address is:

Methodist Rehabilitation Center, 1350 East Woodrow Wilson, Jackson, Mississippi, 39216.

And thanks to many of you, I only have sixteen CDs left.

You continue to be in my prayers. May you and your family enjoy a safe & wonderful Thanksgiving!

JACQUES LASSEIGNE

The Viper Room

If you do a "Google" search for "Viper Room" you get 2,330,000 possibilities. One of the websites is "Wikipedia, the free encyclopedia." The information listed on that web site states: *The Viper Room is a nightclub located along the Sunset Strip in West Hollywood, California. It was opened in 1993 and was partly owned by actor Johnny Depp until 2004. The club is well known for having been the site where actor River Phoenix died of a drug overdose on Halloween morning in 1993. Even following Phoenix's death, the club remained a hang-out for Hollywood hottest young actors. Regulars included Jennifer Aniston and Sean Penn. In Oliver Stone's film* The Doors *(1991), the Viper Room was used as a filming location for scenes depicting the London Fog, also of West Hollywood. London Fog was a lesser-known nightclub next to the Whisky a Go Go where The Doors had their first regular gig for four months in early 1966. The Pussycat Dolls performed at The Viper Room from 1995 to 2001.*

Add to that list, The TERMS. They performed at The Viper Room on January 24, 2006. And they performed quite well.

Our Louisiana country boys were back in California for the first time since recording their album, *Small Town Computer Crash*. That crowd had to be different from what the band was used to. It was, but the reaction was the same—they loved the band. Cassie Smyth wrote about this experience in the May 2006 edition of *SB Magazine*. She titled her article, "Terms of Endearment—Band Gets Ready for Spotlight." She interviewed Scott for this article: ***SB Magazine:*** *You've been touring a lot. Where is that taking you?* ***Scott:*** *We went to Los Angeles in January and New York last September, and we're going back in June. We go to school during the first part of the week and record or play on the weekends.* ***SB Magazine:*** *What's been your favorite place to play? Anything stand out?* ***Scott:*** *Without being cheesy, Shreveport is one of my favorite places to play. We played at the Revel and opened for Kenny Wayne Shepherd. The kids that came out were really into it, singing the words back to us. There's no greater feeling than that. There were 200 kids singing with us. I'm excited when we go to Shreveport, because we know we're going to have a great show.*

E-MAIL CONNECTIONS

Outside of Louisiana, we played The Viper Room in Los Angeles. That was really insane because...everybody liked us. Which was surprising. Everyone in LA is kind of... (Scott hesitates and laughs here in a classic resistance to saying anything rude). They're kind of pretentious. When we got there, the manager said: "Don't be mad if people just cross their arms and look at you funny." We started playing, and we only had about five people there that were friends of ours that came to support us. But the place was full, and everyone was nodding their heads or rocking out. I knew we were winning them over when this 300-pound bouncer with long hair and a heavy-metal T-shirt walked away from the door to listen. He told us, "Thank God for you guys. Everyone around here is just heavy metal or Guns N' Roses wanna-be bands." But at Centenary and the high schools here, the kids have really connected to our sound. When we play Shreveport, we feel like rock stars. And in reality, we aren't.

Well, for not being "rock stars" they were making significant progress in that direction.

Brandon absolutely loved this new experience. He would call his mother during their tours and yell into his cell phone, "Mom, you will not believe where I'm standing right now. I'm at The Viper Room!" or "I'm at The Cutting Room in New York City!" or "I'm at an Air Force Base in Washington, D.C." He was thoroughly enjoying this experience.

As his mother stated, "He was just soaking in every moment. It was truly the opportunity of a lifetime." He just loved to play music and was having a grand time. One of the T-shirts he wore on stage expressed his sentiment. On the front of that shirt were these words: "No Job, No Money, No Car, But I'm in a Band!"

TERMS Group E-mail—November 30, 2006: Brandon Update:

Good Thursday Morning to my Dear Friends & Family! Sure hope you had an enjoyable Thanksgiving Holiday with your family.

Last Wednesday (Thanksgiving Eve) Brandon began TALKING! Sure, it is a whisper, but he IS talking! After therapy, his cousin Blake called. The phone was put to Brandon's ear. Blake asked him: "What are you doing?"

Brandon responded with this word: "Nothing." Later when his girlfriend called and asked him what he was doing, Brandon responded with, "Hanging out." What a GREAT THANKSGIVING! Brandon continues to talk in a whisper, and most of the time, the family can't make out what he is trying to say, but maybe that will change as he gets stronger. And he is getting stronger day by day.

Brandon's trach tube was taken out last week, and a "button" was put in its place. The button just keeps the area open in case Brandon does not respond well to the trach tube being out. So far he has responded well to the trach tube being out. Tomorrow Brandon will have a swallowing test performed. If he can properly swallow, then he can start eating pureed foods and drinking liquids. That will be a nice change for him.

His memory seems to be just fine. So far, everything the family and the technicians have asked him about he remembers! When he fully begins talking then the complete extent of his memory can be known, but so far, so good!

While his right side is responding well, his left side is still lagging behind. His mother could have sworn she saw his left eye open slightly. Maybe it was just a reflex, or maybe it is the beginning of his left side waking up. Angela said: "I am going to pray for the latter!" One thing is for sure—Brandon is working very hard to come back.

Thank you for your support (the CDs have all been purchased) and for your continuous prayers for Brandon and his family and for all our young men—Clyde, Blake, Ben, and Scott. Thank you for being there.

Dane's 40th Birthday Celebration

We observe birthdays. Birthdays are a time to celebrate a point reached chronologically or a year to look forward to. Some have special significance in our society. We make a big deal of a baby's first birthday, our teenager daughter's Sweet sixteen birthday, our own eighteenth or twenty-first birthday

E-MAIL CONNECTIONS

(turning the "legal age"), then the "old" birthdays, such as the thirtieth, the fortieth, and the fiftieth. At times we do make quite a ceremony of the blessed event with as many friends and family around as possible.

Dane Andreeff, owner of Maple Jam Records, was turning forty in the spring of 2006. What does a very successful businessman do when that happens? Throw a party, of course. And what a gala it was. March 11, 2006, was the date. Baton Rouge Country Club was the place. Hundreds of friends and family were in attendance to join in the celebration of Dane's big 40th-birthday bash. There was just about any kind of food there, including Alaskan King Crab. And when you have a Grammy-Award-Winning producer as president of your own record label who has worked with some of the giants in the recording industry, you have a few options concerning a surprise special guest at your birthday party. Sure, some guys have black balloons and gag gifts and maybe a bikini-clad girl popping out of an oversized cake, but very few have a Rock & Roll Hall of Fame artist perform at their 40th-birthday party celebration, and those few included Dane Andreeff.

From this Rock & Roll Hall of Fame artist's website are these comments: *In 2004 this artist was inducted into the Rock and Roll Hall of Fame. He also received in 2004 an honorary Doctorate of Music from Occidental College in Los Angeles, for a remarkable musical career that has successfully combined an intensely personal artistry with a broader vision of social justice....In 1977, his* The Pretender *album was a breakthrough album—his first to chart in the Billboard Top 10, peaking at # 5. On the heels of that success came what stands as his top-selling album, 1977's seven-times platinum, life-on-the-road concept opus,* Running on Empty.

Of course, I'm referring to Jackson Browne.

Before the big crowds that evening, there was a small gathering for dinner. In attendance were Dane Andreeff, birthday celebrant and record label owner, Greg Ladanyi, president of the record label and producer, Starr Andreeff, vice-president of the record label, The TERMS (Ben, Clyde, Blake, Brandon & Scott), Wiley Chris Whitesides, sound engineer, Walter Schmidt, road and booking manager, Jackson Browne's sound crew, and Jackson Browne. It was quite an intimate gathering with a famous artist who has had outstanding success in the music industry. Who would have thunk it—our young men, country boys from rural America, having this type of experience—and in Baton Rouge, Louisiana!

JACQUES LASSEIGNE

Jackson Browne performed five songs for the crowd that evening. The selections were, "These Days," "Doctor My Eyes," "The Pretender," "Running on Empty," and "Stay." He actually asked Ben, The TERMS lead singer, to join him on stage for the song "These Days." Then he was ready to perform the song "Doctor My Eyes." He asked the audience, "Is there a drummer out there?" Scott was quite nervous, but he walked up on stage to accompany this legend in the music industry in a very famous song—and one where they had not rehearsed at all. The song began and Jackson Browne quickly stopped, since as Scott put it, "I messed up the song." He went to Scott to talk about what he wanted Scott to do. Scott knew what Jackson Browne wanted him to do now, although he was not that experienced on that particular type of beat, and he did not know the song (that song was a little before his time), but he proceeded. It worked out quite nicely, and Jackson Browne thanked him for his assistance with that song when he was finished. Who knew a couple of years before when the band was practicing their new songs in a very small, rented room that this amazing opportunity would present itself. Scott simply stated, "That experience was indescribable." What an education they were receiving outside the classroom, and what wonderful memories they were making.

TERMS Group E-mail—December 4, 2006: Brandon Update:

Happy Cool Monday Morning to you! Sure hope you are enjoying this December weather—Cool & Sunny!

Last Wednesday Brandon's button (that covers his trachea-tube hole) was taken out. He is no longer on any type of breathing assistance. There is a small hole in his neck where the button was. The doctor stated that it will close up on its own in a day or two.

Brandon is doing better with his "loud talking." He is working hard to use his vocal cords and not to whisper. He is getting better in that category.

Brandon did take his swallow test on Tuesday. He did not pass that test, so the speech therapist will have to work closely with him to build up his throat muscles so he can have a safe swallow when he begins eating food.

As mentioned earlier, Brandon's left side has not progressed as much as his right side—so far. Brandon has to use his right arm to physically move his left arm. This past week he said: "I can't play like this." He was, of course, referring to being able to play the bass guitar. That seems to have motivated him. Since then it seems that he is "willing" his left side to move. A couple of days after he made the statement, "I can't play like this," he was able to force his left hand to move a bit. It was a lateral-type motion. Then later he made his left leg move. Limited movement, but definite movement! His mother had to do a double take—she could not believe her eyes. She was so excited.

Brandon is moving into the restless and agitated phase of his recovery. He can barely sleep because he is always moving some part of his body. That also means that Brandon's mother is not getting much sleep either.

Speaking of neurologists, the one that is performing Brandon's testing is Dr. Art Leis. Mark Adams, CEO of Methodist Rehabilitation Center in Jackson, Mississippi, elaborated on this doctor. "Dr. Leis and his research team discovered that the West Nile virus attacks the spinal cord and caused paralysis and poliomyelitis." You never know when this type information will come in handy—this might come up in a trivia quiz that I'll give you later.

For those of you in the Monroe area, Blake, The TERMS' percussionist, is organizing a Fund-Raiser for Brandon's medical account. It will be held on Thursday, December 14th at Sixth Street Bar and Grill in Monroe. Yes, that is the place the band was scheduled to perform that fateful night of September 30th. Several bands and some guest singers, including Alan West Brockman and Ben Labat (lead singer of The TERMS) will perform. Ben has written some great new songs—they are really good. Tickets will be $10 each.

Speaking of Blake, he has gone from the hard, plastic neck brace to a softer neck brace—which he does NOT like! He should be returning to the doctor soon for a follow-up visit to check on how he is healing. He has experienced pain and numbness in his arm/hand.

Thanks for all your prayers for Brandon, his family, and for all the young men, Clyde, Blake, Ben & Scott. I really appreciate you.

Centenary College—Gold Dome Performance

Paying your dues. In many professions people must pay their dues before becoming a success. In music it is no different. Paying your dues in the music business for a band consists of daily practice sessions, working MySpace.com, and your band's main website, talking with fans on-line and building that fan base, driving miles and miles on the road from gig to gig, and performing in all kinds of venues. Up to this point, The TERMS had played in bars and restaurants and on riverfronts. They had performed in front of four people, and they had performed in front of a couple of thousand people. Their gig on April 21, 2006, was the kind where they would again perform in front of a couple of thousand people—more than 2,400 people.

The location was on the Centenary College campus—a small liberal arts college in Shreveport, Louisiana, with a student body that numbers just over 1,000. The place was the Centenary College Gold Dome, their basketball arena. Its unique design actually came from Scott's grandfather, Orvis Sigler. The billing was the warm-up act for Better Than Ezra, a former Louisiana band with a pretty decent fan base in Northwest Louisiana. The acoustics in this basketball arena were surprisingly good. The importance of this performance was highlighted with the presence of their producer, Greg Ladanyi. He worked with their sound engineer, Wiley Chris Whitesides, that evening to make sure everything was ready to go on the technical end for that important performance. One reason this concert was of particular significance—their album had been tweaked and was to be re-released nationwide in a few days (April 25, 2006). This event was to help kick off that new release.

My wife and I had seen the band perform live probably twelve times prior to that show. This was absolutely their best performance that we had witnessed. Everyone had their "A" game on that evening. It was a phenomenal performance to experience. It was an hour of the best music that many in the Centenary Gold Dome had witnessed in a long time—many people expressed that very sentiment to me after the show. The old songs worked; the new songs worked; the great presentation worked. It was great getting to see these young men, who had worked so hard and put in so much time, getting a chance to perform on a real stage in front of 2,400 fans without the confines of a smoke-filled bar and a very small stage. They showed just why the accolades coming their way were more than justified.

In The TIMES (Shreveport, Louisiana, newspaper) on August 19, 2007, an article written by Ashley Northington was titled "Centenary is one of 25 Hottest Schools in America." In that article she explains: *The* Kaplan *and* Newsweek *guide list Centenary College on their list of "Hottest Liberal Arts Schools You've Never Heard Of." The guide names America's 25 hottest schools, which all offer top academic programs but are generating extra buzz by trend-setting initiatives or other recent events.*

They must have taken into account the fabulous performance by The TERMS at this small liberal arts college!

Earlier that spring, The TERMS opened for another big-name band, Blues Traveler, at the Varsity Theatre in Baton Rouge. When Scott was just starting out in the band he commented to me on one of my many trips to Baton Rouge, "If we play at the Varsity Theatre I know we will have made it." They did play at the Varsity Theatre a couple of times. One time as the opening act for Blues Traveler. What an opportunity and what a validation to The TERMS' successful progression in the music world. As noted in The *TIMES Preview Magazine* of August 17, 2007: *With eight studio albums, three live albums, a Grammy Award and more than 10 million albums sold worldwide, Blues Traveler is one of the most acclaimed jam bands of its time.*

And on February 23, 2006, The TERMS opened for them. The crowd loved The TERMS' performance that evening. Yes, Dorothy, we're not in Kansas anymore.

TERMS Group E-mail—December 7, 2006: Brandon Update:

Good Morning Friends! Bundle up....it is 20 COLD Degrees this morning in Shreveport! The fireplace was going strong last night!

What will Brandon remember when he fully recovers? People have asked that question. At this time, Brandon can remember things from his past, but it is very hard for him to remember anything that is happening now. His doctors state that he may not even remember his stay in the rehabilitation hospital when he does eventually get better. Even though he is responding and answering questions correctly now, he still may not understand what has happened to him and why he is in that hospital bed and why he is in this condition. That is very hard for Brandon's mother to watch. And she has been at his side since the accident. The rest of his family is able to make it over once or twice a week to the Jackson, Mississippi, facility to be with them.

Another milestone occurred this week. We are so proud of Brandon for working so hard to get stronger every day. On Wednesday, he actually took his FIRST STEPS! Yes, as in WALKING! Now, he had the aid of two therapists and a walking table, but he did walk. He can barely make a step with his left leg, but he is trying. After physical therapy, Brandon is literally exhausted. Brandon has lost thirty pounds since the accident, unfortunately, mostly muscle. But this week he gained back five pounds, so he is on the mend.

He is finally moving out of the extremely agitated state; therefore, he is getting a bit more rest. Before he made it to that state, he, like other similar patients, get fixated on something. In his case he wanted to get OUT OF HIS CERVICAL COLLAR that was around his neck! The staff and Angela had to watch him closely; in fact, they actually had to tape it down on him. Earlier this week, Brandon's mother walked into the bathroom for maybe three seconds. When she came out of the bathroom he had taken off his neck collar and had thrown it at the foot of the bed. Needless to say, the collar is back on him and TAPED DOWN!

He still mostly talks when talked to. It seems that when he wants to talk it is three or four in the MORNING! Maybe he is thinking that he is finishing up a gig, and it is time to relax and talk. Finally last Wednesday night he actually slept from 10 P.M. until 3:45 A.M. His mother said: "It was great! His sleep schedule is almost like having an infant again."

Brandon's mother said this week: "I just continue to be amazed at the goodness of people. I only pray that I can, at some point in my life, give back to others what has been given to our family."

Thank you for your continued prayers for Brandon and his family and for Clyde, Blake, Ben & Scott. You are appreciated more than you can ever know.

Opening Act for Pat Green

The TERMS performed at Centenary College on April 21, 2006. They also performed the previous two nights. They were the opening act for Pat Green on those two nights. Pat Green is a three-time Grammy-nominee. From his website: *Pat Green wins ABOUT.com's Best Male Artist Award. July 24, 2007—Once again, Pat Green's fans prove they are the most loyal fans in country music. The Dancehall (Pat Green's fan club) recently had a hand in helping Pat Green win the award for "Best Male Artist" on About.com. The 5th annual contest began a few weeks ago and included finalists such as Brad Paisley, Joe Nichole, and Trace Adkins. Green ended up with an impressive 45% of the total votes.*

On April 19, 2006, The TERMS opened for him at Rabb's Steakhouse in Ruston, Louisiana, and on April 20, 2006, they opened for him at the House of Blues in New Orleans, Louisiana. Pat Green's music is in the category of country, although some would label it country-rock. Whatever the case may be, Pat Green's fans really liked The TERMS. Their reception at the House of Blues in New Orleans was outstanding. After their performance that evening, The TERMS sold a significant number of CDs to Pat Green's fans. Both my children went through phases in their young life where they liked country music. In fact, my daughter still does. Being a supportive dad, I listened to their music when we were driving in the car together. I commented to Christen and Scott that some of the new country music they were listening to had very similar beats to some of the rock music I listened to in high school. No wonder Pat Green's fans liked The TERMS' music. That great, enthusiastic reception the band received at the House of Blues on April 20th seemed to propel them to a new level during their superb Centenary Gold Dome performance the following night.

After that Centenary performance Scott took Anne and me back stage with his special band-member pass to the room where the band members were hanging out. They were critiquing their performance. They were discussing their good points and where they could have improved. It was very interesting to be a part of that environment and witness this scene first-hand. There were the band members, the sound engineer, the booking manager, and a Grammy-Award winning producer in their special room, surrounded by finger food and beverages. Later they were to spend the night in luxurious rooms at a local casino. No Motel 6 this evening. Now this was the way to perform and to tour. This would be easy to adjust to. Yes, a taste of the good life.

TERMS Group E-mail—December 10, 2006: Brandon Update:

Good Evening Dear Family & Friends,

Hope you had a good weekend break. Brandon continues to work hard to improve. His mother went to check on him at physical therapy last Thursday and did not see him. The nurse said, "He is walking in the hall." Angela then proceeded into the hallway where she saw Brandon walking up and down the hall—with assistance, of course—but walking with determination. As Angela put it, "This time I just could not hold back the tears. I stood there and cried like a baby. He is working so hard—I am just so proud of him."

Later that same day, at another physical therapy session, Brandon was working BOTH arms on a type of bicycle-machine designed to work with the arms. Again the tears flowed from Angela.

When therapy was finished for that day and they were back in his room, Angela was talking with Brandon and asked him who he missed the most. If he could see anyone who would it be? He responded, "My teacher." Angela asked him, "Which teacher?" Brandon responded, "That scientific one." Angela then asked, "Do you mean Ms. Dunn?" He said, "Yes." Angela thinks he had a crush on her back in his school days!

On Friday Angela went to physical therapy and saw Brandon sitting upright WITHOUT any assistance. It was the first time he sat up without someone holding him up from behind.

His next swallow test is Tuesday. Brandon loves speech therapy because he gets pudding and/or applesauce there. When he goes there he just STARES at that food. He is SOOOO READY to begin eating and drinking again. He begs his mother for some water—which she cannot give him yet. But there are signs that he is getting better. Last week after begging for water and continuously getting "no" for an answer, he then asked, "How about a beer?"

As a reminder, anyone in the Monroe area can attend the Fund-Raiser for Brandon at the Sixth Street Bar in Monroe. Cover charge is $10, with all proceeds going towards Brandon's medical account. Ben Labat, lead singer for The TERMS, will be one of the performers. Scott will be there also. He will have finished his finals the day before. Yes, Scott and Ben will graduate from LSU in a week and a half from the College of Business.

Thank you so much for your prayers for Brandon, his family, and all our young men, Clyde, Blake, Ben, & Scott. It is needed and very much appreciated.

The Top 19 Independent Albums of 2005

Performance after performance, practice after practice, long drives on the highway to the next gig, meeting with fans, conference calls with the record label, interviews with media outlets and various websites—it was an exhausting schedule. You do all this and sometimes wonder if anyone is paying attention. Well, yes, people were paying attention. I tried to be as objective as I could during all this process, but I thought their music was exceptional. Many music critics agreed with my evaluation. Their reviews began to come in and it was mostly good, really good.

January 17, 2006, from *HoustonMusicReview.com*, Houston's Best Music Scene Source, by Samuel Barker: *Coming to Terms with the New Year... With the new year comes a lot of new expectations. So far this year, we have a couple shows lined up to cover, a LOT of CD reviews ready to post, and all sorts of new ideas. Until we get to the new, relive one last moment from last year and check out our review of The TERMS, who played the Continental Club's Christmas Party. 12-22-05—The TERMS—Continental Club—Houston, Texas....This year, the Continental Club had a new up-and-coming band from Baton Rouge, La., help spread the holiday cheer with a set of originals and covers to fill the already-packed club with music. A 5-piece band made up of LSU students, The TERMS brought a surprisingly tight and mature sounding set to the audience. While the band has been around a while and worked their way up from acoustic trio to 5-piece rock band, their young age made the professionalism and overall strong song structures come together impressively.*

Vocalist/guitarist Ben Labat has the face to melt the ladies' hearts and a voice to bring their boyfriends into the fold. Everything flowed right for the band. Lead guitarist Clyde Hargrove, who seems to be the most reserved on the stage, tore through impressive solos that actually got a few people to break out of their party mode and pay attention.

It will be interesting to watch this band grow and move up the ladder to venues like the Engine Room or maybe even the Verizon Wireless Theater. The band definitely has the potential to do some great things. You can't help but see it after hearing but a few songs, even through the smoke-filled, tightly-packed Christmas party at the Continental Club.

Check the band out online at http://www.thetermsmusic.com and check for dates in your area. This band is going national. Be one of the select few who can say they were at the first show they played in your area. Hope all enjoyed the holidays. If you're looking for good new music, this is a great place to start.

A few days later, a stunning review appeared on the website *ink.19.com*. The review was dated January 20, 2006. The review was titled, *"THE TOP 19 INDEPENDENT ALBUMS OF 2005"* by Andrew Ellis. From this review: *On the face of it, 2005 was a bad year for the music industry: labels like Sanctuary reported record losses and shed thousands of staff, high profile lawsuits were launched against peer-to-peer traders in attempt to halt the seemingly unstoppable rise in illegal music downloads, and rosters were cut across the board with more and more bands competing for fewer and fewer recording contracts.*

Add to that the depressing homogeneity of radio play lists and music charts and the picture looks incredibly gloomy. However, there is more

E-MAIL CONNECTIONS

to the music industry than the bands you may see on MTV or hear on Clear Channel radio stations. 2005 was a great year for independent artists, with the emergence of new technology giving bands the chance to make records cheaply and promote themselves effectively on online showcases such as MySpace as well as their own web sites.

As a writer for Ink 19, I am inundated with promo albums for indie bands, artists, and singer songwriters and this year the quality level has been amazing. Here's my pick of what I consider to be the best independently released albums of 2005...

 # 13. The TERMS—Small Town Computer Crash

Being a college student is hard enough as it is; recording an album of superb guitar pop with an acclaimed producer at the same time is even more difficult, but it's something The TERMS achieved with top marks on Small Town Computer Crash. *Greg Ladanyi saw enough in the Baton Rouge band to sign them to his fledgling Maple Jam label and that promise has been realized on songs like "Neutron Bomb," the stunning "Outlier," and the hypnotic pop of "There She Was," which really showcase Ben Labat's captivating voice. 2006 could see The TERMS graduate to the big time.*

Of the thousands of CDs that were produced in 2005 and of the hundreds of CDs that Andrew Ellis reviewed that year, he chose The TERMS' *Small Town Computer Crash* to be in his Top 19 Independent Albums of 2005. What an honor, what a step up, what acknowledgment of the caliber music The TERMS were putting out. To make that list was remarkable, and to make number thirteen was even better. Yes, lucky number thirteen. What a stamp of approval. What a vote of confidence. What an accomplishment. What a boost to their music career.

TERMS Group E-mail—December 17, 2006: Brandon Update:

Dear Friends & Family,

Hope this note finds you and your family well.

Blake finally got his neck brace OFF yesterday! He is one happy person!

Anne and Scott were able to travel to Jackson, Mississippi, yesterday (Saturday) and had a good visit with Brandon. More on that visit later.

Brandon failed his latest swallow test; therefore, an Ear, Nose & Throat Specialist came in to check his vocal cords and discovered that they are just fine, but he does have scar tissue built up around his trachea-tube site. Brandon will probably need surgery to remove that scar tissue. It is impairing his breathing somewhat and makes it difficult for him to cough. The lack of swallowing is due to his brain injury. That should come around with time.

Brandon is continuing to work hard and is walking better EACH DAY. In fact, he started on Friday with a rolling walker. His right side is doing fantastic. His left side is coming along. In fact, HE CAN SEE OUT OF HIS LEFT EYE, but his eye lid is not open yet. Brandon opened his eyelid with his right hand to show Scott. Brandon told Scott, "I can see out of this eye; I just can't operate this eyelid yet."

As I mentioned before, doctors state that Brandon may not remember his time in rehab. Speaking of memory, as an example, Brandon does not remember being in a band called The TERMS, but when his mother plays The TERMS' CD, he can sing all the words to the songs! On Saturday Scott asked Brandon to sing his rap song that he has worked on since high school. He hesitated, but when Scott began singing it, Brandon immediately joined in and sang all the words! He has a high-pitched voice at this time, but as his vocal cords receive more exercise, his voice will get more volume to it, and he'll sound like the old Brandon.

When they asked Brandon what age he will turn on his next birthday, he correctly answered twenty-three! That was a breakthrough. His mother was pleasantly surprised.

He is still on a feeding tube for nourishment, so Anne asked him, "If you could eat at any place, where would you go, Brandon?" He

E-MAIL CONNECTIONS

IMMEDIATELY replied: "CANES!" ....as in Raising Canes, the place with those delicious chicken fingers. Scott has commented before, "You can gain two pounds just by walking into that place! But the food sure is good!" And Brandon can afford to put on a few pounds, since he has lost thirty pounds since the accident.

It looks like Brandon will be able to come home for a few days at Christmas! Then he will return to Jackson, Mississippi. And barring any complications he will be discharged around December 29th! His rehab, will, of course, not be finished. He will continue his rehabilitation in Shreveport.

Once again, Angela, Brandon's mother, stated that this will be their best Christmas ever. She is forever grateful to Gary Brooks, who was first on the scene of the accident to begin the life-saving CPR on Brandon, along with the assistance of Dr. Charles Joyce and Ben Labat. And grateful for the SICU doctors and nurses at St. Francis Hospital in Monroe—they kept Brandon alive. As she puts it, "The out-pouring of thoughtfulness and generosity of family and friends and of people we don't even know has been overwhelming. I hope and pray that your Christmas will be as happy as ours will be. We are so grateful."

Anne wanted to take a picture of Brandon and Scott so she asked Brandon, "Would it be okay if I take your picture with Scott?" He almost jumped out of bed! I think that was a "yes." Hopefully attached to this e-mail is a picture of Brandon and Scott. It is amazing how far he has come in a short amount of time, considering the severity of his injuries.

Thank you all so much for your support and your prayers. It has done wonders......and has produced miracles. MERRY CHRISTMAS!

More Music Reviews—Early 2006

More good reviews of the band were coming in. From www.SkopeMagazine.com, dated February 3, 2006: *Southern rockers, The TERMS, are enjoying early success with their debut album,* Small Town Computer Crash, *especially from their home state of Louisiana. With their album set for release, the band was asked to write an original song for the 2006 Mardi Gras national television commercial to help rebuild New Orleans. The song, "Bounce Back," was written by the band over the holidays and can be heard when the commercials begin airing in the next few weeks.*

The TERMS were also recently asked to write the theme song for the new Louisiana State University television commercial campaign, also set to air in early '06. Honored, the band quickly wrote the original tune, "Evo Devo Welcome to the Now," a high-spirited rock anthem.

In addition, two of the songs from the band's debut album, Ransom Groove, *and* Outlier, *have been chosen to appear in the upcoming indie film,* Mini's First Time, *also set for release in early 2006. The movie boasts Kevin Spacey as one of the producers as well as a stellar cast including Alec Baldwin, Jeff Goldblum, Carrie Ann Moss (*Matrix*), Nikki Reed (*Thirteen*) and Luke Wilson.*

Small Town Computer Crash *features 12 rockin' tracks, from the enticing opening guitar riffs of first single, "Neutron Bomb," to the intricate guitar work and soothing vocals of "Ugly."*

The band's music does everything...it cannot be ignored, says The Shreveport Times, while The Advocate declares: *All you need is ears to notice that The TERMS...are the Baton Rouge band most likely to succeed. With tour success and their songs heading to both television and the big screen, The TERMS are also catching momentum through the airways with first single, "Neutron Bomb." Some of the stations currently playing the single are Nashville's "WBUZ," Gainesville, FL, "WHHZ," Wichita, KS, "KAHR," and Baton Rouge, La., "KNXX."*

About a week later, on February 15, 2006, came this review by Aaron Pompey from the web site Mish Mash Magazine (www.mishmashmagazine.com). This was a review of their performance and work at Rehearsals.com in California: *Louisiana natives The TERMS delivered their signature gritty, affective southern brand of rock to a small, private audience in Burbank on Thursday, January 26, 2006—showcasing a cutting-edge sound that has put The TERMS on more than a few Best of 2005 lists and has paved the way for the band to find an even larger audience in the months to come. Sponsored by Rehearsals.com, a new website that showcases the creative energy and evolution of the songwriting process, The TERMS played several songs from their recent release* Small Town Computer Crash, *alongside some new songs the band is polishing up for another new release.*

'The band was fresh...rambunctious,' says their producer, Greg Ladanyi. 'But the first thing I listen to is melody and songs, and they clearly have that.' Thinking The TERMS have something too special to warrant a quick deal with an existing label, Dane Andreef and Ladanyi decided that this was a perfect opportunity to start their own record label and bring in The TERMS as their first signed artists.

Small Town Computer Crash *was released in April of 2005 and is being re-released to coincide with their label's new joint deal with ICON MES, and a tour planned through June of 2006. Although Andreef and Ladanyi have plans to begin bringing other bands into the Maple Jam fold, their present focus is on The TERMS, whose success is nearly guaranteed by a strong presence on the indie radar (INK 19 puts* Small Town Computer Crash *at # 13 in its top 19 indie albums of 2005) and on the LSU campus, where their track "Welcome to the Now" is part of the school's new major marketing campaign.*

Prior to the show, the guys marched through an exhausting day of rehearsals and interviews as Maple Jam's newest and first discovery. But they'll have more than a few more exhausting days ahead as they tirelessly move ahead with the music, the new label, and a schedule that will have its own set of challenges...and expectations.

During their set, the guys made a strong effort to live up to those expectations. The band followed up their catchy first number "Ugly" with the band's war metaphor "Gulf of Tonkin." Songs that followed included "Welcome to the Now," the punk-influenced "Casablanca," their single "Neutron Bomb," and "Ransom Groove"—a song inspired by serial killer Derrick Todd Lee, who stalked LSU students back in 2002. "Groove" also happens to contain one of Greg Chiartano's favorite bass lines.

Labat started off the band's second set with a solo acoustic version of "What's Done is Done" and "Sea and Sky" before the band rejoined him for the final few songs, including the genre-mixing "Big City Concrete Wildflowers," "Love of Lies," and the existential "Langlonglen."

Watch for The TERMS to become more conspicuous once their Rehearsals.com appearance shows up online and the re-release of Small Town Computer Crash gets them more airplay. The TERMS' upcoming tour dates include stops in Florida, Louisiana, Tennessee, Texas, and Kansas.

After reading some of these reviews, one realized that people in the music business thought this band was special. The friends and family of the band members thought so, but these music critics were not relatives! Things were happening—good things. Momentum was starting to build. It was a time of frantic activity. And it was a time of being noticed.

TERMS Group E-mail—December 31, 2006: Brandon Update:

HAPPY NEW YEAR'S EVE! Easy on the Egg Nog!

Just before Christmas, Brandon went into another phase of recovery. He became quite monotone, and his expressions were very flat, almost robot-like. His memory is kind of sporadic. When Angela, his mother, told Brandon they were going home for a short Christmas visit she also asked him what street they lived on. He responded, "Laurie Lane." They did live on that street, but back when Brandon was in middle school. When Angela reminded Brandon they actually lived on Ockley Drive he seemed to remember.

Brandon did make it home for a few days at Christmas time. They pulled up to their home and this is what greeted Brandon: friends and family at the top of the stairs wearing T-shirts that read, "I Love Brandon;" a large banner stating, "WELCOME HOME, BRANDON!" was hung from the top of their front porch; and a first-class wheelchair ramp, that had been expertly constructed by the men's group from Summer Grove

Methodist Church. Angela and Jay were ecstatic that Brandon actually became emotional at that moment. Maybe he was coming out of that "monotone state."

Scott, Anne, and I made it over for a short visit on the evening before Christmas Eve. By the time we made it there, Brandon had had a full day of visiting. He was in his bed resting. One person who visited him that day was Ms. Dunn, the "scientific teacher" whom Brandon must have had a crush on back in middle school. She came over and brought Brandon a lot of Christmas and get-well cards from many of her fellow teachers. He told her, "You are so beautiful." She responded, "Well, thank you. You are so sweet." That was a cute moment.

They returned to Jackson, Mississippi, to the rehab center around 4 P.M. Christmas Day. The plan was to spend four more days there, then return home to Shreveport on December 29th to begin rehab here. As you know, life is what happens to you while you are making plans. Thirty minutes after arriving back in Jackson, Brandon began coughing and having a difficult time breathing. "Respiratory" was called, and they put him on oxygen that evening. The next day an Ear, Nose and Throat doctor from the University Hospital checked him out and decided to have an emergency trachea tube inserted. He went into surgery. The SICU at the University Hospital was real strict with their visiting hours. (The Monroe hospital allowed Angela and the family much more leeway). They could only see Brandon for fifteen minutes four times a day. Unlike Brandon's stay in the SICU in Monroe, he was much more alert and, hence, frightened about what was going on. Since he could not see his family much, he thought they had abandoned him. Finally on Thursday, they allowed Angela to stay with Brandon. She stayed with him until Friday morning.

The opening in Brandon's throat is much larger than the normal trachea-tube opening because the surgeon putting in the trachea-tube tried to remove some of the scar tissue left by the old operation. The incision is quite large and inflamed. It is also quite painful. The ENT doctors tried to see the scar tissue in his throat to determine if they could go ahead and try to remove some of it, but it was way too inflamed. The doctors recommend that the trachea tube not be removed until his neck is fixed. Yes, they are almost positive that he will have to have surgery to stabilize the C6 vertebra in his neck.

Catch 22 situation: The Rehabilitation Doctor cannot release him to get his neck fixed until the neurosurgeon accepts him. The neurosurgeon does not want to accept him until he is discharged by the rehabilitation doctor. Angela is hoping that maybe they can get a neurosurgeon in Shreveport to see Brandon so they can come home for good. Calling Dr. Nanda!

Other than the trachea incident, he is doing wonderful. His left arm is moving more and straightening out more. Also, it seems that his memory and his confused state are improving a bit. To help out with his rehab, the record label allowed us to purchase Brandon's guitar. We will present that to him upon his return to Shreveport. Scott brought Brandon's guitar up from Baton Rouge to Shreveport this past weekend.

Thank you so much for your continued good thoughts and prayers for Brandon and his family, and for all the young men—Clyde, Blake, Ben, and Scott and their families. We had a good visit with Ben and his family (his parents, Reggie & Kathy, and brother, Blake) at Ben and Scott's graduation from LSU a couple of weeks ago. They both graduated from the College of Business with a degree in management. In fact, for the ceremony, they sat on the same row with only one person separating them. Quite appropriate. With their intense experiences of the last three years, it was fitting they experienced this closing of one chapter of their life and the commencement of a new one together, from the same vantage point.

Blake was able to finally remove his neck brace, but he can only lift a maximum of twenty-five pounds at this time. Clyde is still on crutches, but is making good progress.

May this New Year bring many blessing to you and your family.

E-MAIL CONNECTIONS

The Best New Band of 2006

There are many "best of" lists and awards given out each year. There are the Country Music Awards, the Golden Globe Awards, the Emmy Awards and the Academy Awards, just to name a few. In 2006 the Academy Awards proclaimed Forest Whitaker as Best Actor for his work in the movie *The Last King of Scotland*, they proclaimed Helen Mirren as Best Actress for her work in the movie *The Queen*, and they proclaimed *The Departed* as the Best Picture. Also, in 2006, "the best new band of 2006" was named. The winner of those accolades was a band called The TERMS.

John Frank, from the website *TheMediaFix.com*, wrote on March 13, 2006: *When you think of the places for a rock band to be born in, New Orleans (Baton Rouge) isn't usually at the top of that list. However, coming from a place with so many different music styles present isn't always a bad thing. The TERMS have found the perfect mix of pure energy rock and the relaxed southern style twangs. Without even a full length release they have already started to make a name for themselves. The TERMS recorded a song for a promo video for LSU and shot some footage for a new web-based video distribution company.*

I was able to catch them playing a couple of their first Los Angeles shows, and was beyond impressed. While the record sounds good and polished, their live show blows it away. Ben Labat (lead vocals and guitar) carries so much of a presence on stage that it seems as if he was born for this life. While the band has replaced a member (Brandon Young replaced Greg Chiartano on bass guitar), it is not apparent. Their show is seamless and carries the crowd energy from the opening note.

The music is surprisingly great. I am definitely not a fan of country, and am not usually moved by southern rock. However, Small Town Computer Crash *blows my mind. The opening chords of "Neutron Bomb" (the first single) completely set up the album by providing an energy that no one can resist the urge to love. The album does slow down a bit after this, which could leave some listeners wanting, feeling drained. However the final version of the disc will have two new songs, one being "Welcome to the Now (Evo Devo)" which is a very energetic, electric college rock anthem (written for LSU); this change will undoubtedly add the missing piece to this album....the album is full of great tracks. It is definitely interesting to hear some of the added percussion on songs such as "Gulf of Tonkin," as it changes the sound without really disrupting anything. The lyrics are very deep, but maintain a fluidness to them that is reminiscent of pop songs. Look out for a DVD from these guys and get a hold of it if you can. They have great personalities that really come through in the behind the scenes footage, and provides a good background on the guys themselves.*

The TERMS is definitely the best new band I have heard in a long time. They manage to bridge the gap between fans of different genres and even different generations. This album is one that a baby boomer parent can enjoy just as much as the twenty-something college kid. The final release of Small Town Computer Crash *is scheduled for mid-April, and will be worth every minute of waiting. The band should be touring over the summer and into fall, which is not to be missed. While there is still a lot of time left in the year, I have no problem picking these guys as the best new band of 2006, with their debut album being one of the top albums overall. Raw energy, fresh sound, fluid melodies...what isn't to love about these southern boys?*

Wow, what a write up! The special characters of this band were being noticed. Yes, they performed very well in person and put on a great live show. Music industry executives have told the band before, after hearing them perform live, "You sound just like the album!" That is difficult to do. Some bands are "studio bands" and cannot put it all together in a live performance. The TERMS could do that and so much more. They had that something special. One thing special was the guitar riffs that came from lead guitarist, Clyde Hargrove. As Blake Oliver once stated in an interview, "Clyde's guitar riffs are one of the main reasons our music is so different." And as Greg Ladanyi once stated, "Clyde has so much music in his head." Fans knew all this and band members' families knew all this, but it was exciting to see that people in the music industry from all over the country were also realizing this. What a year 2006 was shaping up to be.

E-MAIL CONNECTIONS

TERMS Group E-mail—January 7, 2007: Brandon Update:

Hi! Sure hope you enjoyed the Weekend Break!

Brandon has received clearance from Dr. Bernie McHugh, Jr., Brandon's original neurosurgeon, to have surgery on his throat to clear some of the scar tissue. Surgery is scheduled for tomorrow (Monday) at the University Hospital in Jackson, Mississippi. Sometimes this procedure has to be repeated in order to get all of the scar tissue removed. But it is much less invasive than having to totally remove the section of the trachea that contained the scar tissue and suturing it back up. The doctors feel that this is the best way to proceed right now. Angela, Brandon's mother, does not yet know if they will keep the endotracheal tube in or take it out. If things go as planned, Brandon should get to come home later this week.

The "old" Brandon is coming back. Recently, Brandon has begun to make jokes as more and more of his personality, or the "old" Brandon, returns. In a picture he took last week, as the picture was being taken, he stuck his tongue out on one side of his mouth. In the past, in most pictures that were taken of him, Brandon was almost always making some kind of off-the-wall face. That aspect is coming back. That is extremely reassuring to his family.

Another example of Brandon coming back occurred in one of his physical therapy sessions. At times, the therapist that works on him is of the opposite sex and is quite cute. That was the case last week as she was having Brandon balance himself on two bars as he was practicing standing and walking. The cute therapist told Brandon, "Work hard and concentrate because I don't want you to fall." Brandon responded, "Well, I wouldn't mind falling on you." She just laughed. Yes, Brandon seems to be coming back!

And on New Year's Day, Anne called Angela to see how things were coming along. As Angela was on the phone in the hospital room, Brandon asked, "Is that Ms. Lasseigne?" Good cognitive work!

Angela, again, wants to thank everyone for their kind thoughts and prayers. As she recently stated, "It has meant so much to us. I don't know how we could have come this far without all of you."

Thanks again, and have a joyous week.

This Band Is Something New and Great

Good reviews kept coming in during the spring and summer of 2006. From the website sidelink.net on April 20, 2006: *"Spotlight Album Review—The TERMS—Small Town Computer Crash (Maple Jam Records). This band is something new and great... Good music to me is a band that can create music that changes and ranges to something new sounding on each track, and The TERMS have done this."*

From the website StealtheSpotlight.tripod.com: *"Steal the Spotlight—June 11, 2006—The TERMS' Small Town Computer Crash Review. The sound of the music has a way of attracting you to listen more... This album is a killer one... A very well put together album, both lyrically and musically."* His favorite tracks from this album were "Welcome to the Now—Evo Devo," "Neutron Bomb," and "Heartstorm Rescue."

And to get a small glimpse into the Ben Labat's head, this interview by Lance Scott Walker in the February 2006 issue of *002 Magazine*. THE TERMS—*A conversation with lead singer/songwriter Ben Labat.* **Question**: *The TERMS are setting up to be one of the most successful bands ever from Baton Rouge—if not the most. Has that affected the music scene there at all?*

Ben: *We certainly hope we have affected the music scene. There are many talented tune-tribes in Baton Rouge that people don't know about. Some of my favorites are Elsah, The Myrtles, and The Eames Era. If The TERMS can interest the people of Baton Rouge in original music, then it will give other artists and musicians the opportunity to be more creative knowing that someone is listening.*

Question: *Do you feel like too much is made of the fact that you're all LSU students, or is the school a really important part of what you do?*

Ben: *It's where I am STILL going to school, so people can make* *however big or little a fuss about it as they want. LSU is a huge part of all our lives. It is where we met, it is what we see every day, and LSU has somewhat shaped who we are as people and as musicians.*

Question: *You do a lot of regional touring—in finding a way to balance the two, do you just have to tune out one (school or rock 'n' roll) in order to get anything accomplished with the other?*

Ben: *We have to study on the road, and think about writing great songs while in class, that's how we balance. It's not really a balancing act though; most of us like learning, so we kind of just do it.*

Question: *Did (Grammy-winning producer) Greg Ladanyi do anything to permanently shape the way you play as a band?*

Ben: *Of course! We used to all play as fast and as hard as we could just to be heard. Greg let us hear the music in soft, in silence, and in each other's instruments. He made us play more like a band, not like five individuals competing to be heard, and we are very grateful to him for opening our eyes to that.*

Question: *How about as a songwriter?*

Ben: *Greg brings us back down to earth. We like to experiment with ideas and sounds. Greg has helped us decipher which ones are good, and which ones are crap. Lyrically speaking, I get off on these strange tangents sometimes that make no sense to anyone else but me. Mr. Ladanyi tries to get me to write so others can understand also, which is obviously an important part of any song. But like I said, he tries; he doesn't always succeed. I can be a bit of a pill sometimes. I love being strangely vague.*

Question: *And finally, back to the issue of school—how much do you all have left, and will you be ready to do this full-time when that happens?*

Ben: *Clyde and Blake have already graduated, Brandon is taking a semester off, and Scott and I are seniors. What do you mean do this full-time when we're finished school? We're doing it full-time right now! Just kidding! It will be nice to have a little breathing room when we are finished though.*

Life was fast. Each day was full. But at least the school semester would be over with soon, and that would be one less burden for Ben and Scott to have to deal with. As Ben stated—they were basically doing the band full-time. Their time commitment was definitely full-time.

TERMS Group E-mail—January 15, 2007: Brandon Update:

BRRRRRRRRRRRRRRRR! Hope ya'll are keeping warm—this Cold Blast is, well, COLD!

Brandon is back home! He returned home last Wednesday evening.

They stopped at the hospital in Monroe to pick up Brandon's X-rays, etc., in order to provide that to the doctors in Shreveport. His neurosurgeon in Monroe, Dr. Bernie McHugh, Jr., stated that he felt Brandon's neck was stable, and he would not recommend surgery. He also told Brandon that he could take his neck collar off. Brandon IMMEDIATELY liked this doctor a lot! Of course, he did not remember Dr. McHugh, since Brandon was in a coma most of the time he was in the Monroe hospital, but that doctor is on his GOOD LIST, especially when he stated: "Well, if Brandon can swallow his own saliva, then he should be able to eat."

Brandon REALLY, REALLY wants to eat…he told his parents to order two pizzas for him! They will see about that when Brandon visits his new Ear, Nose and Throat Doctor this week, Dr. Cherie-Ann Nathan. Angela has heard many wonderful things about her. It must be tough not being able to eat. Brandon thinks about it all the time. As a business seminar speaker once stated: "Who thinks more about water: A person who just drank a gallon of it or a person in the desert?" We will see how this part of his recovery progresses.

Brandon's first two nights home were eventful. When Brandon's home equipment (suction machine, heat/moist humidifier apparatus, etc.) was delivered, there should have been a respiratory therapist on hand to help with setup, including going over the functions of the equipment, but the therapist was off that day. Sooooo about 1:30 that next morning the equipment stopped working. Phone calls were quickly made. Someone did come out to help them at 2:30 that morning and fixed the equipment. On Brandon's second night home he experienced a horrible coughing episode. It was so bad and scary that his parents called 911. By the time the 911-emergency crew arrived, Brandon's condition had gotten better. Yes, the roller-coaster ride continues.

But they are home and they are around friends and family. Sunday afternoon Scott and a friend went to visit with Brandon. They sat on the front porch and had a great time. Much laughter accompanied this visit. During this visit Scott presented Brandon with the guitar he played while in the band. My wife's family and The TERMS' parents got together to give Brandon's family a very special Christmas gift. Part of that gift included buying back Brandon's guitar from the Maple Jam Record Label. Brandon was VERY EXCITED to receive that guitar yesterday. Angela and Jay thought that visit was just the right therapy for Brandon.

Last Saturday, Dr. Nanda's office called Angela to tell her he had agreed to follow Brandon's case as his neurosurgeon. She was so excited and grateful to hear that. She just cried and cried on the telephone.

Anne and I had a great visit with Brandon and his parents this evening. Brandon looks great. He is moving his legs at will and is being VERY FUNNY! Yes, the old Brandon is coming back.

Thank you so much for your continued support of Brandon, his family and all the guys, Clyde, Blake, Ben, and Scott and their families. It has been tough as you can probably imagine. Some of you knew that the band was scheduled to play live on national television on the Megan Mullally show the week of December 20th. Megan Mullally won an Emmy for her supporting role as the high-pitched friend on the Will and Grace television show. The TERMS had already performed for her show, taping an "evergreen" segment that would be used in case it was needed (for instance, if Megan was sick one day or an earthquake hit, etc.). The band made a great impression with Megan Mullally and the show's producers; therefore, they were invited back for two more shows…the next one being the week of December 20th. Ben and Scott would have had to skip their LSU graduation ceremony, but that would have been fine. That national exposure could have catapulted them to the next level and to the next national television program and onto the national stage in their musical quest. Oh well…

We are looking forward to a good 2007. And thanks to good people like you, it will be a good year. Take care.

BillBoard Magazine

Billboard Magazine is the Bible of the music industry. Most book stores do not carry that magazine since it is designed mainly for people working in the music industry. I remember in high school listening to people on television and radio talk about the latest big record hit on the *Billboard* Charts. Here is a little background on *Billboard* Magazine from the website, Wikipedia, the free encyclopedia: *Billboard magazine was founded in 1894….The magazine began coverage of motion pictures in 1909 and of radio in the 1920s. It was the development of the juke box during the 1930s which led Billboard to begin publishing the music charts for which it ultimately became famous. This also began the process which would lead the magazine to gradually cede coverage of other parts of the entertainment industry to such publications as* Variety *and* The Hollywood Reporter. *From 1961 until 2005, Billboard was devoted entirely to the music industry.*

The TERMS were one of thousands of bands in the music industry, but their band was beginning to make its mark in that world. It is a very tough business. Could The TERMS ever make it into the Bible of the music industry? In the spring of 2006 the answer was an unequivocal yes. They would actually make it into that famous magazine not once but TWICE!

On March 11, 2006, an article concerning the joint venture with Icon and Maple Jam Records appeared in *Billboard* magazine along with a very nice picture of The TERMS! Hard to believe—these young men were in *Billboard* magazine.

Just two months later, The TERMS were listed in *Billboard* again. It was the May 13, 2006, issue. The TERMS had re-released their revised album on April 25, 2006. The record sales for their album that week were outstanding. Those sales propelled them onto the *Billboard* Charts! In the *Heatseekers* category (independent albums) they were ranked 11th nationwide. Imagine, of all the albums released that week they ranked that high. Even more amazing was their ranking in their geographic region of the country. In the "South Central" region The TERMS' album, *Small Town Computer Crash*, was #1 that week! From a group of guys at a college in South Louisiana who got together in a very small, rented room to practice for several months before playing before a live crowd in Baton Rouge, Louisiana, to making "the charts" in *Billboard* magazine. What a journey they were on.

Back to the website, Wikipedia, the free encyclopedia: *To this day, the most successful acts on the Billboard charts are The Beatles, Elvis Presley, Madonna, Michael Jackson, The Rolling Stones, Elton John, Stevie Wonder, Mariah Carey, Janet Jackson, The Supremes, George Strait, The Bee Gees, Bing Crosby and Whitney Houston.* If there had not been a car accident on September 30, 2006, one could ponder if The TERMS could have been added to that list of legends one day.

TERMS Group E-mail—January 29, 2007: Brandon Update:

Winter is back with us, my Dear Friends & Family! BRRRRRRRRRRR!

The roller coaster ride continues: Brandon went for a MRI last Tuesday morning. He returned home for only an hour when Dr. Nathan's office called and instructed them to go immediately to the emergency room at LSU-Medical Center. The MRI showed that Brandon had a subdural hematoma (bleeding) in his head. After hours of waiting, the neurosurgeon said the bleed was small, but they had to perform other tests to determine if it was new or old. A decision would have to be made if surgery would be necessary to drain the blood/fluid. Once they discovered that Dr. Nanda already had some of Brandon's x-rays, the hospital decided to admit Brandon. They also immediately put the neck collar back on him. Bummer.

Around 1 P.M. the next day, Dr. Nanda saw Brandon. During the visit he mentioned to Brandon that he had seen the band perform last year at a benefit in Shreveport—good bedside manner! Back to medicine—

he felt that the hematoma would NOT require surgery at this time. They would monitor it and have another CT-scan in about a month. He did express some concern that surgery was not performed at the time of the accident on Brandon's neck. His neck healed with a slight curve. On the positive side, he did say that the neck was stable and would not require surgery—AND that he did NOT have to wear that neck collar. YEAH! Dr. Nanda was back on Brandon's good list.

Dr. Nanda would order Brandon's rehab and have his office set it up. That is what Brandon's family has desperately wanted since they returned to Shreveport, although Dr. Nanda stated what the Rehab Facility in Jackson, Mississippi, stated: "Time is really the only healer in a brain injury." They both said a person could have 8 hours/day for a full year in rehab, and that might not help. Everyone heals differently. But in Brandon's case, he has made amazing progress in the last few months. His improvement is truly a miracle.

Some of you watched the program (that has played on the local cable TV access channel) called the "DEW DROP INN." It features bands. It showed The TERMS performing in Baton Rouge last year. Jay, Brandon's father, was recently playing that video tape with Brandon watching. Brandon commented, "That guy has a guitar just like mine." His father then asked Brandon to look more closely at the video. Brandon then stated, "That's me." He still does not remember his time in The TERMS, but maybe this will help some.

Some of you are new to the e-mail list so you may not know a lot of the history of the band. One tidbit: Their 1st CD went to a music critic/website that ranks albums/CDs. They literally listen to hundreds of CDs each year. This website ranked *Small Town Computer Crash* by The TERMS in the TOP 19 BEST INDEPENDENT ALBUMS OF 2005. Amazing....I knew they were good—now a lot more people knew that. In fact, they were ranked # 13 on that list.

Speaking of The TERMS, Ben and Blake came in town Saturday afternoon to meet with Scott in order to pay a visit to Brandon Saturday evening. I will get more details from Scott this week, but it was a good visit. One thing Brandon said was, "Tell everyone I love them, and I appreciate everything that everyone has done for me." Anne says, "What a sweet guy."

Thank you for your continued great support and prayers for Brandon, his family, and all the guys (Clyde, Blake, Ben, and Scott). It has made a huge difference.

Have a good week.

Chapter Six
The Travails of Touring

A Taste of Sushi

In the early days of The TERMS, my job with the Louisiana Department of Labor had me traveling to our administrative office in Baton Rouge on a regular basis. I would check Scott's schedule to see if we had time to get together. If so, I would take Scott out to eat. He would determine the place. He did not pick my normal places to eat such as Subway, Burger King, Taco Bell, or McDonald's, but restaurants where you sit down to eat with nice cloth napkins. With no dear mother to prepare and cook his meals, he would eat out frequently. In the process he was becoming quite the food connoisseur. In fact, on one trip he demonstrated his new-found fondness of sushi. Needless to say, I did not try any. As Terry Bradshaw once stated in a commercial, "That is what I call BAIT!" I am of the same opinion.

The band was in Los Angeles in January of 2006. They had performed at the Viper Room, Rehearsals.com and at The Mint. The night of January 27, 2006, the band members ate dinner. Scott ordered his new favorite food, sushi. No problem. The band performed their gig that evening and finished around midnight, which was early for them. They began packing up to drive back to Baton Rouge. This was going to be one of those long trips; no overnight hotel stays, just driving, driving and more driving till you reached the destination of Baton Rouge, Louisiana. In other words, a *long trip* with drivers desperately trying to stay awake, and their buddies riding shotgun asking them every few minutes, "Are you *awake*?" and "You okay?"

Unfortunately for the first part of this trip, Scott was not any help. At thirty minutes past midnight he became sick. The expression, "He was sick as a dog," is not quite strong enough since he was as sick as *two* dogs. He stated later that was one of the worst feelings he has ever had. Food poisoning is no fun. This episode fits that description. It was a long trip back to Baton Rouge. Towards the end of the trip he finally was able to help drive. When it was his turn to drive Scott normally drove the nineteen-foot box van with all their equipment in it. Ninety-nine percent of the time Brandon Young rode shotgun with Scott when he drove the box van. The rest of the band rode in Dane's SUV. They did make it back to Baton Rouge safe and sound—Anne and I did make a couple of phone calls to them during that long trip back. I don't think Scott has eaten sushi since. A person learns two ways—from the experience of others and from their own experience. This was one experience Scott wished he had learned from someone else.

Changing gears from raw fish to another music review. On August 10, 2006, a review by William Michael Smith on the Houston Press website stated: *Looking for something that rocks hard, has plenty of ticks, interesting rhythms, several great voices, and smarty-pants lyrics with hooks galore? Look no further than The TERMS. These Baton Rouge young guns make all the right moves on* Small Town Computer Crash, *which was produced in Los Angeles. The title track is an oh-so 21st century love song with a hook ("She's not ready for your love system") that's sharp as a tuna gaff. Other stellar tracks include the tightly wound, push-me-over-the-edge "Welcome to the Now, Evo Devo" and the explosive "Neutron Bomb," which rocks as hard as anything out there right now. The TERMS' musical oeuvre is such that they should appeal across the invisible lines that divide the indie rockers, the roots rockers, and the MTV crowd: the coiffures, clothes, and poses are perfectly video-ready, the lyrics jibe with the indie vogue, and the ticks and attitude fit the roots rock scene. Quite a heady combination in such a young band. I suspect we'll be seeing a lot of these guys in H-town.*

That music review should help Scott feel better.

TERMS Group E-mail—February 9, 2007: Brandon Update:

Greetings Dear Family & Friends!

Sure hope you are staying WARM….it is BRRRRRRRRRRRRRRRR outside! A bit chilly for a 20K race in the morning, but what the heck.

Anne had a great visit with Brandon and his parents this afternoon (Friday). Brandon is looking great. He is looking more like himself every day. He is back in therapy—physical, occupational and speech therapy—and that is great news. In fact, his therapist gives him HOMEWORK to perform, so there is no rest for the weary! Today, his physical therapist informed Brandon that this is his last day with the wheelchair! He has "graduated" from the wheelchair to the walker! Brandon is walking quite well with his walker. His balance is improving greatly.

Speaking of getting better, Brandon is EATING some. At first, it was pudding, then mashed potatoes then milkshakes. This week it was EGGS and PIZZA and CANE'S CHICKEN FINGERS! His doctor wants him to eat as balanced a diet as he can. Yes, milkshakes, pizza and chicken fingers seem pretty balanced to me. Now, he does not "eat" at every meal, but it is becoming a fairly regular occurrence.

The roller-coaster ride continues: Brandon did have a visit to the emergency room a couple of days ago due to complications with his trachea tube. It was bleeding. The doctors changed his trachea tube. Angela & Jay have to clean out his tube and change it every day (he has a couple of them). It seems that his scar tissue is causing problems. A future surgery may be in the works to address that situation—soon.

A fellow Saturday-morning runner of mine, Teresa H., who ALWAYS has a smile on her face, is a nurse of Dr. Cherie-Ann Nathan, Brandon's ear, nose, and throat doctor. She told me last Saturday morning some comments that Brandon had made the week before. He told her quite excitedly: 'My band members are coming to visit me this weekend!'

Yes, Ben, Blake and Scott were able to visit with Brandon a couple of Saturdays ago (Clyde was not able to make it since he was still out of state). It was a good visit. Ben stated, "Brandon was looking good. He was talking and laughing! Blake, Scott, and I were jogging his memory with some silly stories and tall tales from our exhaustingly awkward, but worth-every-second, 4,000 mile trip this past summer! It hit me like a herd of elephants that we had done some pretty amazing, almost superhuman things together!"

Brandon has been informed that there are no more TERMS, so he told Ben that night: "You better not stop writing and singing, okay?" Ben almost lost it....the tears and emotions were building up, but Ben managed to compose himself. Yes, they did so many things together. They had been through so much. They had bonded so well. They have overcome so many obstacles.

These young men have gone through many episodes and phases since the September 30th accident. Of course, some had pretty significant physical injuries, but they have all gone through mental and emotional anguish. We all have problems, and these young men are no exception. They are working through this ordeal they have experienced. They have all grown up quite a bit since that fateful night.

Yes, some of you know that The TERMS are no more. Now, the rest of you know. I was depressed for a week! They are soooo talented and accomplished so much in their short time together. A California music critic last year wrote his review of the band and named The TERMS *"THE BEST NEW BAND OF 2006!"* They had that something special. But life has many twists and turns, and it moves on. Ben flew to New York last week, Blake just moved to Austin, Texas, Clyde just came in from Atlanta to map out his future plans, Scott is working at Enterprise Car Rental in the Shreveport area, and Brandon is making great progress.

Brandon is able to open his left eyelid some now. It will just take time for the nerve to recover from the damage it sustained, but the improvement is encouraging. And, just to let you know, Brandon's birthday is coming up on March 12th. If you would like to send him a note or a birthday card, send to 133 Ockley Drive, Shreveport, La. 71105.

Thanks to all of you so much for your continued thoughts and prayers for Brandon, his family, and for Clyde, Blake, Ben and Scott. It is greatly appreciated.

JACQUES LASSEIGNE

Highway Adventures

Trips are fun; they are a chance to get away for a while from the regular routine; they are an opportunity to see different places, different sights, different sounds; and they are a chance to explore new worlds. But driving the highways and by-ways of this country also gives one an opportunity to experience that unpleasant occurrence known as "car trouble." In this case, it was "truck trouble," as in a nineteen-foot-box-van kind of trouble.

On one trip the band had already performed at a number of gigs in Texas and was traveling to El Dorado, Arkansas, on a Saturday, to perform at a place called Einstein's. Some of the parents were hoping for a quick visit from their rock-and-roll sons on this trip before they returned back to Baton Rouge. That visit occurred earlier than we expected. At 3 A.M. that Sunday morning Anne and I suddenly realized that a few band members were in our home. It seemed that their truck broke down on the way to El Dorado, Arkansas. They spent a few hours on the side of that road as a large tow truck company was being contacted to tow the nineteen-foot-box-truck to Shreveport. While waiting on the side of the road, they were joined by our fine highway patrolmen. A nice conversation ensued. One of the officers even agreed to put one of the band members in handcuffs in order for Wiley Chris Whitesides to take pictures for future use. They figured if they could not perform on stage that night at least they could make it interesting and memorable. Finally the wrecker arrived and towed the box van, with all of the band's equipment in it, to the street on the side of my house. It was a good location for the wrecker to drop off. It was easily accessible to the next wrecker to hook up and haul the box van back down to Baton Rouge. The problem was diagnosed—transmission.

During the summer of 2006, the band embarked on a 4,000 mile tour that took them up and down the East Coast. That tour included many miles in between performances. They drove in heavy city traffic, on deserted highways, and on many miles of Interstate highways during those six long weeks. A lot was demanded of them that summer, and a lot was demanded of their nineteen-foot box van. The van did a magnificent job. Towards the end of that six-week tour they were more than ready to get home, but, again, life is what happens to you as you make plans. They planned to be back in Baton Rouge, Louisiana, by a certain date and time. That schedule was not quite met, as their truck broke down again. They were only 150 miles from Baton Rouge. So close, but yet, so far away. The problem again was the transmission. These trips were straining the limits of their nineteen-foot box van; therefore, the band began to look at alternatives in the transportation arena.

Speaking of transportation departments, The TERMS were driving back from a successful performance in Florida, when, once again, they found themselves on the side of the highway. It was not mechanical failure this time, but a failure to communicate. They were driving on a highway in Florida in a driving rainstorm when they realized they were being followed by a Florida State Trooper with his lights on. Being followed by a state trooper with his lights flashing is not a good thing, especially when you were not speeding. The officer asked the guys for the reason they did not pull in at the truck-stop weigh station a couple of miles back. Their reply: "We did not know we were supposed to." One of the laws in Florida deals with imported fruit, or rather, smuggled fruit. Let's see. We have an unmarked, plain-white box van driving on the highways of the state of Florida. That truck just skipped a designated weigh station. State Trooper thinks, "This truck does not want to be inspected; it must be hiding something."

Throughout this episode, the rain was pouring down. The band members responded nicely and politely to the state trooper, which is exactly what you do in that situation. They calmly explained that (1) They did not realize they were supposed to stop at that Florida weigh station, and (2) They were members of a rock band. Of course, the officer wanted to see what was in the van so the guys got out in the torrential rain to open the back of the van. The officer did not see any contraband, but he did see a lot of evidence of a rock 'n roll band! All was right with the world at that point. In fact, the band gave the officer one of their new CDs! And, yes, they did stop at the next Florida truck check point. Stories to tell the grandkids one day.

TERMS Group E-mail—February 26, 2007: Brandon Update:

Dear Family and Friends,

And a Good New Week to you! Sure hope you made it through all the bad weather we experienced this past weekend!

Anne and I visited with Brandon and his family a week ago, and he is looking great. We walked in and saw Brandon sitting at the dining room table with three stacks of paper in front of him, a pencil in his hand, and a calculator within his reach. We asked him, "What are you doing, Brandon?" He replied, "My homework." His therapist gives him homework to work on—from math problems to comprehension to whatever! He was working diligently on them while we were there. His therapy sessions are taking place at Willis Knighton-North. They are performing a fabulous job.

He is not only working hard on his homework, but also on his eating. Yes, he has not been fed through his peg tube (feeding tube) in a week. As most of you know, Brandon had lost thirty pounds since the accident, but now that he is eating "real food" again he has gained back fifteen pounds! I asked him if that was the result of Raising Cane's Chicken fingers. He replied, "Dutch Chocolate Ice Cream." Angela confirmed that he has taken a strong liking to that ice cream—she has to watch that now!

It was just amazing to watch him—how much better he looked, how much better he was working his body, especially his arms, and how much better his speech was. It is remarkable when I compare that with what he looked like lying in that hospital bed in Monroe only four short months ago. Brandon sometimes gets down since he thinks he should be walking on his own now (without a walker), but Angela and Jay just explain to him how well he is doing and how far he has come in such a short time. Anne and I see him every couple of weeks so we get to see dramatic changes in him.

And finally he was able to meet Bratton Frierson. Bratton also sustained major brain trauma a couple of years ago. He goes up to the rehabilitation department of Willis Knighton Hospital to visit with similar patients. He encourages them and just tells them that it took him two years to get where he is today. What an inspiration he is.

Brandon's left arm has 90% of its normal range of motion at this time. Pretty soon, he will be tearing up his guitar strings again!

E-MAIL CONNECTIONS

Brandon's new neurosurgeon is Dr. Ravish Patwardhan. His observation of Brandon's hematoma (a localized collection of blood, usually clotted, in an organ, space or tissue): it is much smaller than it was. Eventually his body would reabsorb it—Great news! The pain that Brandon is experiencing in his right upper leg is a blood clot, but because Brandon had that filter put in, Dr. Patwardhan does not think he has to worry about that one. More good news.

Since Brandon's bleeding episode (in his trachea area), the doctor changed him to a metal trachea tube to see if that would help. Dr. Cherie-Ann Nathan did another scope of Brandon's throat and unfortunately, the surgery performed in Jackson, Mississippi, did not accomplish the needed results. The scar tissue grew back, and Brandon's next surgery will address this situation. That surgery is scheduled for March 12th—Brandon's birthday. When the doctor realized that day was Brandon's birthday she was going to delay surgery, but Brandon would not hear of it. He REALLY wants that endo-tracheal tube out!

He did get one tube out. Brandon was eating well, and he had not been fed with the peg tube for two weeks. This past Friday his peg tube was taken out! Dr. Nathan also informed Brandon that there was no reason for him to still be in a hospital bed at home. He could sleep in his OWN bed. Brandon LOVED that. He was extremely happy. In fact, he called practically EVERY friend in his cell phone directory to tell them the news. Angela stated, "No lie, he was on the phone for HOURS!"

Progress is being made. Angela and Jay know how lucky they are and how fortunate to have so many friends supporting them. Angela stated, "Brandon has some of the most caring, attentive friends." And she has so many other supporters that she has never met—people like Tammy in Lafayette, one of my sister-in-law's (Paula) friends. It is amazing how many people have been touched in a positive way by Brandon's situation. I thank you from the bottom and top and side and front and back of my heart.

May you have a blessed day.

Chapter Seven
University Support

LSU Today

The spring semester of 2006 was coming to a close. A lot of summer touring was on the horizon. Just before the semester finished, an article about The TERMS appeared in *LSU Today*, LSU's Biweekly Newsletter for Faculty & Staff. The article was in the April 21, 2006, issue and was written by Michelle Z. Spielman. The article was titled "Education and Entertainment Unite to Fulfill a Dream." Here are some excerpts from that article.

LSU E.J. Ourso College of Business instructor Carol Carter knew back in the spring of 2003 that her student Ben Labat was on the fast-track to stardom. Labat, who is currently an LSU senior and the lead singer/songwriter of the five-member Baton Rouge-based rock band, The TERMS, took Carter's Small Business Management class during his junior year.

In the class, students were required to pick a business they would be interested in starting and to create a comprehensive business plan that would help bring it to fruition. Labat wrote a business plan for his band, the Sidewalks, which would eventually become The TERMS.

Carter, who is also assistant director of the Entrepreneurship Institute within LSU's E.J. Ourso College, said she remembers the day Labat presented his business plan. "Ben had the class captivated. Not only did he present a grade 'A' business plan, he had us rocking in the classroom with his musical talent."

Labat is not the only member of The TERMS with an LSU background. Lead guitarist Clyde Hargrove received a mass communication degree

E-MAIL CONNECTIONS

from LSU in 2005, and bassist Brandon Young is continuing his academic pursuits at LSU this fall. Drummer Scott Lasseigne, a senior in business management in the E.J. Ourso College, said he often uses lessons learned in his management classes when working with the various personality types he encounters in the music industry. Percussionist Blake Oliver said he draws on his 2005 LSU degree in agricultural economics when deciphering the band's financial statements. "If we hadn't been educated in the business field, I don't think that we would have gotten this far so fast," Oliver said.

Indeed, it was Labat's 60-page business plan, along with great timing and the band's unique talent that impressed local entrepreneur Dane Andreeff, president of Baton Rouge-based Maple Jam Records.

Since signing with Maple Jam Records, The TERMS have enjoyed local success and catapulted onto the national music scene, performing in Los Angeles, Houston, New York, and other U.S. cities.

This month, the band's education in the music industry continues as Small Town Computer Crash *is set to be released nationally on Tuesday, April 25, through Maple Jam Records/ICON MES.*

The album includes "Welcome to the Now: Evo Devo" *which was written for LSU to use as an anthem in its national image and recruiting campaign. LSU has used* "Welcome to the Now" *as the campaign's theme and has prominently displayed it in printed materials, on the Web and in a 30-second national television spot. The song is the first single track on the album and includes back-up music and vocals by the LSU Tiger Band and the LSU Choirs. These LSU groups, along with the LSU Cheerleaders and a number of LSU students, appear in The TERMS'* "Welcome to the Now: Evo Devo" *music video, which was shot entirely on the LSU campus. Those familiar with the LSU campus will recognize shots of the LSU Law School, Parade Ground, Tiger Stadium, and the LSU Union Theater within the video. Free downloads of the* "Welcome to the Now: Evo Devo" *song and music video, as well as an interview with The TERMS can be found at www.lsu.edu/now.*

Later this month the band will visit Baton Rouge's Episcopal High School to perform a live concert for students and speak to them about the importance of attending college. Labat said that the band's message to students will be simple. "You can apply what you learn at LSU to a dream you have," Labat said.

It's just the message that LSU's Carter wants her students to take away from her class.

That was a nice way to end the spring semester and to kick off a busy summer.

TERMS Group E-mail—March 7, 2007: Brandon Update:

Dear Family & Friends,

Good Wednesday Evening to you. Hope you are enjoying this SUNNY, Mild Weather! Perfect Spring Weather!

Brandon is continuing to make progress. He goes to speech, physical and occupational therapy three times a week. He is continuing to work on his homework that he is assigned each week.

I was able to visit with Brandon for a short time last Saturday. When he shook my hand it was a good, firm handshake. That young man is working on his strength! I told him that soon I will have to challenge him in arm wrestling. He responded, "I'll be ready."

Brandon's left eye lid is beginning to open some. That is actually messing up his balance when he walks! The doctor does not want to have surgery on that nerve until a year has passed. At that time the doctor will re-evaluate the eye's progress to determine the course of action.

Just before I came by last Saturday, Brandon's junior high science teacher (yes, THAT one! The one he had a crush on years ago) had come by to say "hello" and to bring him some DUTCH CHOCOLATE ICE CREAM!

His surgery is still set for Monday, March 12th (his 23rd birthday). If you wish to send him a birthday card or get-well card send to this address: 133 Ockley Drive, Shreveport, La. 71105. Brandon's last name is Young.

E-MAIL CONNECTIONS

For those of you in the Shreveport-Bossier City area, you may have seen an article by Brandon's mother, Angela, in *SB Magazine*. She wrote that article last summer. She did not have any idea when they were going to run that article. It just ran. Pretty good article!

Speaking of *SB Magazine*, it is time for their Annual Readers' Choice Awards. That is where you vote for "the best whatever," i.e., Best Italian Restaurant, Best Mexican Restaurant, Best Florist, etc. Well, it has an entry for Best Local Band! Sooooooo, all you folks in the Shreveport-Bossier City area, why not submit The TERMS as the Best Local Band? If you do not subscribe to this magazine, you can pick it up at local stores such as Brookshires. Let's see what kind of impact we can make. THANKS!

Ben is up in New York. He has a second interview this week with a music company in their marketing department. Blake is in Austin, Texas. He has interviewed with a firm this week. Clyde is in Shreveport setting up a music studio. Scott is in Shreveport working with Enterprise Car Rental. He was the Top Salesperson at his store again in the month of February—Thanks to people like Mark Porter, Bruce Allen, and Henry Bernstein!

Thanks again for all your prayers and support. It is very much appreciated. Take care.

Chapter Eight
East Coast Summer Tour of 2006

The Storm

The East Coast Summer Tour of 2006 was here. It would take The TERMS on a 4,000 mile odyssey. A new addition to the group was Jeff Riley, sound engineer. He took Wylie Whitesides' place. Wylie had business interest in the video world, and those contracts were calling him. The bond between him and the other band members was strong, but it was time for him to move in a different direction. He missed out on this summer adventure. Jeff did not. Those memories will be utmost in his mind in the years ahead.

The TERMS' schedule included the Peppermint Beach Club in Virginia Beach, Virginia, the Lucky Dog in Worcester, Maine, the Knitting Factory in New York, the Hudson Beach Café in New York (an LSU fund-raiser), the Bitter End in New York, The Cutting Room in New York, The Saint in New Jersey, the Continental in New York, Langley Air Force Base in Hampton, Virginia, The Purple Moose Saloon in Ocean City, Maryland, Grog & Tankard in Washington, D.C. (Georgetown), the Downtown in Morristown, Tennessee, and other venues in between. It was a lot of performing, a lot of driving, and a lot of staying in less-than-desirable hotels along the way. Yes, their education in the music industry was continuing. As in many things in life, there was the good and the bad. But the band pressed on.

Some performances on any tour are not always too pleasant. In fact, sometimes it can be downright dangerous. That was the case on July 4, 2006, for The TERMS. They were scheduled to play at Bolling Air Force Base in Washington, D.C., on July 4th, along with another band. This particular military festival was located by the Potomac River. The view of the site included a lot of grass, many tents, food booths and children running around. That day saw lots of sunshine, hot temperatures and no clouds in the sky. The band was scheduled to begin playing at 5:30 P.M. Blake stated, "How cool a thing to perform at an Air Force Base in your nation's capital on the fourth of July with Air Force One and Marine One flying overhead!"

Around 5:00 P.M. a HUGE, BLACK CLOUD placed itself over this festival site. Clyde suggested that they take down their speakers and put them up in their cases in order to protect them from the pending rain. Scott was against this idea, but relented. Good move, since the bottom fell out from that enormous black cloud a mere thirty seconds after they finished putting up the speakers.

The wind began whipping up at ferocious speeds. The band, using quick thinking, moved their nineteen-foot box truck to the back of their stage to prevent the wind coming from the Potomac River from blowing their tent away. At this point the band had $30,000 worth of equipment on that stage under the tent. While the truck was doing a fine job, Ben and Scott were trying to hold down the tent as well as pulling all of the electronic equipment under a make-shift tarp to protect it from the pouring rain. Suddenly Ben screamed in pain and fell to the ground. It seems that he had received a pretty good shock from the lighting that was hitting all around the festival site. Unfortunately, he was holding onto a metal pipe at the time. When he recovered from that shock he began holding the tent again, but this time he was touching the material and not any metal. That was too close for comfort.

Shortly after that incident a man in an Air Force uniform ran over to their tent and shouted to them: "Hold on, guys. You're experiencing 80 MPH Winds! HOLD ON!" Scott turned to see Jeff, Clyde, Blake, Brandon, and a fourteen-year-old teenager, who joined in to help them, holding onto the tent that was protecting their sound board, interface, compressors and mixer—another $20,000 worth of equipment—from being ruined. Then the tent blew, taking Brandon and Clyde and the teenager with it. Blake estimated that teenager flew about fifty feet in the air. They ran to him, and miraculously, he was fine. Luckily, the storm stopped as quickly as it had started.

As the band members walked around the festival site they noticed that their tent was the only one that had not blown down. I guess their truck was not worthless after all! They were able to "air out" their equipment on a racquetball court on the base overnight. Despite some cosmetic damage to the sound board and a few bruises, the band escaped this frightening episode with surprisingly little damage to their equipment and with little physical harm to them. At the time it was very scary. They were out in an open field with this deluge of rain and lightning all around them. That is one Fourth of July that will remain etched in their memory banks for a very long time.

Blake commented, "I know how scary this all sounds; it was scary, but with the group we had, nothing was too much for us to handle. We handled everything the best we could in any situation that came up. That's what made us a great band, and more importantly, best friends."

The Purple Moose Saloon

The TERMS were booked for three consecutive nights at The Purple Moose Saloon in Ocean City, Maryland. Don't you just love that name? The dates were Friday, July 7th through Sunday, July 9th. Ocean City is a major tourist getaway in that part of the country, especially being so close to Washington, D.C. The band was scheduled to play for three hours and forty-five minutes each night. That is a lot of singing. Ben's voice was not in the best shape when we caught up with the band that Sunday evening. My wife, a speech therapist, instructed Ben to get some vocal rest after their commitment with The Purple Moose Saloon was fulfilled. He would not have any voice left soon if his present pace was continued. A few days later his voice returned to a much more acceptable tone for the first-class singer that he was.

Anne and I scheduled our vacation that summer around the band's east coast tour. We planned to see them perform in Ocean City on July 9, 2006, and in Georgetown on July 11, 2006, at Grog and Tankard. Our daughter, who had just finished getting her bachelor's degree in nursing, flew up from Texas to meet us for the Ocean City performance. We also brought some old friends with us from Maryland, Bill and Karleen, and their children Christina and William, for that performance. What a great vacation—visiting with good friends and family and watching your son and his good buddies embark on another chapter in their lives as a touring rock band.

The TERMS' first night at The Purple Moose Saloon was rather interesting. They were a long way from friendly faces in Baton Rouge, Shreveport, and Houston. They were performing before a brand new crowd that, at times, were more interested in the available gambling machines then their unique brand of music. That first night displayed quite a bit of friction between the band and the crowd. The crowd kept yelling, "Play cover songs," or "Cover, cover!" meaning play songs that they knew—songs that played on the radio. The TERMS complied and played one of their original songs then followed that with a cover song, then an original song followed by a cover song. Not a warm-and-fuzzy crowd that first evening.

During the next night's performance, a woman walked up to the band in between songs and told them: "Put the DJ on; ya'll suck!" Yes, she had consumed a large quantity of adult beverages, and she wanted to strut her stuff on the dance floor to music that she was accustomed to. I had to laugh when Scott told me this. Being the kind of person that I am, my first reaction to her would have been, "Why, THANK YOU SO MUCH!"

I sent this story to my TERMS' group e-mail and received a reply from my good friend Jim O'Brock. Jim, in his younger days, had toured with a band for seven years and had many stories from that adventurous chapter in his life. He related this story concerning one of his experiences: "The TERMS' experience reminds me of one of ours in Indianapolis, Indiana. We also played our own music. We would tell people who requested, say, Creedence Clearwater, that Creedence Clearwater did not play any of our music, so we were not playing any of theirs! But I digress... In that city there was a waitress who HATED us. She would walk in front of the band holding her ears! We were going to be at that establishment for a whole week, so I thought I would try to break the ice. I started talking to her and she warmed up a little.

"Now, at the time I looked a little like a television star named Bobby Sherman. The waitress asked me, 'Do you know who you look like?' I told her that I was trying to make it in music without using my actor fame. I let the whole band in on the ruse, and by the end of the week, we had her so convinced she had met Bobby Sherman that, had I told her before we left that we were just kidding, she would not have believed us! Ah, life on the road!" Yes, life on the road can be quite interesting.

Back to Ocean City, Maryland. The third night came, and reinforcements entered the realm of The Purple Moose Saloon. Anne, Christen and I, as mentioned, brought our good friends to that establishment. After every song The TERMS performed, we clapped and yelled our approval and, generally, made any favorable noise we could generate. That helped guide the crowd that evening into a more receptive mode. As the evening went on we noticed more of the crowd "getting into it" by also clapping, tapping their feet to the music, and dancing on the dance floor. That crowd just needed a little encouragement from us groupies! It is amazing how such enthusiasm can be contagious!

That vacation trip to visit with the band and with old friends reminds me of our short time on Earth. When it is all said and done it is our relationships that are of lasting importance. A good friend and fellow runner, Bill Peatross, once stated in a weekly e-mail to our Saturday-Morning-Run Group, the importance of friendships. On June 14, 2007, he wrote, "A friend of mine came home a few weeks ago. He left on an unwanted trip several months ago and returned stronger and wiser than before. Separation offers the opportunity for introspection and reflection and, while I missed him, I knew he was living the running mantra of, 'Pain is temporary, and pride is forever.' Good friendships are easy things; comfortable, warm and regrettably, easy to take for granted. My friend's absence reminded me that something as delicate and special as a friendship should be remembered and appreciated each day. Friendships are the icing on the cake of life." So true.

The Dancer

Christen flew back to Texas while Anne and I met up with some other dear friends from the Washington, D.C., area, Joey and Lynnette. They were going to accompany us to Georgetown to watch the band perform at Grog and Tankard. The band members did what they are supposed to do to promote the band's many performances. They called and e-mailed friends of their scheduled dates on the East Coast, and their friends graciously responded. Grog and Tankard was filled to the brim the night of July 11, 2006. During the band's performance Ben asked the crowd, "How many of you are from Louisiana and came to hear The TERMS?" Eighty percent of the crowd cheered. That information came in handy. After their performance, Scott talked to the manager about the crowd they had generated and the many adult beverages this crowd had consumed in his business establishment. Since The TERMS were an unknown quantity in this part of the country, they agreed to perform that night for no fee, but Scott was explaining to the manager the very good revenue they could generate for his establishment. You produce a good product, you sell the product, you close the sale, and move on to the next location. Yes, life on the road in a place far from home.

The band played a forty-five-minute set that evening at Grog and Tankard. That establishment is a long, narrow building with a raised stage in the middle. Along with Joey and Lynnette, we were also joined there by Christina and one of her friends. We were seated a mere ten feet from the stage. As the band rocked on that evening, a young lady with an extremely short dress began dancing, by herself, right in front of the stage. It was obvious that she wanted an audience. Then the young lady grabbed a young man by his tie as he was walking by and began dancing with him. I believe the term used is "dirty dancing." She had other moves also, which I do not have any special titles to categorize them. We all thought, "Well, this is interesting."

Christina (22 years of age) leaned over to Anne and said, "The way she is moving we are going to see some panties soon." Well, Christina was wrong. The young lady kept on moving her body, lifting her arms high in the air and around her male dance partner and gyrating in many different ways. Yes, Christina was wrong. We did not see any panties. We all soon discovered that she did not have any undergarments on at all.

The dancer was right in front of the stage. One result of this dancing exhibition: the band did not end their song in a nice, clear, emphatic manner that is normal for them. Ben soon composed himself and said over the microphone, "Sorry about that rough ending. I was a little distracted." A few of us laughed out loud. I called Scott on his cell phone the next day as they were driving to their next destination and told him to instruct Ben to *focus*!

The band thought this young dancer may have been a "working woman." They were smart enough not to find out if indeed this young lady was a business entrepreneur. One has to be careful out on the road.

The Four Seasons Hotel

During The TERMS' five-and-a-half-week East Coast Tour there were many days of driving eight to nine hours to get to their next performance, staying in cheap hotels, and eating subsistence meals, but one stop was different. I asked the band members to send me any thoughts they had about their experience in The TERMS. It could be on any subject, it could be two sentences, two paragraphs, two pages or more. Ben wrote about The Four Seasons Hotel experience. The following story is his with a few comments from Scott.

Ben Labat: "When I think of the time I spent traveling, laughing, and doing all those other things that came along with being in The TERMS, it is hard to grasp just one memory. There are so many good ones and so many unusual ones that my head feels like a slot machine anytime the wheels start turning. Now, there is one particular story that still makes me smile in partial disbelief whenever I think of it or tell it, and with that said, I would like to tell it once again.

"Picture if you will, six grungy young men traveling around the northeast Unites States in an SUV and a cargo truck. When I say cargo truck I mean a cross between a 1950s milk truck and the Oswald's station wagon from *National Lampoon's Family Vacation.* We have stayed in the cheapest of cheap motels, played the dirtiest of dirty dive bars, had ourselves and our equipment soaked and nearly washed away by a tropical storm, broken down twice on the side of the Interstate, and had our cargo truck towed to a 'lovely neighborhood' in Queens. We were towards the end of our five-and-a half-week East Coast tour, and as you can imagine, we are feeling good about life, no one is feeling any pain, no one is getting on another's nerves, and we are always smiling as the sun is always shining....NOT!

"We are driving into Philadelphia, rough and road ready, a little cranky, but nonetheless still laughing at one of Brandon's jokes or the weird smell coming from the back of the car. For some reason instead of pulling into our regular $29.95 luxury motel we continue to the heart of downtown Philly and drive our mutant something-out-of-a-cartoon-version-of-*Mad-Max* vehicles' into the Four Seasons Hotel. For those of you not accustomed to the lavish lifestyle of being a rock star, the Four Seasons is a five-star hotel frequented by celebrities such as U2, Elton John, and tonight, by The TERMS.

"The reason for turning into the Four Seasons hotel instead of our normal roach hotel was our friend and fellow band member Clyde Hargrove. Clyde, in a valiant, borderline overzealous, effort to win a girl's heart, spent half of his life savings for a room here. (Clyde's parents probably are not aware of this, so please don't tell them—Thanks) When the charmingly weird and chivalrous gesture was not appreciated by the young lady, Clyde split the one penthouse suite into four regular rooms for his band mates. That's right, courtesy of Mr. Clyde, The TERMS are living like royalty, even if for only one night.

"We were not the only mega-rock-superstars gracing the Four Seasons with our presence that day. Crosby, Stills, Nash, and Young had the same idea. I spent the better half of the afternoon waiting in the lobby to catch a glimpse of a real living legend. It's kind of funny; you feel like a stalker, the friendly kind of stalker, of course. Security guards also feel like you are a stalker, but not necessarily the friendly kind.

"Once I caught my split-second glimpse of Neil Young and Gram Nash, I retreated back to the room. There I found the entire crew gearing up for a late afternoon trip to the world-class spa in the Four Seasons basement. Yes, not only were six road-worn gentlemen going to sit in a hot tub, but they were also going to snack on chocolate-covered strawberries and sip champagne. The phrase is CHILL OUT!

"After two or so bottles of champagne, a couple of trays of strawberries, and a series of annoyed waiters who were not sure of what to think, we trekked through the lobby, soaking wet, to the concierge desk to make reservations at a 'nice' restaurant. When I say 'nice,' I mean swanky, upscale, posh, and ritzy—you get the picture. A 'nice' restaurant according to The TERMS' definition is quite a bit different from the Four Seasons' standard of a 'nice restaurant.' Nonetheless, we made our reservations, and were instructed to be back in the lobby thirty minutes early to meet our driver. Yes, we were going to have our very own driver to drive us to and from here, there, and everywhere.

"It is eight o'clock, and it is time to go. Our driver picks us up in a brand-new Jaguar; yes, a Jaguar. The driver proceeds to whip and whirl through the streets of Philadelphia like the floodwaters from hell before he eventually drops us off at this crazy, modern-looking building. I cannot remember the name of this place to save my life, but it had the word 'Buddha' somewhere in the name. Scott, Brandon, Clyde, and I walk through twenty-five-foot doors with the same looks on our faces that we all had when we saw our first issue of *Playboy*.

"There is a waterfall in the middle of this place and an elevator to four different dining floors. We sat at our table and just laughed, then we laughed some more. I can still see Clyde walking around and exploring the restaurant like he was in Willy Wonka's Chocolate factory, and I can still hear Brandon casually flirting with our waitress, whom I vividly recall being dressed all in white. We were so out of place, and we knew it. Sometimes when you are out of place you tend to completely let go and have the most fun. Good times! Notice that I am skipping the part about the restaurant bill...ouch!

"Dinner is over, and we are zooming back to our hotel with our NASCAR-wanna-be driver. Call it a night? Wrong! There is a very 'nice' lounge in the Four Seasons hotel that was calling, no, screaming our names, "Ben! Scott!

Brandon! Clyde! Come here, come here!" If you are wondering where Blake is, he has uncharacteristically retired to his bed. Too many strawberries will do it, that is, if accompanied by too many glasses of champagne. Back to the nice lounge. In the lounge were none other than Neil Young, his wife, and his band, Crazyhorse. If we got too close to Neil Young the security personnel would ease in and cut off access. I guess after John Lennon's tragic death, a rock star just can't be too careful. After I nervously told Mr. Young what an honor it was to meet him and that his work on *The Painter* was some of his finest work and what a huge stalker, I mean, admirer I was, he simply said, "Thanks," and retired to his room, accompanied by his three personal security guards.

"Mr. Young was the only one who retired early. His wife and band stayed in the lounge sharing life stories with five starry-eyed guys from Louisiana. Yes, we are five again. Blake miraculously awoke from his beauty sleep (see also 'hangover'). It seems that anytime someone is having a good time or something interesting happens, Blake is there, like some sixth sense."

Scott: "We had a very nice conversation with Neil Young's wife and learned that they have been married for twenty-eight years. The band all knew who The TERMS' producer, Greg Ladanyi, was. We may have been some country boys in a no-name band from Louisiana, but being associated with a Grammy-Award-Winning producer helped give us credibility in their eyes. It was an evening of great conversation and great stories. That evening we gave Neil Young's wife a copy of our CD, *Small Town Computer Crash*, and she gave us an autographed Neil Young CD."

Ben: "After we all had our fill of beer, last laughs, and tall tales, we really did call it a night, but man, what a freaking day.

"As cool as this story is, and as much fun as it was being there, it's not the Four Seasons or the fancy restaurant or even getting to meet Neil Young that made it worth remembering. It is a group of friends that have fun together, no matter what, that makes anything worth remembering. Thank you, Gentlemen."

TERMS Group E-mail—March 18, 2007: Brandon Update:

Dear Family & Friends,

Sure hope you enjoyed a nice weekend break. The weather in Shreveport was GORGEOUS!

E-MAIL CONNECTIONS

Brandon's surgery last Monday went well. They arrived at LSU-Medical Center at 6:00 A.M. and returned home at 11:30 P.M. Yes, a long and exhausting day. Brandon's actual surgery lasted two hours. It seems that the trachea problems are not with the scar tissue, but with a calcification problem. Dr. Cherie-Ann Nathan used a new type of bendable laser/probe-type thingy (I stop at nothing to provide you with the latest in medical terminology) for this surgery. She did laser the "granulation tissue" that was blocking Brandon's airway. Since the surgery Brandon has not experienced any pain in that location, but did have some issues with the medicine (one was steroids) for a few days. He missed therapy for a few days last week due to his body's reaction to all that medication, but that has subsided somewhat.

Brandon's left eyelid is opening more and more, but his left eye is not cooperating yet. That eye tends to drift to the left and not follow the movement of his right eye. That condition is called "third-nerve palsy." That is one reason Brandon has experienced balance problems when he walks. The doctors normally wait a year to see if the condition corrects itself before recommending surgery. With that said, Brandon continues to make progress with the walker. His parents have high hopes that with the progress he continues to make he will be walking on his own soon. That is truly remarkable, as I vividly remember visiting with him in his hospital room only five short months ago. Modern medicine, great care by doctors, nurses, therapists, and other medical personnel, great therapy techniques, a strong will to move forward, a network of family and friends that just would not give up on him, and many prayers have all helped to produce a true miracle.

Memories from Brandon's past continue to emerge. Brandon's family will be driving around or just sitting at home when Brandon will say, "I just remembered who my Gateway teacher was at Byrd High School," or "Mom, I just remembered what the studio looked like in Los Angeles." At this time it is just random memories that pop up.

Anne and I stopped by after church last Sunday to give Brandon a birthday card (THANK YOU—So many of you sent Brandon a birthday card. He and his family really appreciated that thoughtful gesture). He had a tough time that weekend with coughing. Maybe it was all the pollen in the air, maybe it was the blockage in his trachea area, but as a result of that occurrence, he did not do too much talking that weekend. A birthday party was planned for Brandon that day due to his surgery the next day. Many friends and family stopped by to wish him well. One person was The TERMS' original production engineer/sound guy, Wylie Whitesides. He brought all kinds of video footage of the band from their summer tour and a music video the band produced in Shreveport. Maybe that will spark some memory flashbacks.

And Thank You for submitting The TERMS as your favorite Local Band in the SB Magazine's Annual Reader's Choice Award Voting. If you live in the Shreveport-Bossier City area, you can go to http://www.sbmag.net and send in your ballot. It is very easy to do. Thanks!

Brandon continues to work on his "homework" from rehab daily and is doing well. If he continues to make progress with that, his parents hope that he can return to college in a year or so to finish his degree.

Angela has just returned to work part time. Her boss, Robert Dunkelman, has been great to her in this difficult time. Angela said, "Thank goodness I have a job to return to and that will work with me concerning my schedule with Brandon." Her boss continued to pay Angela all the time she was at Brandon's side in the Monroe Hospital and in the Jackson, Mississippi, Rehabilitation Center. There are good people and good employers in this world. He is one of them.

Brandon is making great progress with personal functions. He can now shave himself—no help needed, thank you—and can almost completely dress himself, although he is not totally self-sufficient yet. My dear wife says, "What man is?" I will ignore that comment…for now…it is Lent so I will have to wait until AFTER Easter to reply….

Thanks for your great support and prayers. Hope your life is blessed.

The TIMES, "American Tragedy, Group Reunites on stage Saturday. PREVIEW," Top Right Corner Headline on Friday, December 28, 2007, newspaper issue.

UpBeetMusic.com, by Robert Velasquez, October 14, 2005.

Wikipedia, The Free Encyclopedia, Page name: Metronome, Author: Wikipedia contributors, May 29, 208, page version ID: 215744843.

Wikipedia, The Free Encyclopedia, Page name: Sushi, Author: Wikipedia contributors, January 12, 2008, page version ID: 183804368.

Wikipedia, The Free Encyclopedia, Page name: Viper Room, Author: Wikipedia contributors, December 24, 2006, Page Version ID: 179599558.

Wikipedia, The Free Encyclopedia, Page name: The Wizard of Oz (1939 film), Author, Wikipedia contributors, January 22, 2008, Page Version ID: 186029750.

Wikipedia, The Free Encyclopedia, Page Name: Academy Award for Best Actor, Author: Wikipedia contributors, December 24, 2006, Page Version ID: 183512803.

Wikipedia, The Free Encyclopedia, Page name: Billboard (magazine), Author: Wikipedia contributors, January 5, 2008, Page Version ID: 182356065.

Wikipedia, The Free Encyclopedia, Page name: Mors (mythology), Author: Wikipedia contributors, September 23, 2007, Page Version ID: 159735261.

Wikipedia, *The Free Encyclopedia*, Page name: Afroman, Author: Wikipedia contributors, Jan. 31, 2008, Page Version ID: 188725659.

Wikipedia, The Free Encyclopedia, Page name: Megan Mullally, Author: Wikipedia contributors, January 10, 2008, Page Version ID: 183432283.

Wikipedia, The Free Encyclopedia, Page name: Selma Blair, Author: Wikipedia contributors, May 10, 2008, Page Version ID: 211528405.

Wikipedia, The Free Encyclopedia, Page name: Timothy Olyphant, Author: Wikipedia contributors, May 10, 2008, Page Version ID: 211433690.

Wikipedia, The Free Encyclopedia, Page name: Danny Kortchmar, Author: Wikipedia contributors, January 15, 2008, Page Version ID: 172053145.

E-MAIL CONNECTIONS

The Daily Reveille, Issue Date: September 28, 2006, Letters to the Editor, by Holly Houk Cullen, APR, Interim Assistant Vice Chancellor, Public Affairs, Originally Published: September 28, 2006.

The Daily Reveille, Posted: November 30, 2006, "Uncertain Terms, Band Finally Speaks out after Controversy, Tragedy and Success," by Travis Andrews.

The Daily Reveille, Posted: January 6, 2007, "End of the Now, University to Cancel Marketing Campaign," by Michael Mims.

The Free Dictionary by Farlex, Hematoma, http://www.thefreedictionary.com/Hemotoma, June 11, 2008.

The Free Dictionary by Farlex, Unction, http://www.thefreedictionary.com/unction, December 24, 2007.

TheMediaFix.com, "The TERMS," by John Frank, The Media Fix—Music—The Scene! March 13, 2006.

The Music Edge Website, themusicedge.com.

The NIV (New International Version of the Bible) Study Bible, Zondervan Publishing House, Grand Rapids, MI 49530, General Editor Kenneth Barker, 1995 Edition, page 988.

The Quotations Page, Published by Michael and Laura Moncur, October 15, 2007, Quotations by Author: Theodore Roosevelt (1858—1919), 26th president of U.S., pages 1-3.

The *Quotations Page*, Published by Michael and Laura Moncur, October 15, 2007, Quotations by Subject: Criticism, pages 1-4.

The TIMES, "The TERMS, Driving to Make it Big: Three Locals Part of the New Band," by Alexandyr Kent, page 12E-13E, April 29, 2005.

The TIMES, Music Review, by Alexandyr Kent.

The TIMES, "Centenary is One of '25 Hottest Schools in America,'" August 19, 2007, Ashley Northington.

The TIMES Preview Magazine Insert, "Blues Traveler to 'Hook' Fans at Horseshoe," August 17, 2007.

The TIMES, Sunday Living Section, June 3, 2007, "The TERMS, Car Crash Ends Band's Climb up the Charts and Today, at Different Beats, Its Members Recover," by Stephanie Netherton, page 1D, 3D.

The TIMES, "TERMS Guitarist Carves New Path with New Music," Friday *PREVIEW* Section, June 29, 2007, page 5E.

MishMashMagazine.com, "The Terms, Rehearsals.com—1.26.06—Burbank, CA," by Aaron Pompey, Photos by M'Lou Elkins, February 15, 2006.

Pat Green website: www.patgreen.com, homepage, October 15, 2007.

Rehearsals.com website, by Doug Miller.

RobinsonFilmCenter.org website, Robinson Film Center Online.

SB Magazine, May 2006, Volume 7, Issue 5, "Terms of Endearment, Band Gets Ready for Spotlight," Cassie Smyth, page 75-77.

Sidelink.net website, "Rock Stars for Hire," April 20, 2006, "Spotlight Album Review."

S*kopemagazine.com*, Music Review of their April 2005 CD Release of *Small Town Computer Crash*, February 3, 2006.

Skopemagazine.com, "The Terms Music Chosen for New Orleans' Mardi Gras 2006 Television Commercial Campaign," February 3, 2006.

Steal the Spotlight website, StealtheSpotlight.tripod.com, June 11, 2006, "The Terms' 'Small Town Computer Crash' Review."

The Advocate (Baton Rouge, La., newspaper), by John Wirt, June 10, 2005.

The Daily Reveille, Issue Date: January 31, 2006, "Public Affairs hopes to Reinvent Image," by Justin Fritscher, Section: Campus Life, Originally published January 30, 2006.

The Daily Reveille, Issue Date: February 10, 2006, Section: Off the Cuff, Originally published February 9, 2006, with Jay Melder.

The Daily Reveille, Issue Date: February 22, 2006, "University not helping image, Cheney, 'Evo Devo' earn little respect," by Sevetri Wilson, Originally published February 21, 2006.

The Daily Reveille, Issue Date: March 15, 2006, "Chat with the Chan over Coffee," by Ginger Gibson, Originally Published, March 14, 2006.

The Daily Reveille, Issue Date: March 29, 2006, "Selling LSU, University's Image Campaign Seeks to Drive a Quest for More Private Donations," by Ginger Gibson, Originally published: March 28, 2006.

The Daily Reveille, Issue Date: June 15, 2006, "Our View: University Fundraising Effort Is Ill-Advised," Originally published: June 14, 2006.

The Daily Reveille, Issue Date: September 18, 2006, "LSU's Media Campaign Lacks Focus," by Mathew Sanders, Originally published: September 17, 2006.

Bibliography

002 Magazine, "The TERMS, A Conversation with lead singer/songwriter Ben Labat," by Lance Scott Walker, Photography by Amber Perley, February 2006.

225 Magazine, Spring 2006 Issue, www.225batonrouge.com.

Billboard.com, May 13, 2006, "Top Heatseekers," # 1 Small Town Computer Crash, The Terms—South Central. # 11 Nationwide for week of April 25, 2006.

Bill Peatross' e-mail on Friendship, June 14, 2007. (Part of weekly SMR e-mail).

Hi & Lois ©King Features Syndicate, Cartoon June 2006.

HoustonMusicReview.com, "Coming to Terms with the New Year…," January 17, 2006, "The Terms—Continental Club—Houston, Tx," 12-22-05, by Samuel Barker.

Houston Press.com, "The Terms, Saturday, August 12, at the Continental Club, 3700 Main, 713-529-9899," by William Michael Smith, August 10, 2006.

Ink19.com website, "The TOP 19 INDEPENDENT ALBUMS OF 2005," by Andrew Ellis, January 20, 2006.

Jackson Browne's website, www.jacksonbrowne.com, December 23, 2006.

LSU Today, LSU'S Bi-weekly Newsletter for Faculty & Staff, "Education & Education Unite for Fulfill a Dream," by Michelle Spielman, April 21, 2006, pages 2-4.

LSU Today, LSU'S Bi-weekly Newsletter for Faculty & Staff, "Football Finishes No. 3 in Final Major Polls," by www.LSUsports.net, January 9, 2007.

LSU Today, Bi-weekly Newsletter for Faculty & Staff, "LSU Public Affairs Wins Top Honors for Crisis Communication," by Kristine Calongne, August 11, 2006.

If you would like more information about Maple Jam Music Group go to http://www.maplejammusic.com/

If you would like more information about Ben Labat and his music go to www.MySpace.com/benlabat or www.MySpace.com/happydevilmusic

If you would like more information about Clyde Hargrove you can contact him at clydehargrove@gmail.com.

If you would like more information about Blake Oliver you can contact him at blake222@gmail.com.

If you would like more information about Scott Lasseigne you can check out the company website, www.apspayroll.com, or contact him at his MySpace page

E-MAIL CONNECTIONS

TERMS Group E-mail—March 4, 2008: Brandon Update:

Dear Family & Friends,

Sure hope you are enjoying this new day.

Brandon has been dismissed from Dr. Nathan, his ENT doctor. She had been dealing with his tracheal stenosis. In dismissing him she stated that everything looked good. Brandon would not have to return to her unless a problem came up.

Brandon has also been dismissed from Dr. Richards, his eye doctor. He went for his follow-up visit last week to check on his progress since his recent eye surgery. His eyesight is better, but he still has double vision, although if he holds his head a certain way and the stars in the sky are in alignment, he does experience single vision. He has been prescribed glasses, and maybe that might help some. We shall see.

Dr. Richards has given Brandon the green light for Dr. Vekovius to perform the eyelid lift surgery. That should be his last surgery. Hard to believe: his last surgery. In visiting with Brandon last week, he looked quite good. His spirits are great.

That shows in his plowing through his college courses. He has three courses: all senior-level courses. He is taking physics, physics lab, and advanced Spanish. So far he has 2 Bs and 1 C; pretty outstanding accomplishment for someone recovering from a severe brain injury. And LSU-S has always had a reputation as a difficult school, making those grades and his effort even more significant.

Life is not a bed of roses for Brandon and his family and not for you and me. We deal with what life dishes out to us and move on. Well, some people move on while others complain and feel sorry for themselves. Brandon teaches us, by his example, that there is no time for the latter; he is moving on.

May you and your family be blessed.

Till later.

laugh, a time to mourn and a time to dance, a time to scatter stones and a time to gather them, a time to embrace and a time to refrain, a time to search and a time to give up, a time to keep and a time to throw away, a time to tear and a time to mend, a time to be silent and a time to speak, a time to love and a time to hate, a time for war and a time for peace."

For The TERMS, this past year was not a time to die, but a time to be born, or rather, to be re-born; a time to plant seeds for a new course in their lives; a time to heal; a time to build a new life; a time to weep (yes, we all did plenty of that) and a time to laugh (we did plenty of that also); a time to mourn what they once had, but also a time to dance and celebrate what they have now; a time to embrace family and friends each and every day and never to take them for granted, because you just never know what tomorrow may bring; a time to search for the meaning of life; a time to contemplate their place in this world; a time to be silent in deep meditation and prayer, and a time to speak up and tell one another how much you care for them, how much you love them, and how much they mean to you; and it is a time for peace—a time to slow down life's hectic pace and just be still. It was a time to enjoy the moment. It was a time to enjoy the company of your family and friends; after all, tomorrow is not guaranteed.

Life moves on, and so will Ben, Blake, Clyde, Brandon, and Scott. They are moving forward with their new lives, and we are very thankful for that. The TERMS' parents are very grateful that their sons survived the accident, emotionally and physically. Clyde, Blake, and Brandon are not paralyzed from their injuries, which is truly astounding. Brandon continues to make amazing progress. His recovery is truly nothing less than a miracle. With his grit and determination it will be quite interesting to see where that takes him. The last sixteen months have been an incredible ride. Yes, there have been ups and downs, but that is what the journey called life is all about. They are looking forward to tomorrow, but living their utmost today. Who knows what tomorrow may bring—a college degree, a medical degree, a future wife, a new job, a new career, a newborn baby, a move out of state, new music collaboration, a sold-out reunion concert—who knows? But for now it is time to put together another "Brandon Update" for my TERMS' group e-mail lists of friends and family.

I shared these heartfelt e-mails with Brandon and Angela. Their response:

From Brandon: "Wow. That's all I can honestly say. Wow. I am just overjoyed that my determination and will power has reached another person. God has done many wonderful things for me in the past and will continue to in the future."

From Angela: "This one nearly made me cry. Jacques, thank you so much for keeping Brandon alive in so many people's hearts. If it wasn't for your 'Brandon Updates,' they would not even know about Brandon and his struggles."

On a lighter note, as Brandon and I were exchanging e-mails the last few days, he mentioned that he will probably need to purchase a new computer for school. His was fairly old and slow; not what he needed to return to college with all the demands of college course work. He asked me for my recommendation on which computer to buy. I responded that he might want to check with someone more knowledgeable than me in that arena—someone like Brandon McGovern.

Brandon Young responded: "Thank you again, sir. I really didn't even think about Brandon McGovern, but I should have because he is one of my really good friends. I think my memory is back in Monroe somewhere. Maybe we should plan a trip to go and look for it."

Yes, maybe some of Brandon's memory is back in Monroe, but that can be filled in by friends and family. He obviously does not need all of his lost memory to move forward. He is just taking what he does have and moving on. And if that is not enough, he goes around the obstacle or through it to press on. What a journey he has taken us all on.

Coming to Terms

One of my wife's favorite Bible verses is from the Book of Ecclesiastes. Many of you are familiar with that passage. It goes like this: "There is a time for everything, and a season for every activity under heaven: a time to be born and a time to die, a time to plant and a time to uproot, a time to kill and a time to heal, a time to tear down and a time to build, a time to weep and a time to

Unwavering, Heartfelt Support

The support for all these young men, especially for Brandon and his family, since the accident, has been phenomenal. Their concern has not wavered. Listed below are examples of that care and support via a few e-mails received in response to this latest "Brandon Update."

E-mail from Flo B: "Brandon has helped me in overcoming my struggle with my accident. I have prayed many a day for God to give me the strength and outlook on life that Brandon has. I hope one day I may get to meet this incredible young man. If anyone ever doubted there is a God—they need to meet Brandon."

E-mail from Annette B: "Can you imagine how many people that have not been through half as much as Brandon are sitting at home feeling sorry for themselves? I hope someday Brandon will be able to reach out and tell his story to those people and let them know what determination and the will to live can do for the human body. What a guy—to jump from one stepping stone to another without quitting. He just builds a bridge over the obstacles he encounters, crosses over it, and continues forward. His never-give-up attitude is what so many of us need. What a guy, and what an inspiration!"

From Judy M: "Even though I have never met Brandon, I feel like I know him through the e-mails you have sent since the accident. If you think it is appropriate, please pass on to his family that I pray for him very often and have since the accident. I prayed for all the other young men of The TERMS, but Brandon has been stuck in my heart during this whole recovery process. Please tell his mother that I pray for her and her family also. Brandon is an inspiration to me on days when I think my life isn't going so well. I think of him and how brave he is, how determined he is, and how he perseveres through all the challenges he has encountered. He gives me hope concerning my own life. It's odd, but I feel much love for this young man that I don't even know."

In the past, Brandon had performed quite well in school; in fact, when he graduated from C.E. Byrd High School in 2002 he was ranked 24th in his senior class of several hundred graduates.

To accommodate this new situation, Brandon dropped his computer science class and added another math class. Yes, he now has two math classes, Discrete Mathematics and Linear Algebra. I did not realize that you could be discrete with math, but then again, I graduated from college in the Stone Age.

Concerning this latest struggle, I told Brandon that he has made tremendous strides and come very far. This is just a blip in the road. He will work through this—he just will have to work harder than before and maybe work in different ways—but he will be able to do this. I told him, "I keep you in my daily prayers and I know you will persevere." Brandon responded, "Perseverance is my new middle name—next to Determination."

In asking Angela about all this, she responded with, "The first week was very overwhelming. The second week was better. There has been a few bumps in the road this third week, but you know Brandon; he just manages to overcome whatever obstacle is in his way."

Terry Bradshaw wrote a book years ago titled *No Easy Game*. That can also be applied to our everyday life with the title, *No Easy Life* or concerning Brandon's new challenge, *No Easy College Course* or *No Easy Semester*. The struggle is what makes us who we are: our outlook on life, our view of life, the intensity of our fight, our very being, our character. I have no doubt that this latest "blip" in Brandon's recovery will be just that, a blip. His struggle to improve has made him extremely strong, mentally, emotionally and physically. His comeback is still a work in progress, but what a magnificent piece of work it is.

Have a great week.

Till later

morning around 7 A.M., as Anne Flynn, a friend and co-worker, was driving to work, she had her radio tuned into 99.9 KTDY, a Lafayette FM radio station. That station was playing a collection of LSU music in preparation for the big game that evening. The songs ranged from pop to rock to country. One of the songs in that mix was The TERMS' song, "Welcome to the Now, Evo Devo." The music lives on!

Sure hope your new year started out on a positive note also.

Till later.

A Blip in the Road

TERMS Group E-mail—February 2, 2008:

Dear Family & Friends,

Exhilaration and Realism—those two words express Brandon's first week back at college. What a vast array of emotions those words conjure up.

Brandon was very excited about returning to college a couple of weeks ago. Less than 16 months from his devastating brain injury he was attending college classes. For icing on the cake, he was also driving himself back and forth in his own vehicle. No help needed in that department, thank you! Simply amazing.

Then reality struck. Sometimes the second year of recovery from a brain injury is harder than the first. That is when a person comes to the realization they are just not quite the same person as before the accident. As Brandon puts it, "The input is the same, but as I try to process that information and let that knowledge out, it is a different story. My brain is processing information differently now. I kinda had a meltdown on Thursday of my first week back at school. I was really discouraged and overwhelmed with how classes were this time."

and made an opening for Brandon last Friday at Willis Knighton-Pierremont. Woo Hoo!

On January 10, 2008, Brandon sent me an e-mail that stated, "Tomorrow will be the big day. Soon I'll be able to see one computer in front of me while writing e-mail instead of two. Yeah!"

Brandon looks like he has been in a heavy-weight boxing match due to his latest surgery. His eyes are black, blue, and red, but he doesn't mind that temporary look if he can eliminate his double-vision. You may recall that Dr. Richards already operated on Brandon's left eye. This latest operation was on his right eye—his "good eye." The doctor tried to align them as best he could in order to eliminate Brandon's double-vision.

In class today, Brandon turned to look at his professor and became quite excited. He only saw ONE professor and not two. Now his vision is not perfect yet, and he still has double-vision at certain angles, but his doctor stated that his vision will continue to progress with each passing day.

As Brandon wrote in another e-mail to me, dated January 13, 2008, "My mother says my vision will clear up soon enough. It has only been two days since my eye surgery, so I am confident that my vision will be clearing up soon. I just have to live by my key word—Determination."

Yes, Brandon can teach us all about determination, resolve, grit and the will to improve.

Another band member returned to college this week—Ben. He is working as a veterinarian assistant while taking various science classes. He may want to pursue veterinarian medicine as a career. Hmmmmmm—the singing vet. It is said that music soothes the savage beast. Maybe it will soothe dogs, cats, and horses also, not to mention their owners.

Another TERMS' song sighting: January 7, 2008, was the date of the BCS National Championship Game between Ohio State and LSU. That not played his drums since the accident. He wanted nothing to do with that part of his life, but now that Brandon was coming back strong it was okay to enjoy playing the drums again; it was okay to enjoy music again; it was okay to live again. Since that reunion jam session, Scott has taken his drum sticks in hand, walked into his garage, and has happily practiced drum beat after drum beat on his drum set almost every day since. That weekend session with his band mates and especially with Brandon seemed to give Scott's conscience the permission to move forward and once again, enjoy music with the same passion that existed before the accident. It was okay to smile, it was okay to be happy, and it was okay to beat those drums again; and beat them he has.

The "Reunion Concert" that Brandon and I envision has not occurred yet, but this "reunion jam session" was just what the doctor ordered. It was a chance to get together once again not to create a new song, but to re-create their bond—to cement their relationship the accident of September 30, 2006, suddenly disrupted. After lunch at Strawn's they said their good-byes and went their separate ways. They plan to meet again and have more jam sessions; maybe in the future there will be a Reunion Concert with several hundred fans and friends in attendance. That will be an awesome event. But until then, one thing is for sure; this weekend started another phase of their healing process. This medicine was just the right dosage. It was just what the doctor ordered.

TERMS Group E-mail—January 14, 2008: Brandon Update:

Dear Family & Friends,

Today, all across this great country, many students began their Spring Semester classes at their chosen college. Among those thousands of students was one person you know well—Brandon Young.

His two classes today were Physics and Advanced Spanish. Personally, I had a difficult time in college with my Advanced English class. Brandon is very excited about this new phase in his recovery.

Speaking of recovery, his eye surgery that was set for Tuesday, January 8th, was put off again. That was the fourth time this surgery has been re-scheduled. Dr. Alan Richards was very sorry about all these delays

Scott: "The experience was magical. I could not imagine how good Brandon felt. I really could not imagine the joy Brandon's parents felt. They have seen him grow each day since September 30, 2006, to where he is now. They must have experienced an awesome and indescribable range of emotions. I kept putting my own ecstatic emotions aside just to empathize with how Brandon felt. It was one of those moments you'll never forget, and it is an emotion I don't want to forget."

Ben: "One thing that really made me smile, besides actually playing and smiling at everyone, was when we were all getting our instruments out of the back of our cars. The walk up to Clyde's door with Scott holding his drum sticks, Blake holding his djembe (pronounced "Jim-bay," it is a type of bongo drum) and Brandon holding his bass was picturesque; and, man, did it strike a chord. Some of the most fun we had touring was unpacking and packing our equipment for shows. While it sucked at the time, that was when we goofed off and told jokes. Good times!"

Brandon: "The reunion jam session was a very long-awaited joy. I enjoyed every second of it. The first couple of songs seemed a bit 'lacking' in certain places, but that is definitely understandable considering the guys had not played the songs in 14 and ½ months. After those first couple of songs, it was like we were back in sync. I had been learning the songs since January of 2007. I had been practicing a lot; that showed that night, as I was able to play along with the guys in this performance. It was really a beautiful experience for the guys from what they told me. I quite enjoyed myself."

Ben, Blake, Clyde, and Brandon joined together the next morning for another jam session. Blake's father and step-mother were able to make that session. She was very moved by that experience. Alise, Blake's step-mother, sent me this e-mail: "Felt so good watching them interact and play once again. I teared up with the first song—then, finally, felt at peace. I called Morgan at work to let her hear the jam session over the cell. It's been a tough year of worries. Sure, they've had to regroup and go separate ways, but they'll always have that bond. It was a perfect way to start the new year." Obviously, the band members felt the same way.

Later Scott and his young son joined Ben, Blake, Clyde, and Brandon at one of Shreveport's favorite family restaurants, Strawn's, for a hearty lunch meal. His son needed to meet all of his "uncles." During that lunch session, his son seemed to have bonded with Clyde, and the band had bonded again. Scott had

Finally it was time for the band's jam session that Friday evening. Originally I thought this might be a time for just the band members, but thankfully it wasn't. As we arrived at Clyde's home, there was a beehive of activity. Band members were hooking up their equipment to available electrical sockets; amplifiers were put in place. The spectators, Jay, Angela, Khanh, Tiffany, Anne, and me, gathered in Clyde's dining-room area. The band members filled up Clyde's living room.

The guys were a little tentative in the beginning. Fifteen months had passed since they had performed together. It seemed like a lifetime ago. So much had happened in the interim. Of course, Ben, Blake, Clyde, and Scott wanted this to be a positive experience for Brandon. Yes, Brandon had been practicing some of The TERMS' songs, but how would he do in this setting? A song was mentioned for them to play. Brandon said, "I don't remember that one. How about this one?" The first couple of songs were a little rough. But as the saying goes, "The third one is the charm," and was it ever.

It was a special evening watching them perform together again. It was a special evening watching Jay and Angela, as their heads nodded approvingly as Brandon played very well and kept up with his band mates. It was a very special evening watching Brandon standing up to perform and watching his fingers dance on his guitar strings. He even sang the words to a couple of songs. Maybe he thought Ben needed help with the words. Then again, maybe he wanted to show his parents that he could multi-task.

Two of the e-mail responses from the latest "Brandon Update" that included this wonderful occasion:

12-30-07, from Mel B: "This was the best news we've had all year!"

12-31-07, from Dane A: "That must have been a wonderful reunion for the boys. I wish I could have been there."

After that weekend, I asked the band members to comment on that experience. Below are their comments via our e-mail connection:

Blake: "From just waiting for Brandon to move one finger in the hospital to seeing him rock out on the bass in perfect form still has me in shock—and very thankful."

In visiting with Ben he mentioned that he was talking with Greg Ladanyi monthly. Although he was no longer performing for Maple Jam Records, he had signed an agreement with their new company, Maple Jam Music Group. He would continue writing songs for them. As Ben stated, "I may write two songs a month or twenty songs a month. There is no set quota." One thing is for sure, other performers may be able to sing Ben's songs, but they will never belt out those tunes as only Ben can. They will never be able to capture his essence, his style, his passion, his tremendous vocal range, and most definitely, not his stage presence.

While Ben was working on his solo career in New York earlier this year he had the great fortune to collaborate with Danny Kortchmar. In an e-mail from Ben, dated March 3, 2007, he wrote, "As far as the music goes, I have been meeting with a gentleman named Danny Kortchmar (Jacques, Google him if you get a chance). We have been writing a bit together. This is the guy I will most likely be collaborating with if I continue with Maple Jam/ICON. He is very easy to work with and loves the way I write. He didn't get it at first, but I've brought him over to my side! He has worked with the likes of James Taylor, Neil Young, Billy Joel, and Carol King. He also plays in a band with Steve Jordan (Scott will know who he is)." And from Ben's e-mail of January 14, 2008, "It was really cool working with him. He was very knowledgeable and passionate about many different genres of music. He was also tired of generic radio, much like me. I wish we could have gotten some material released, but hey, things just don't always work out the way you think they will."

Back home, Ben had been putting in some time as a substitute teacher. That experience confirmed one career path he will NOT be pursuing—teaching. He did mention that he was contemplating a career as a veterinarian. He would be working with a local veterinarian soon as an assistant to investigate if that is a career field he might wish to pursue.

We had a great visit with Blake's father, Mac, and step-mother, Alise. They are such nice people. After a good visit and a few pictures they were off to eat dinner at Superior Grill. Even with superb directions from us they still got lost, but eventually made it to the restaurant. In fact, the next morning they went to Clyde's home/studio to watch the band in another jam session. Yes, they got lost again. Alise wrote in an e-mail, "Still laughing about our round-and-round lost driving trying to find our way!"

Chapter Eighteen
Emotional Healing Process Has Begun

Weekend of December 28, 2007

Plans are made and plans are changed. Events happen, but sometimes they are postponed. One event that did happen was the band's reunion the weekend of December 28, 2007.

Angela had been thinking about getting the band members together during the Christmas break, but she wanted to surprise Brandon, so she kept things rather low key. Phone calls and e-mails were sent to Ben, Blake, Clyde, and Scott concerning the semi-secret event. Finally, things came together. Angela informed Brandon of the happenings on Wednesday, December 26th. Items on the weekend agenda included a visit with everyone at Jay and Angela's home and a jam session at Clyde's home/studio.

Anne and I parked on the street in front of Jay and Angela's home. We walked towards their house and greeted Clyde first. He was talking on his cell phone and standing on the front steps where a wheelchair ramp had been just a few months before. Inside were Jay, Angela, Brandon, Ben, Khanh, and Tiffany. Joining us later were Mac Oliver, Alise, Blake, McVea, and Ashley. It was a time to visit, make small talk, catch up on the latest news, and take pictures; yes, plenty of pictures.

That evening I discovered that Blake is steadily making progress in the world of commercial insurance. Friday, December 28th had been quite a stressful day for him. He stated, "I was working on the computer, talking on the phone, and running back and forth from the fax machine. It was a wild day." An insurance proposal that he had worked on for the past two and a half months had culminated in a frenzy of activity that day. He stated that it could be a tough business, but he was getting more comfortable in that business environment.

Brandon's next surgery (eye surgery) is set for January 8th. He is anxious to have that performed.

Enjoy your New Year's Break—easy on the Egg Nog. May your 2008 be great.

faces, the intensity of their performance, the glances made amongst them were a sight to behold. Seeing Brandon standing up in Clyde's living room with his band mates, performing with his brand-new bass guitar that Santa had just brought him, as his fingers busily worked that instrument—What a moment to treasure, and treasure we did. Anne whispered to me during that performance, "Scott can't stop smiling."

It was a magical evening. Ben and Khanh had driven up from Raceland that day with a stop at Eddie's BBQ Smokehouse in Alexandria, Louisiana, where they had a chance encounter with their former sound engineer and friend, Wiley Whitesides. Blake had a very intense day in the world of commercial insurance, as a deal he has been working on for the past two and a half months finally came together. Clyde was busy getting everything together as he worked around his various business meetings scheduled for that day and evening. Scott worked his normal 12-hour shift with Enterprise Car Rental and was still in his coat and tie as he joined the group that evening. Blake's father, Mac Oliver, and his step-mother, Alise, and McVea, Blake's brother, along with Ashley, one of Brandon's sisters, also joined the reunion at Brandon's home.

Another TERMS' song sighting. Morgan, Alise's daughter, was shopping at Kohl's in Monroe last week when The TERMS' song, "There She Was," began playing on the store's piped-in music. She immediately called Alise!

Also last week, Brandon was home reaching high for an item, with his right hand. His arm was straight up over his head. Jay suggested that he try to reach that item with his left arm and hand. Just a few months ago, Brandon could not raise his left arm over his shoulder, but that night his left arm and hand went up as high as his right arm and hand had done. Jay said, "That's when we lost it. We cried a river of tears."

Today a few of the band members should be visiting with Scott and Sara and Dixon. They wanted Dixon to see his uncles from The TERMS, and his "uncles" wanted to see if Dixon had any potential to be a drummer like his Daddy.

E-MAIL CONNECTIONS

members of The TERMS that would be the start of their emotional healing process; for others it would complete their healing process. The next day would truly begin a new chapter in each of their lives. What a performance that would be. What a night to remember. It would be a tribute to the determination of Brandon and his indomitable will to recover from his devastating injuries, a tribute to Blake and Clyde to recover from their physical injuries, and a tribute to Ben and Scott for moving forward and not wanting to perform again until all their buddies were ready. It may never come to pass, but wouldn't it be grand if it did.

TERMS Group E-mail—December 29, 2007: Brandon Update:

Dear Family & Friends,

Sure hope you and your family are enjoying this Christmas Season!

At the top of *The TIMES'* (Shreveport newspaper) front page yesterday was this title "AMERICAN TRAGEDY—Group reunites on stage Saturday." Little did they know of another reunion that occurred this weekend.

Angela Young had been trying to surprise Brandon by getting the band together during the holidays so they could visit and perform once again. That is just what happened last night. After visiting with Brandon at his home for a couple of hours, they ventured to Clyde's home and studio. Around 9:30 Friday night The TERMS commenced a jam session that we witnessed for the next hour.

The "we" included Jay and Angela, Tiffany, Brandon's girlfriend, Khanh, Ben's girlfriend, Anne, and me. Scott and Blake had not played in 15 months, and, of course, the band had not performed together in the same time period. They were a little rusty. The first couple of attempts were a little awkward as everyone was trying to get their rhythm with one another, and, of course, they were anxious to make this work for Brandon.

By the third attempt at a song, they were rocking. The looks on their

JACQUES LASSEIGNE

Closure—Not There Yet

There will continue to be "Brandon Updates" to my TERMS E-mail Groups as new steps are taken by Brandon and the rest of the band members. There will be many things to report to dear family and friends. New surgeries, stories about Brandon's return to college, progress made by other band members in their new endeavors, and Brandon graduating from college will be some of the topics to be relayed in future e-mail updates.

One topic that would be great to report on would be "The TERMS announce their Reunion Concert!" That would be a huge event generating phenomenal interest. The television broadcasts of Brandon's recovery have mentioned just such an occasion. If that ever comes to pass it would not only generate extraordinary interest and exceptional media coverage, but it would give Ben, Blake, Clyde, Brandon, and Scott the closure they need to move on with their lives. In late September 2006 they were going strong in the music world, and they were on the upswing concerning their personal harmony with one other. A couple of months later they were to perform their single, "Big City Concrete Wildflowers," on nationwide television in the United States and Canada, courtesy of The Megan Mullally Show. That should have been a great springboard to bigger and better things. The sky was the limit. But a cruel twist of fate would end that abruptly on a neighborhood street in Monroe, Louisiana, on September 30, 2006.

Physical wounds will heal, thanks to great medical attention, superb medical professionals, wonder drugs, time, and prayer. It takes a bit longer, sometimes a great deal more time, to heal the emotional wounds associated with such catastrophic events. That was one thing that made Ben such an outstanding lyrics writer. He had deep, emotional feelings he could tap into. That was clearly evident with the new songs he wrote after the accident. Adjectives are lacking in describing those songs, but some are excellent, well-written, superb, outstanding, phenomenal, personal, heartfelt, inspired, brilliant, stunning, marvelous, and exceptional. If these young men ever get together to practice again for one last reunion concert that would help their healing process. They would be getting together in order to say good-bye—good-bye to a fantastic past they shared together. They could tell their many fans and friends good-bye from The TERMS and thanks for an absolutely glorious journey. For some

Speaking of removal, Brandon is being removed from his daily ritual at home. In January, he will be returning to college! Yes, he is scheduled to return to LSU-S in January. He is excited about the opportunity and the challenge.

What a difference a year makes. At this time last year, Angela was going through one of the hardest times in her life. She was with Brandon 24 hours a day at the Methodist Rehabilitation Center in Jackson, Mississippi, last December, and he was just beginning to awaken from his brain injury. He had to learn to talk again, to swallow again, and to walk again.

Last week, that hospital held a "reunion" for their former brain-injury patients. Brandon definitely remembered the physical layout of that wonderful, healing place, although he could not remember his gifted therapists who helped to bring him back out of his mental and physical fog.

Mark Adams, CEO of the Methodist Rehabilitation Center, stated, "At last Thursday's brain-injury patient reunion it was great seeing Brandon again. I definitely remembered Brandon, although in Brandon's mind he was meeting me for the first time. That exchange also occurred with others who were involved in Brandon's rehab. He played his acoustic bass guitar to two TERMS' songs. By doing so he reminded all of the Methodist staff in attendance, including me, why we work here. I followed Brandon's recovery more closely than I've followed any patient's recovery. It was and it continues to be a blessing for me to have been contacted and able to help Angela and Brandon."

As Angela states, "When I try to express my thanks to all of you for your wonderful support and for you standing by us in this most difficult time, there are no words that really say what I feel inside. But you need to know that I hope that you have a very Merry Christmas. I know we will—Jay & I have our son back."

blend in…But don't give up on me yet…I might be running on fumes, but I ain't running on empty yet, No, I ain't running on empty yet." Things have definitely changed. No matter what, life moves on. We do not know what tomorrow may bring, but one thing is certain: change is constant. Ben, Clyde, Blake, Scott, and Brandon knew about change, whether it was a change in the lyrics or melody in a song or a change in their schedule or a change in their personnel or a change in their compensation package or a change in their marketing strategy.

These young men grew up quickly after the accident. The emotional pain is still there; in fact, for Blake, Clyde, and Brandon, the physical pain is still there at times, too. You are thankful you had a once-in-a-lifetime adventure that few people ever have a chance to experience. Yes, you are sorry that it ended so abruptly, not giving you the chance for closure. It helps that you are busy making a new life and dealing with new issues and new challenges. After all, it could be worse. But, every once in a while you think of those times and what might have been.

TERMS Group E-mail—December 18, 2007: Brandon Update:

And a Good December Evening to you!

Another month, another surgery planned, another delay. Brandon was scheduled this month for eye surgery. He was hoping to have his eyes aligned. That would accomplish two things: (1) He would no longer have double vision, and (2) His balance would greatly improve when he walks. As you can imagine, it is difficult to walk the straight and narrow line when you are seeing the world with double vision. To compensate, Brandon mostly uses his right eye when he walks.

It seems that the hospital resident set Brandon's surgery with the wrong surgeon! They found out this discrepancy four days before surgery during their pre-op visit. In addition to that set-back, the surgeon and the hospital are now requiring a statement, in writing, from Brandon's doctor that it is okay for him to have this surgery. Hmmmmmm, this has happened before! Oh well, Angela is taking this latest obstacle in stride by remarking, "This provides Brandon another month to heal from his recent stent removal."

E-MAIL CONNECTIONS

What's done is done, what's done is done
What's done is done, what's done is done

Woke up on the wrong side of bed,
got off on the wrong foot
and walked to the wrong side of town
Later than soon I'll shape up and settle down

Found myself in a sticky situation somewhere out on a limb
And for just that one moment I could both stand out and blend in

What's done is done, what's done is done
What's done is done, what's done is done

What's done is done, what's done is done
What's done is done, what's done is done

But don't give up on me yet, don't give up on me yet
No don't give up on me yet, don't give up on me yet

My circuits may be a little fried
My batteries are almost dead

And I might be running on fumes, but I ain't running on empty yet
Oh no, no! I ain't running on empty yet

Oh, I might have more than a couple of screws lose
Always burning that candle at both ends

And I might be running on fumes, but I ain't running on empty
No, I ain't running on empty yet.

Yes, as Ben sings, "I'm well aware things have changed…What's done is done, What's done is done…I didn't write the script to life and I've got no clue how the story goes…And for just that one moment I could both stand out and the night and watched a rerun of the news. Sherri Talley was doing the *Miracle Worker* segment on Brandon. It was so good to hear his voice. Up till now I had only seen pictures. Oh, I just returned from the Credit Union Service Center on Line Avenue, and the 'Wildflower' song was playing! The TERMS are still with us. Thanks for including me on the updates for Brandon."

That is the kind of support you have shown to all of us these past few years. It is so good to have you on this journey with us. We could not have made it this far without you. Thanks.

What's Done Is Done

The title of The TERMS' song, "What's Done is Done," is prophetic. What has happened has happened. It has been said that not even God can change the past. Read and ponder the well-written lyrics to that song written by Ben and composed and performed by The TERMS, well before the accident:

I might not always say what I mean, but I always mean what I say
Sorry doesn't cut it this time, and I'm well aware things have changed.

Sorry I wasn't there for you like I would've, should've, could've been
I could have been a better lover; I could have been a better friend.

Now I've done some pretty stupid things, and I'm sure I'll do a couple more
Let a lot of good people down and left a few true hearts on the floor

What's done is done, what's done is done
What's done is done, what's done is done

I'm pretty good at holding my tongue and then stickin' my foot in my mouth
Some say better safe than sorry, but I've still got my doubts

I know, I know, I know, I know you told me so,
I didn't write the script to life, and I've got no clue how the story goes

broadcast and this morning during their early morning news show. Obviously, from the video, Brandon is walking much better, and his balance is quite good, even though he still has double vision. His eyes are not quite aligned at this time, but surgery to correct that is on the horizon. That surgery is set for December 4th. Approximately six weeks later he will have a procedure to lift his left eyelid.

His eye surgery was delayed a couple of months due to Dr. Nathan's concern about another surgery and a tube being placed down his throat. Brandon really wants this surgery, and, of course, Angela is concerned with all the ramifications that are involved with this upcoming surgical procedure.

Brandon's trachea-tube site has closed up, and he continues to breathe well. He does have a pretty deep hole in his neck where the stent/trachea tube was located, but that can be "fixed" at a later date. If you saw the TV interview, you were able to get a quick glimpse of that area.

Brandon's determination to get better and to move forward strikes you every time you visit with him or every time the TV station runs another update on him. His motivation to do what it takes to get better and improve is truly inspiring.

Concerning our other young men, Blake continues to do well in the world of commercial insurance in Austin, Texas; Clyde is teaching art and music to elementary students in nine schools in the Shreveport area and is loving it; Ben moved back home and is substitute teaching as he considers his options, that may include returning to school to obtain his master's degree. Scott is continuing to progress with Enterprise Car Rental Company and is trying to teach his four-month-old son important lessons, such as smiling and laughing when his grandparents come to visit.

Thanks for being there these last few years. Another example of your tremendous love and support came today from a good friend and co-worker. Emmy sent me this e-mail today. "I woke up in the middle of that heartbreak, that misfortune, that adversity. It has been said before that a person does not drown if they fall into water; they only drown if they stay there.

A good support system, a team comprised of family and friends, can do wonders to help one navigate the pitfalls of this thing we call life. Personal visits are great, phone calls are great, cards and letters are great. E-mails joined that list a few years ago.

About nine weeks after the accident I traveled back to my hometown to visit with my father. His health had been deteriorating. My plan was to work that Monday then drive the three hours and forty minutes it took to make that trip; visit with him that evening and the next day. I would drive back to Shreveport the next afternoon or evening then return to St. Martinville the following weekend for another visit. As I drove up to my parents' home that Monday night, the front yard was full of cars. That was not a good sign. I did not realize his condition had taken a turn for the worse that day. He passed away an hour and a half later with his family by his side, at home, just as he wanted. I am so thankful I made it to his bedside before he died.

It was late, but I wanted to tell Anne the news. I tried to compose myself during that phone call but was not too successful. At least she knew the sad news and that I would not be returning home the next day. Unknown to me, the next morning Anne got on our home computer to e-mail the news to our friends. Four of those dear friends met me at the funeral home a couple of days later to offer their condolences and just to be with me during that time. Three friends drove down to St. Martinville later that week to attend the funeral and to be there for support. Two of those drove four hours—one way—to be there. Yes, funerals are not for our dearly departed family and friends; they are for the people who are left behind. The support of those dear friends was initiated by a heart-felt message by my wonderful wife via a simple e-mail. By hitting the "send" button on e-mail, wonderful things can happen. It did in this case, and it did in the case of The TERMS' car accident e-mail sent in the early morning hours of October 1, 2006.

TERMS Group E-mail—November 6, 2007: Brandon Update:

And a cool evening to you, Dear Family & Friends,

The local ABC affiliate, KTBS-Channel 3, filmed an update on Brandon on Halloween and aired it last night during their 10 o'clock news

Chapter Seventeen
What Does It All Mean?

A Journey Called Life

Life is indeed a journey. That journey takes many twists and turns and detours. At times, the path of life is monotonous, and at other times it is thrilling. It is dull and exciting; it is a breeze, and it is extremely difficult; it is filled with warm relationships and it is filled with loneliness; it has moments of great joy and moments of extreme sorrow and hurt; it has a sense of peace and balance, and it also has a sense of disappointment and loss. It is like riding a wild roller coaster. Strap on your seat belt because it will be a wild and bumpy ride with its ups and downs, its thrills, its breath-taking dips, and its sudden stops.

For some, the sudden stop of a roller coaster can equate to their dropping out of school or the ending of a relationship or the loss of a good job or the relocation to another area of the country or the diagnosis of cancer or a car accident. People react differently to life's sudden stops. Some dust themselves off, learn from that painful episode, and move on. Others never seem to move beyond that point. That is truly tragic. Nobody said it was going to be easy, but it can be extremely worthwhile, even rewarding, to move forward and live your life to the fullest; a life with new meaning, a deeper meaning.

What does it all mean? Now *that* is a very good question. The "why" question has been studied and meditated on by philosophers, writers and theologians throughout the ages. The "why" question is "Why do bad things happen?" or "Why do bad things happen to good people?" or some version of that theme. We don't really know why bad things happen; all we know is they do, and they will continue to happen. There is a lot of hurt in this world; always has been and always will be the situation. The difference is how we react to

JACQUES LASSEIGNE

Yes, there will be more surgery in the future (eye surgery) and more steps to make in his recovery, but he and his family are moving forward. It is a wonderful thing.

Thanks for being there. May you be blessed.

E-MAIL CONNECTIONS

Car accidents happen every day. In this country, 40,000 people are killed on our highways each year: a heart-breaking statistic. Cancer is diagnosed, heart disease is diagnosed, loved ones pass away. It is a part of life. We don't have to like it, but that is just the way it is.

This past year has been quite a journey for many of us. You have been a big part of that journey. Your love, your prayers, your support, and your kind words have been with us every step of the way. The band members and their families could not have made it to this point without you. Thanks for being there. You are such wonderful friends and a superb support group. You are ministry in action.

We all have issues in our lives, but you took the time to add this to your important-things list.

Anne and I ventured to Brandon's home after church today. It was so much different from our visit there last September 30th. Angela greeted us at the door today as she did on that fateful evening, except today was tears of joy instead of uncertainty and pain. Brandon's family is marking today as his new birthday, since he literally was reborn a year ago at the accident scene. Therefore, Anne and I presented Brandon with a birthday gift today—a frame with a Bible passage written on it that surrounded a picture of Brandon and his band members, his friends, Ben, Blake, Clyde, and Scott, who joined him together for the first time since the accident a few months ago at his home to say hi. Brandon does not remember the times they had together being in a band called The TERMS, so his buddies are there to fill his mind with those special memories.

Brandon is looking real good. He continues to make progress in all aspects of his life. His speaking is stronger, and he is still working out at the fitness center in Bossier City. One of the last aspects of his physical therapy was getting him to put on his pants standing up rather than sitting down. Many of us do not give that kind of thing a second thought, but in Brandon's world it is another step in his magnificent progress.

Whether The TERMS will return to the stage remains to be seen, but Lasseigne says the past months have strengthened their bond. "I don't think our friendship will ever die. What we've been through makes us stronger because the only thing holding us together before was music. Now we've experienced life together and come close to death. It's indescribable, but while we used to bicker about music, now we realize more of what we mean to each other."

I wrote the following e-mail to Stephanie Netherton the day the article appeared in the paper (June 3, 2007): "EXCELLENT ARTICLE! Very well done, my dear. Nice blend of the past and the present. Appreciate your time and effort on this article and on Brandon and his family. His mother has been through the wringer. It is amazing to see Brandon's drive. It is so much stronger than before the accident.

Yes, it is also my dream for The TERMS to have a reunion concert in the future. That would be grand. Have a good one!"

Her e-mail reply, also on June 3, 2007: "Thank you. Meeting Brandon and hearing his story and the story of the band was very moving for me. I couldn't imagine what everyone has been through in the past months, but I can only hope the story will show Brandon's spirit. Thank you for your help and kind words."

Indeed, in her article, Stephanie showed not only Brandon's spirit, but the heart and soul of his family and friends and of band mates in a rock band called The TERMS.

TERMS Group E-mail—September 30, 2007: Brandon Update:

Good Evening Friends & Family,

A year, 365 days, 52 weeks. It is a measurement we use to designate the passage of time. Some years seem to go by fast—as we get older...; some years seem like time is dragging and it is taking forever, especially when you are in high school and just waiting to get your driver's license. This past year has been a little of both. A lot has happened this past year. For it was around 6 P.M. on September 30, 2006, that The TERMS were in that devastating car accident. That changed everything.

recovered he would not be the same son she'd previously known. She questioned whether his sense of humor and colorful personality would be the same. For several months, Angela's only wish was to see her son smile again and to hear the sound of his laugh. Her wish was granted while she and Brandon watched "Chappell's Show."

"I couldn't believe he was smiling and laughing, and now that's all we do. His sense of humor is there, if not a little more. I truly thank God for his attitude every day, because it could be so different."

Brandon often watches music videos recorded by The TERMS. Questions of what could have been sometimes jog through his mind, and watching the videos is bittersweet for the musician, but his happiness far outweighs the sadness.

"I am sad, but that's very, very small compared to my happiness just to be here, happiness for my future and for everything I'm still able to do," Brandon said.

While Labat wasn't in the vehicle with his band mates on that Saturday, and he never felt the physical pain his friends endured, the emotional scars run deep.

"Your entire ground is pulled out from underneath you. Everything you've worked for over the past four years has gone bye bye," Labat said. "Slowly you learn to carry on, but you don't move on."

In February, with the blessings of his band mates, Labat moved to Brooklyn, N.Y., to pursue his solo career in music. "This is a whole new ball game. We used to sit in our studio, all facing each other to come up with a rough song. Now I'm here doing it all by myself without Brandon and Clyde's creativity and without the backbone of Scott and Blake."

Oliver moved to Austin, Texas, and is selling commercial insurance. Hargrove recently bought a house in Shreveport and built his own recording studio. Lasseigne, who visits with Brandon each Sunday, says the accident forced him to do a lot of growing up over the past several months. In January, Lasseigne married his girlfriend, Sara Milner, and says he couldn't be happier. Brandon hopes to finish his final year of college.

"I don't know if it would be possible or happen, but I'd like to have a reunion gig with The TERMS. That's obviously something I'd love to see happen," said Brandon.

"The neurosurgeon told us how critical (Brandon) was, and I just knew when he looked me in the eye he wanted me to understand. He said, 'He is very, very bad,' like he might not make it," Angela said. "So we had our little goals then—if he makes it through the night, then 24 hours and then 72 hours. He just kept fighting and hanging on."

For seven weeks, Angela sat by her only son's bedside in the Intensive Care Unit at St. Francis Hospital. "I was told numerous times by numerous doctors that the majority of it would be left up to (Brandon) on how well he did," Angela said. "Different people want to get well, and they have that drive and some people just can't, and they just don't."

Brandon developed complications from staying in ICU for so long. Multiple infections prolonged Brandon's stay in ICU and kept him from moving to in-patient physical therapy. "I knew if he continued to stay in ICU he was just going to get infection after infection, which is what happened," Angela said.

Mark Adams, a former Southwood High School classmate of Angela and CEO of Methodist Rehabilitation Center in Jackson, Mississippi, was contacted, and within hours a nurse manager was sent to Monroe to evaluate Brandon. After nine weeks in Monroe, Brandon was transferred to Jackson, and in the first days made great strides in recovery.

"During a brain injury recovery, there is a time when everything is trying to reconnect. He was trying to get out of the bed, but he couldn't walk yet," Angela said. "It was almost like his brain was working overtime to reconnect, and that was the hardest part. There were days when I didn't think I could make it during that (stage)."

Brandon's first miraculous moments came while at Methodist Rehabilitation Center. His first steps were taken and his first words were spoken. Angela said, "When Brandon got there he couldn't sit up, there was nothing left in him, and within a week of being there the change was incredible. He'd been so ill and seemed so defeated, and it was such a turnaround."

Brandon knows his recovery is not just for himself but for his entire family and especially his mother. "The better I do, the better she does," said Brandon.

One of Angela's greatest fears was the possibility that as Brandon

What followed was an exceptional article by Ms. Netherton. Below are excerpts from her article:

Brandon Young's eyes fix on the television as he watches The TERMS perform. He leans to the edge of the couch as his right hand gently taps out the bass line on his leg. His motions appear memorized from watching the recording rather than something he remembers doing as a member of the band.

As his face appears on the screen, Brandon smiles and laughs a little to himself about the life he once lived, and the life nearly taken during a car crash in September. The cane resting next to him symbolizes the moment the 22-year-old's life changed and where the past eight months have taken him.

"I still can't remember very much of it, but I remember bits and pieces like being in Los Angeles, but I can't remember any of the places we played," Brandon said.

Starr Andreeff, vice president of the label, said the band was on the verge of stardom, having already sold more than 15,000 albums, when a near-fatal car crash brought their dreams to an abrupt halt.

"We had records in stores across the country. Our single was playing on 90 radio stations around the country. We were being played on stations in New York, Philadelphia, and Nashville," Ben Labat, lead singer for The TERMS, said. "You feel like you're making some headway, and when the accident happened, at that point, you just want things to go back to normal."

Clyde Hargrove suffered a fractured pelvis and cuts and bruises and was treated at St. Francis North Hospital in Monroe. Blake Oliver was treated at St. Francis Medical Center in Monroe for a fractured bone in his neck.

Brandon sustained a severe brain injury to the right side of his head, his ear was almost completely torn off, his neck was fractured in three places, and his arms were covered with scrapes and cuts.

"His injury was global. It wasn't like it was just one little place. The way he hit it caused his whole brain to shake in his head," Angela said. "You could see on the X-ray the damage and where it was bruised, but they didn't know the extent of the injury. All injuries came secondary to his brain injury and secondary to him being kept alive."

On October 17th, Brandon will return to Dr. Nathan for a follow-up visit. During this visit, a scope of his throat will probably be performed. Brandon was scheduled to have another eye surgery later this month, but Dr. Nathan thinks it is too soon for him to be put under anesthesia again and to have something put down his throat.

Brandon is still working out at Fitness Twenty-Four and is continuing his therapy at Willis Knighton North. He continues to work to get his body stronger, especially his left side.

Angela and Brandon attended a healing Mass at St. Mary's of the Pines last Thursday. Brandon was anointed with healing oil and a priest laid hands on both Brandon and Angela while praying a special prayer for mother and son. It was a very special ceremony for both of them. It touched them dearly.

And you, dear friends and family, are very special to all of us. You are The TERMS' family. We could not have made it this far without your incredible support. Have a great week.

Local Print Media Coverage

The local Shreveport newspaper, *The TIMES*, has also been very supportive of The TERMS. They gave them good ink as they were working their way up in the music business, and they gave them good, sensitive coverage after the accident. An excellent example was the article in the Sunday Living Section on June 3, 2007, written by Stephanie Netherton. We were all astonished by the wonderfully written article and the two full pages given to this story. Five color pictures adorned this two-page spread. There were pictures of the band, of Brandon playing his guitar at home, of Brandon walking on a treadmill in a swimming pool with his physical therapist, as Angela sat in a chair with her watchful eye on her son, of Brandon with a wide grin, and of a "Get Well Soon" and "We Love You" poster made for Brandon. The caption read: *The TERMS, Car Crash ends band's climb up the charts and today, at different beats, its members recover.* On page two the caption read: *The TERMS: Broken Record, New Song.*

stopped at Wendy's in Shreveport as he was on his way back home to Lafayette from a Dallas trip when his young daughter excitedly said, "It's the Flower Song! It's the Flower Song!" Leigh, physical therapist daughter of a good friend, heard the song as she was visiting a music store in St. Louis; and Emmy, a co-worker, heard the song in a credit union office in Shreveport. She asked the credit union staff what radio station they was listening to. They replied, "We're tuned to a satellite station." As Annette, a close friend, states in her 11-21-07 e-mail to me: "WOOOOO HOOOOOO! My favorite song…I still listen to it in my car when traveling…WOOOOO HOOOOOO!" I think she likes that song.

The band is no more, the band members are moving on with their lives, Brandon is still coming back from his devastating injuries, they are all still dealing with life's daily challenges and the lack of their once close-knit association, but the music lives on. The result of their hard work and their creative talent is still there for everyone to witness and experience. All one has to do is turn on the right satellite radio station or venture into the right store. Now that will brighten anyone's day.

TERMS Group E-mail—September 17, 2007: Brandon Update:

Good Evening!

Hope you are enjoying a taste of Fall—we are, at least in these cool mornings.

Brandon is doing well, although his steady progression had a couple of hiccups recently. Those hiccups came in the form of a cough. It has been three weeks since his stent/trachea surgery, and Brandon has been experiencing tickling sensations in his throat that makes him cough. The day after surgery, he was eating lunch with his father, Jay, and he started to cough and choke. Jay had to call 911. The paramedics arrived and calmed Brandon down, and things turned out fine. Brandon had another coughing incident on September 11th, of all days. He feels something in his throat that his senses tell him to cough up. Dr. Nathan will see Brandon this week to perform a swallow test to make sure everything is okay.

Many of you have sent nice comments to me, as Linda O. did recently. She wrote on 8-30-07: "Thanks for these updates. It seems as if I know Brandon. I am always interested in how he is doing. You have been so supportive of Brandon, his family and all the young men in a band we fondly remember."

I will update you on the other members as soon as I receive word from them. Scott, again, made the top sales award at Enterprise Car Rental. Last month he made "Top Gun" for the 3rd consecutive month. Recently he took an oral interview with five different department heads—an hour each. He received a call that evening to inform him he had passed that 5-hour test. Last week he interviewed for the assistant manager position at the Bert Kouns location, the region's highest-volume store. He did receive that promotion and started that new responsibility this week. His twelve-week-old son is excited since his Daddy will be able to buy him bigger diapers and more formula. His son stated just last week, "After all, I am a growing boy."

Thanks for all your prayers and support. You have been a tremendously wonderful support system. Enjoy the cool front coming in this week. It should be in the low 60s this weekend! Hope you have cooler weather in your neighborhood.

The Music Lives On

There have been many "Big City Concrete Wildflower" sightings in the last few months. I'm referring to the playing of that single by The TERMS on the radio. Anne & I heard it for the first time on FM 96.5 KVKI, a Shreveport radio station. It was 4:55 A.M., and I should have been out of bed getting ready for my morning run when Anne hit me and almost shouted, "The TERMS! It's The TERMS! Turn the volume up!" Later other friends and family heard the song "Big City" in various parts of the country. Anne also heard it in Bed, Bath & Beyond in Shreveport, Louisiana, in the spring of 2007 over the store speakers; Adam, a fellow runner, was in Home Depot in New Jersey during the 2006 Christmas Holidays and heard it; Jade, my niece attending Auburn University, heard it in one of the stores in an Alabama mall; Alvin, one of my brothers,

E-MAIL CONNECTIONS

What breathtaking news! Prayers continue to work wonders. Angela thanks you from the bottom of her heart.

Two hours later, after recovery, Brandon was wheeled back to his room. His family was waiting in the hallway to greet him. Angela relates the story, "Brandon looked at us and his eyes were filled with tears and his lips were trembling. He said, 'Mom, it's gone.'"

He will have to be watched closely for a while to make sure no more scar tissue/granulation forms, and he does return to Dr. Nathan next week for a follow-up visit. But what a day yesterday was!

TERMS Group E-mail—September 10, 2007: Brandon Update:

Good Evening to you, Dear Family & Friends!

Brandon went for his follow-up visit with Dr. Cherie-Ann Nathan on September 5th. Everything is going great! His next follow-up visit with Dr. Nathan is in a MONTH! The no-trachea-tube situation: so far so good.

Brandon's speech therapist is releasing him this month because, as she puts it, "I can't find anything challenging enough for him." As Angela said, "What an AWESOME statement!"

Speaking of challenging, Brandon does want to finish his college degree, but he does not know if he will be ready by the spring semester of 2008. Angela thinks he will be ready. Ah, the gentle encouragement of a mother! Because of Brandon's condition I was informed by Ken Ebarb, a good friend and fellow e-mail recipient of all these "Brandon Updates," that Brandon may be eligible for assistance to return to school by the various programs of Louisiana Rehabilitation Services. It is people like Ken who step up to the plate time and time again to provide needed help to Brandon and his family. It has been amazing to watch all of this unfold these past eleven months. Thanks to each one of you.

From Dane A: "Thank you for keeping us up-to-date on his progress. It means a lot."

TERMS Group E-mail—August 28, 2007: Brandon Update:

Good Tuesday to You!

KTBS-Channel 3 did a real nice TV segment on Brandon recently as most of you know. After that piece aired, TV Anchor Sherri Talley received a call from Bob Morgan, owner of the new Fitness Twenty-Four facility in Bossier City. It is a new twenty-four-hour fitness center. He asked her if she could connect him with Brandon and his family. Phone calls were made. Angela and Brandon met with Bob Morgan. He offered Brandon the opportunity to work out at his fitness center at no charge and to receive fitness training FREE of charge for as long as Brandon wanted. Brandon's response, "How amazingly awesome is that?" Isn't it nice to know that there are some really good people in this world?

Another day, another surgery. Dr. Cherie-Ann Nathan performed surgery on Brandon yesterday to have his stent removed. He was first on the surgery schedule. After forty-five minutes, Dr. Nathan called Angela to tell her there was some granulation that had formed, and it would have to be lasered. She needed consent to perform that procedure. During this conversation Angela asked, "Does this mean he will have to keep the trachea tube?" Dr. Nathan would not know that answer until she lasered the tissue.

Yes, one important aspect of this surgery centers around the important issue of Brandon's trachea tube; would it be removed? He has had a trachea tube since the accident. An hour and a half passed when Dr. Nathan called back to inform Angela the granulation was not as severe as last time, and his airway looked good. She told Angela, "I'm taking out the stent and will just place some gauze over the opening." The words sunk into Angela: The stent is out and there is NO trachea tube!

Chapter Sixteen
Favorable Media Coverage

KTBS-Channel 3's Coverage of Brandon's Progress

KTBS-Channel 3 did another follow-up video segment on Brandon in November of 2007. It was just under four minutes long. It showed Brandon working out in a fitness facility under the guidance of a personal trainer and his physical therapist. His physical therapist was amazed at how far he had come since she last worked with him. The video featured Brandon walking and talking and working out. That segment caught me by surprise, but Brandon sent me a video link that I forwarded to my TERMS E-mail Groups. A few comments are below, all dated November 7, 2007:

From Gayle F: "Wow! Very moving…I will share this with my children. Together, we have watched and read about Brandon's progress as we have kept him in our thoughts and prayers and as we have continued listening to The TERMS' CD in our car!"

From Barry B: "I just watched the video about Brandon's recovery. Great story! What an inspiration he is to all of us. Thanks again for keeping us all posted on his continuing recovery."

From Sarah P: "Oh, what a great story! You have been so good about keeping us all up to date, but to actually see his progress, and hear the determination and thankfulness in his words was absolutely awesome! I can't wait to share this video with the kids, because we have continued to pray for him—especially Matthew!"

his "concert," and she took a few pictures of the occasion. Of all the songs he played, he mentioned a "disclaimer" on only one song. Brandon told the therapists, "This is a fast song, and I can't quite keep up with the pace on this song yet, but here we go." Besides that song, he performed magnificently.

Yesterday as Brandon, or as he called himself for his performance, "One Rock Star, Brandon Young," was performing, Scott received a phone call from the local ABC Affiliate, KTBS-Channel 3. They wanted to do a follow-up on Brandon's recovery and of the band. The filming took place this afternoon at Brandon's home. Scott was able to take his lunch break then in order to make that filming session. Unfortunately, Clyde was not able to make it. Scott provided a picture to the film crew with all the band members. That picture was taken at Brandon's home a few weeks ago when they were all in town. That was the first time they were all together since the accident.

Sherri Talley, long-time anchor with KTBS, did the interview. Things could change, but right now that segment will air on Monday, August 6th, at 10 P.M., and Tuesday, August 7th, during their early morning broadcast (5 A.M.-7 A.M.). For those not in the local viewing area, you can view the video from their website on Tuesday, www.ktbs.com.

May you have a blessed week.

experienced the last three years. We sat near Ben's parents, Reggie and Kathy, and Ben's brother, Blake, during the ceremony. It was great visiting with them in person again.

After hearing a short speech the graduates walked up to the stage to receive their diplomas and a handshake or two from the faculty and administration. After Scott received his diploma, one of the handshakes he received was from the Dean of the E. J. Ourso College of Business. In that brief exchange, the Dean commented to Scott, "I am really impressed with you and all that you accomplished. You should be very proud." He probably made the same comment to Ben. He obviously knew of Ben and Scott trying to balance a full-time college course load with a full-time commitment of a touring band with a recording contract to fulfill and of the intense criticism by many for their involvement in the "Welcome to the Now" image campaign by the Public Relations' Office and the song they composed for that campaign and of the recent horrific accident the band was involved in. With all these distractions and events, Ben and Scott were still able to complete their course work on time and graduate with good grades. Indeed, what an accomplishment. That comment was not expected, but it was a touching tribute to the end of an intense chapter in their lives.

TERMS Group E-mail—August 1, 2007: Brandon Update:

Good Evening to You!

As you may know, Brandon is about to "graduate" from his therapy. He has come an awful long way in a short amount of time and had done amazingly well thanks to your good thoughts and prayers, the superb care he has received from the medical profession and his family, the great support from friends and family who call him, visit with him, e-mail him on a regular basis, and from Brandon's tremendous drive to get better.

To thank his many therapists and to show them how far he has come in his recovery, he performed a "concert" for them yesterday at Willis Knighton Rehab Center! He played a TERMS' CD in the background and played his bass part to go along with the songs. He invited Anne to towards the band so he had the band perform the song's ending again so she could walk in a different way this time. That was a wrap. As Ben recalls, "It was cool being in front of a studio audience. I remember the audience clapping for an extended period of time—long after we had finished the song. Wow…then I realized that this is Hollywood, and there are applause signs blinking all over the building! Ecstasy and humbleness—all in the same few minutes!" Ben continues, "We finished the song. As the audience is still clapping, Megan came over to greet us. Clyde and I gave her a hug. That's what Southern gentlemen do. I think we surprised her. The hugs were a bit awkward."

Speaking of Hollywood stars, in the "Green Room" the band met two more. One was Selma Blair. She starred in the film *Cruel Intentions* and has had notable roles in such films as *Legally Blond* (2001), *The Sweetest Thing* (2002), and *Hellboy* (2004). The other was Timothy Olyphant. As Wikipedia, the free encyclopedia, states, "He is perhaps best known for playing Sheriff Seth Bullock on *Deadwood* and the villain Thomas Gabriel in *Live Free or Die Hard*." These two Hollywood stars treated the band members with courtesy and respect. Being with three Hollywood stars, having make-up and wardrobe people attend to you, having a studio audience watch you perform and cheer you on—it was easy to see why Blake later stated, "That was one of the moments where I said to myself, we have truly made it."

The band was invited back two more times to the show, except the next time would be the real thing—no evergreen session, but a nation-wide audience to perform for and to win over. They had won the hearts and souls of the cast and crew. Now it was time to do the same to the show's audience in the United States and Canada. There was one conflict with the scheduled date: LSU's fall graduation. The taping of the Megan Mullally show and LSU's fall graduation fell in the same week. Scott and Ben would have to miss their graduation ceremony. It would be a small price to pay in the great scheme of things in exchange for national exposure. But with the accident and with the dissolving of the band this date was never kept.

The day of LSU's fall 2006 graduation was a rainy day. Since LSU is so large, each college has its own graduation ceremony in the fall. As is typical, the graduates were lined up in alphabetical order by last name. As chance would have it, Scott and Ben sat on the same row for the graduation ceremony, separated by only one person. That was very fitting considering all they had

E-MAIL CONNECTIONS

series, was also nominated for that award in 2001, 2002, 2003, 2004, and 2005, and also won four Golden Globe Award nominations for the show. *Will & Grace* was a very popular show with a very popular cast.

According to Wikipedia on-line, Megan Mullally's new syndicated program averaged about two million viewers in Canada and America. Now, The TERMS would be appearing on her new talk show that debuted in syndication on September 18, 2006. Starr had done good!

The TERMS were scheduled to perform at The Joint in Los Angeles the evening of August 25, 2006, but they had an early call to the Megan Mullally Show that day. The band would be at the studio from 8 A.M. until 4 P.M. They spent an hour and a half in make-up. Ben recalls, "The hairdresser was kinda cute. I think we all took turns flirting with her. It seemed she was used to it." Blake remembers Ben running out of the dressing room in a wet suit that he found hanging up in there. It was there for David Spade to put on during the next Megan Mullally Show. Blake stated, "It turns out they are the same size. I think they ended up having to destroy that suit…those were good times indeed."

Concerning the actual TERMS' performance, the band members did not want to lip sync; it had to be a live performance or nothing. It was a live performance. The band members had been in pressure situations before where they absolutely had to perform well; this would just be another one of those times. The band actually performed their song, "Big City Concrete Wildflowers," twice. Scott had a "click track" programmed in his iPOD for their performance that day. It would play the role of a metronome for this performance. Scott recalls, "The production coordinator was counting down until it was their time to perform, but he obviously did not have my iPOD 'click track' in his earphones! It would have been nice to have been synchronized with the production coordinator, but that is show business. You just improvise. My first hi-hat strike, the part of the drum kit used for keeping time—the count off I do before every song—was not on the correct click, so I adjusted the next three strikes. It went something like 1…2…3…4: song begins. Your heart is already beating a hundred times a minute being in front of a live studio audience, but you adjust as fast as you can, look professional while you are doing it and move on. The performance of the song actually went quite well."

Upon the song's conclusion, Megan Mullally walked towards the band to officially greet them. The director of the show did not like the way she walked

Chapter Fifteen
Almost There, but Not Quite

The Megan Mullally Show and LSU Graduation

In the summer of 2006, The TERMS received a huge break in receiving an invitation to perform on the new Megan Mullally Show. Starr Andreeff, Vice-President of Maple Jam Records, has worked tirelessly on many angles in trying to get exposure for The TERMS. Some worked out, and some didn't. This one worked out. On August 25, 2006, The TERMS were in California to tape an "evergreen episode" for The Megan Mullally Show. That episode is normally never shown to the public unless it is really needed in an emergency, such as in a power outage that prevents a new show from being taped, or Megan Mullally is sick and is unable to tape a new show. The producers loved The TERMS, the crew loved The TERMS, and Megan Mullally loved The TERMS. Everything went very well: so well, in fact, that they were invited back for two more shows. Next time it would be the real thing. That show would air on nationwide television in the United States and in Canada. Earlier in their career, influential members of various television shows told The TERMS they liked them very much and would love to have them on their program, but they needed their music to be played on more radio stations and to be more visible. Well, this was the opportunity they were looking for. At this time, their music was playing on many, many radio stations nationwide. This show could springboard them to the next level and provide them with a much larger audience, a national audience.

Megan Mullally had been in show business for quite a while when she was cast as Karen Walker on the television show, *Will & Grace*. She won Emmy Awards in 2000 and in 2006 for outstanding supporting actress in a comedy

E-MAIL CONNECTIONS

on July 8th and performed in Greenwich Village on July 9th. His new songs are going over well, but we knew that would happen.

Clyde continues to compose and write music. In fact, he ventured to Austin, Texas, a big music destination, to check out the music situation there.

Blake lives in Austin, Texas, and continues to make his mark in the commercial insurance business. He is a commercial-lines coverage specialist with Hertel Insurers Group.

Scott continues working his 12-hour days at Enterprise Car Rental and trying to make a good impression in the business world. Last month he was named "TOP GUN." To get that recognition a person has to excel in many areas of the company's business.

Thank you for your wonderful support and prayers for these young men. They are very special to us. And keep enjoying your summer.

Group TERMS E-mail—July 18, 2007: Brandon Update:

Greetings Dear Family & Friends.

Brain injury recovery is an interesting thing. Brandon continues to make progress in his rehabilitation, but one example shows how varied it can be. The Topic: Random Memory. Brandon REALLY wants to return to college and finish his degree. To help out, Brandon's mother, Angela, found a practice ACT test on the Internet in order for Brandon to get a feel for what he remembers academically.

In working on a math problem that involved trigonometry Brandon did remember the formula to solve that problem. (Personally, I had a difficult time remembering how to SPELL trigonometry). But on another math problem, Brandon had difficulty remembering how to multiply 4 times 4. Now once Angela reminded him how to perform multiplication, he could easily complete those math problems without any further complications.

He is venturing out more. Recently he went to see his old band, Better Than Cornbread, play, and he also went to see Better Than Ezra. They performed at The Horseshoe Casino recently. He was wishing The TERMS would be opening for them again as they did at Centenary College last year.

More big news: Last week on July 10th the handicapped ramp in front of Brandon's house was taken down; yes, taken down. Brandon was very happy to see that. I can remember pulling into their driveway just a couple of months ago as Brandon was walking up the ramp, by himself, slowly. What a difference a couple of months can make in the life of a person who is determined, heck, who is DRIVEN to get better.

Other News:

Ben continues to work in New York. He played his first gig in Brooklyn

Chapter Fourteen
On the Lighter Side

Amniocentesis Test

Yes, after the accident Scott moved on with his new life. He graduated, got married, and now has a son—made me a grandfather. His wife had a difficult pregnancy; in fact, she was ordered to the hospital for complete bed rest and was there about three weeks before my dear grandson was born. People were asking how Sara and the baby were doing during this time so I sent an e-mail to a few friends and family. That update went like this: "Good Friday Morning to you! The amniocentesis test performed on Wednesday showed that 'little Scottie's' lungs were not quite ready yet. That test has four rankings: (1) Immature (2) Transitional (3) Mature with Caution and (4) Mature.

"The test showed 'little Scottie' with a range of between 2-3. If it had shown a range of between 3-4 the doctor probably would have gone ahead and induced. The hospital staff will probably run this test again early next week.

"On that scale, Anne said my score was between 1-2."

Two of the responses to that e-mail:

From Fern H: "I always wondered what the problem with you was….now I know."

From Anne F: "I think I would like your Anne."

With friends like these…

set for him he has surpassed. His physical therapist wants Brandon to continue to work on the fluidity of his motion. He still has a slight jerkiness to his walk, but she feels certain that will improve with practice and time. He can't wait to begin working out again. That is why I stopped doing my crunches. I did not want to have an advantage over Brandon in the six-pack department.

Slowly, but surely, he is venturing out more and more. He went out a couple of Saturdays ago to see his old band play. Their name is Better than Cornbread—the name is a winner! He loved hearing them play. Brandon just loves music. Angela has stated many times to me that he loved every minute that he was in The TERMS. Unfortunately, he still can't remember those times, and he may never be able to, but at least he lived that experience, and his family and band mates can fill in the blanks.

Those of you in Shreveport may have seen the nice write-up in *The TIMES'* Friday *Preview* section a week ago on Clyde Hargrove. It was titled, "TERMS Guitarist Carves New Path with New Music," by Shane Bevel. A nice, large picture of Clyde strumming his guitar accompanied the article. The article mentions the 80-minute piano composition he wrote that is on his new CD titled *Lost Cities* and a new group he has formed called Band of Clyde. The group plans to release their CD titled *Swimming in Rain* in late November. For more info on all this visit the website www.MySpace.com/bandofclyde.

Many of you know that four members of The TERMS' became uncles recently. That is because Scott's wife, Sara, delivered their new son. He came a bit early, but mother and son are doing fine now, except for the lack of sleep that new parents have to deal with. Dixon Cade went home last Sunday after thirteen days in NICU. He weighs 5 lbs and 9 oz. Scott was almost double that weight when he was born—shortly after being born, Scott walked out of the delivery room looking for a serving of steak and potatoes.

Thanks for your wonderful support. It continues to lift us all up.

E-MAIL CONNECTIONS

From Rick T: "I listened to the live TERMS CD on my way to Concordia Parish yesterday and really enjoyed it. It's just a shame that these boys had the 'gold ring' in their hands, and it was suddenly snatched away. Life seems unfair at times, but then later you see God's plan unfurl, and you're grateful that things happened the way that they did. At least that's what I've discovered as I have become older. Could not see it though when I was Scott's age. That 'Sympathy for the Devil' performance really blew my windows open! I don't sympathize with him though. He's never had any sympathy for mankind, huh? But still a rockin' song!"

From Tammi A: "This is very nice of you. Yes, I remember the 'Sympathy for the Devil' performance at The Cutting Room. THE PLACE WENT CRAZY!"

From Jack W: "Thanks for The TERMS' CD. The TERMS really sound great. Whoever recorded the tracks did a great job. The 'live' performances are very clear and well-balanced. The sax is great on track two. This is a really great CD. I'm glad I didn't miss this one. Thanks."

TERMS Group E-mail—July 4, 2007: Brandon Update:

HAPPY JULY 4TH TO ALL OF YOU!

Speaking of our nation's history, I recently finished the book *1776*, by David McCullough. It is a stirring book that tells the intensely human story of those who marched with George Washington in the year the Declaration of Independence was written. The beginning of this nation, the few brave men who kept the vision, how fate helped form a new nation—it is all there. I highly recommend it.

Brandon went for a checkup with Dr. Cherie-Ann Nathan last Wednesday—so far, so good. His next visit with Dr. Nathan will be on August 22nd. At that time she will schedule the surgery to remove the stent.

Brandon's family had a conference with his rehab counselors last week. They should be releasing him at the end of August. Every goal they have

JACQUES LASSEIGNE

More TERMS Music

A few months after the band was officially dissolved, I was having withdrawal symptoms for lack of new TERMS' music. I asked Scott if they had recorded some of their other songs. He said yes, so I asked him to burn me a CD. It was mostly music of their live performances. What a gift that was to mend my broken heart.

That CD has twelve tracks. They are "The Night is Young," "Sympathy for the Devil" (This Rolling Stones' song was recorded during their performance at The Cutting Room in New York in the summer of 2005. They were accompanied by Richie Cannata, sax player for Billy Joel, and Gerado Velez, percussionist for Jimi Hendrix. This is some of the finest live rock music you will ever hear. It is nine minutes and forty-four seconds of an outstanding live performance. It brought down the house!), "Casablanca", "Isthmus" (This was recorded in a Baton Rouge studio in one take! When Greg Ladanyi heard this recording he told the band, "Well, you don't need me anymore." A compliment like that—coming from Ladanyi—said volumes. He did give the band compliments, but as Ben said, "Only after we worked hard to make significant improvements on whatever we were working on. He was not an easy person to please, but I did appreciate the work ethic he brought to the table and instilled in us." Personally, I think this was their best song.), "Good Morning," "Laugh," "Balancing," "Love of Lies" (Ah, the wonders of live music. During this song, Brandon's bass guitar stopped working, but the band improvised quite well. A classic piece of music.), "Big City Concrete Wildflowers," "Turn," "What's Done is Done," and "Shotguns and Sunshine." Fifty-three minutes and forty-six seconds of terrific memories.

I burned a few CDs to give to family and friends so we could all enjoy what once was an up and coming group called The TERMS. Here are a few of their comments:

From Gay V: "Oh, my God—this CD is FAB! WHAT A TREAT! I miss that group and still play their CD all the time. I think they are so talented, and I am so proud that I got to hear them in person! It makes me so sad that all this had to happen!"

anesthesia he asked his mother, "Is that Ms. Lasseigne?" How's THAT for cognitive recognition?

Dr. Cherie-Ann Nathan was able to laser Brandon's trachea, enlarge it, and place the stent. There seems to have been NO adverse neurological effects with the arms, legs, neck. Everything works like it is supposed to!

Brandon's whole family wants to thank each and every one for your tremendous support and prayers these last eight months, and especially for the surgery today.

Brandon will have the stent in for four to six weeks. If that goes well, then he returns to Dr. Nathan for surgery to take it out. She will put a trachea tube back in and monitor it to insure that no more scar tissue forms and that the opening is sufficient for Brandon to breathe on his own. Later she will begin to downsize the trachea tube. He now has a size six; he will then go to a size four, then the trachea tube will be plugged off for a week or so, then voila, it will be gone!

Brandon stated this afternoon that he can already tell the difference and is breathing a lot better. The downside (well, the news can't always be all good) of this stent is it is a little harder to take care of. Angela will have to suction him more frequently and make sure the stent is as clean and moist as possible so it does not "plug off." NERVE WRACKING! But with what Angela and Jay have had to do these last eight months they can surely handle this new wrinkle in Brandon's treatment.

I'll end with Angela's comment. "I have said so many times that I know it is all of the prayers for Brandon's recovery that have brought him this far. I truly believe that." Amen.

each of us, and it's always for our good when we are close to Him. I know that the boys are very down, but they will find their places in the world."

From Karen P: "I just read your e-mail with the disappointing news about The TERMS' end. I am so sorry it did not get a postponed second chance to make it big, since the guys seemed to be well on their way. They were so dedicated and working so hard at it. Sometimes you wonder about turn of events, and I think then you just have to trust that something better may be further along in life. Please remember that your friends empathize with you and are keeping your family and the rest of the young men from The TERMS in our prayers."

From Jane S: "Please tell Scott that Brandon chose to join the group and would do it again in a heartbeat! What a great experience for anyone! Accidents happen, and there is nothing we can do to make things happen differently. Scott is a sweetheart. You and Anne taught him to be caring and that is good, but he should not beat himself up over something that was out of his control."

From Dorothy K: "Life is a constant process, and the only thing permanent is change. So much change—so fast."

From Gay V: "I am so disappointed about The TERMS. I LOVED them! I thought they were GREAT!"

From Corinne P: "I am so sad to hear there will be no more TERMS! I know that you were so proud of them. What great memories, though; and what a great experience for all those young men!"

TERMS Group E-mail—June 18, 2007: Brandon Update:

HAPPY NEWS UPDATE! Brandon was taken today by the surgery team around 10:00 this Monday morning and was wheeled back to his recovery room around 3:00 P.M. Anne called Angela to see how things went. Angela responded with, "Surgery was a SUCCESS!" In fact, when Anne called, even though Brandon was a bit groggy from the

E-MAIL CONNECTIONS

All this time, friends kept e-mailing me about what the band could do while Brandon was recuperating. I had been passing some of these e-mails onto Scott, but finally stopped when he said it was just too painful to read. A couple of months later I finally informed the TERMS' group e-mail lists about this news. Many wrote back with heart-felt messages. A few examples:

From Bill P: "Chapters of life open and close. I'm confident the band members will do fine in that combination of work, opportunities, setbacks and friendships we call life."

From Wendy T: "What a whirlwind you all have been in this last year! Keep us posted. Forever a 'TERMS Family member.'"

From Dale C: "I'm sorry the band could not stay together. I felt they had a great musical future. Thanks for thinking to include me with this news. You are a good friend and lifetime family member."

From Jeannie B: "I am so proud of Scott for having gotten his degree. He will do well."

From Arnie F: "Wow, that's a lot of news in one report. We never know what lies around the corner. Thanks for staying in touch."

From Emmy H: "Wow, how life can turn you around and send you on a different road. My blessings to you, your family and the TERMS' family."

From Kathy C: "I am sorry to hear about the band. Just support them with all of your heart."

From Rhonda S: "Life can really throw us some curve balls. It's up to us how we play the game. There were times in the past five years that I thought I would not survive, but by the grace of God and a positive attitude, my husband and I have not been happier. Keep me posted."

From Rick T: "I am sorry about the loss of the band. Life's circumstances are continually changing, but it is comforting to know that God has a plan for

Scott had been feeling very guilty about the accident and had thought the very same thing that Ladanyi had verbalized in that meeting. When Greg Chiartano decided to leave the band, Brandon was the first person Scott thought about and he was the first person Scott called to ask, "Would you like to join the band?" Anne and I told Scott that he just can't beat himself up over this. Who knows what tomorrow will bring? The future is unknown. Who knows what Brandon's life would have been had he not been in the band? We could explain this to Scott, and he could understand it on an intellectual level, but it was a different situation on an emotional level.

In mentioning this to Angela Young, she replied, "It saddens me that Scott would ever feel any type of guilt for what happened to Brandon. He should look at it as he made it possible for Brandon to have one of the best years of his life. Brandon loved every minute he was with the band. Not Scott nor anyone else had any idea that accident would happen. It was just that, an accident. There is no reason why and no one to blame. We love Scott and don't ever want him to be anything but happy."

Scott did not respond to the opening comment by Ladanyi. Then it was announced that the record label had decided to disband The TERMS. Ben was to travel to New York to work on a new solo career, and if a band was ever formed again, Scott was offered the opportunity to be in the new band. Scott waited a couple of seconds before responding to all this news. He looked at Greg Ladanyi, President of the record label, and Dane Andreeff, founder and owner of Maple Jam Records, and said, "I want to thank you for the opportunity to be in this band, for all the experiences you have afforded all of us; it has been a hell of a ride. I was able to be a part of something very special and did things that some people only dream of. I thank you for that, but I must decline your offer."

Though the band was disbanded, Dane continued to pay the band members their monthly stipend through the end of the year. That was very gracious of him. He had tried to run a professional and first-class record label. He sure did exhibit a first-class gesture with that parting gift of generosity.

Scott finally told Anne and me the news a couple of weekends later. He was in town to visit Brandon at the Methodist Rehabilitation Center in Jackson, Mississippi. The news hit me like a ton of bricks. I was depressed for a week! They had the talent, they had the drive, they had the work ethic, and they had great opportunity come their way, but now it was over. That was a bitter pill to swallow.

Chapter Thirteen
The Accident's Aftermath—The Business Side

The TERMS Are No More

Six weeks after the accident the record label called a meeting. Ben and Scott attended, since Brandon was still lying in a hospital bed, and Clyde and Blake were recuperating at home. The record label had already cancelled all gigs for the months of October and November 2006, but there were some important performances coming up in December, including one at The Continental Room in Houston, Texas, and one on The Megan Mullally Show. Yes, they were scheduled to be on a national television show. What great exposure. That performance would, undoubtedly, open more doors for the band and probably help them reach the next level. The TERMS' original bass player, Greg Chiartano, had already contacted the band and offered his services on an interim basis to help out.

Greg Ladanyi opened the meeting by looking at Scott and saying, "It's your fault that Brandon is in that hospital bed." Ladanyi had wanted to bring in a different bass player when Greg Chiartano expressed his desire to leave the band. This bassist could also sing back-up vocals and was quite proficient on the organ. Ladanyi's thinking was to bring in a true outsider that would bring his unique talents and thoughts to the band as well as adding a new musical dimension to their music. Scott lobbied hard to have Ladanyi consider Brandon. Scott felt Brandon would fit in well with the group. Of course, Brandon brought with him excellent bass guitar-playing skills and a good singing voice for back-up vocals. Brandon did his part by learning all the songs before his audition was held. Ladanyi finally relented and put Brandon on a three-month, probationary stint. After two months the probationary status was removed. He then became, officially, one of The TERMS.

boys. One of the girls in my classes is IN LOVE with Scott and has spoken to him on the phone once when Walter called. It's hilarious. I have my own little promotion area here at school, and one of my students is making a flier to post concerning The TERMS' April 21st appearance at Centenary. One student bought 20 tickets for herself and her friends. They are very popular here."

E-mail from Brandon's mom dated April 4, 2006: "Just wanted to let you know that it will definitely be Monday morning before I have a final count on my order. Now that I have told people the price of the CD and of the Monday deadline, I have had people doubling up on their orders."

All the parents worked diligently on this promotion. What a superb effort on everyone's part. Of course, the band members were e-mailing their friends and fans on their personal e-mail and on MySpace.com and on their TERMS' website. It was a frenzy of activity. Anne and I met our goal; in fact, we sold just under 300 CDs. When one counts all the CDs the parents helped sell, the total count reaches over 900 CDs. What an amazing effort by everyone. With the parents' effort, with the band members' effort, with the behind-the-scenes effort of the record label, especially Starr, and with the incredible support of family, friends, and fans nationwide, the goal was reached. The sales put The TERMS in *Billboard Magazine's* Charts! They were ranked # 11 nationwide that week and # 1 in the Southeast Region. Yes, the power of e-mail can be an amazing thing. With good effort, a good plan, a good product, and help from a few key people, one can work wonders. It sure did in this instance.

E-MAIL CONNECTIONS

So if you would like this new version of their CD just let me know. I do not want your money now, especially since I don't know how much our discount will be. I just need to know how many to order when the time comes. Our window of opportunity is three weeks before the official release date of April 25th.

So, if you would like one, great!
If you and your significant other would like one (one for each vehicle), great!
If you would like to give them as birthday presents, graduation presents, etc., great!
If you would like to have one for your co-workers, nieces, nephews, etc., great!

The band keeps making progress, and this will greatly help push them more into the national realm. People like them when they hear their music, from California to Texas to Louisiana to Kansas to Tennessee to Florida to New York and Boston, and this successful promotion will help push them further onto the national scene.

Any questions, please let me know. You can call me or contact me via e-mail.

Thanks very much for your consideration!

Word starting spreading among the parents of the band members.

E-mail from Scott on March 21, 2006: "Dad, The news about your CD promotion is going around the studio. Walter wants his mom to join the effort…so does Clyde. Keep rocking, Dad. Everyone is excited about your sales."

E-mail from Walter's mom dated March 22, 2006: "Thanks so much for the promotion info. Hi, I'm Walter's mom, Pam. I'm excited about the parent pre-release promotion and definitely want to be a part of it. I'm so proud of the

JACQUES LASSEIGNE

You may or may not know that our son, Scott, is a senior at LSU, and he is also in a band. They were "discovered" in October of 2004, signed a recording contract the next month, and flew to Los Angeles the next month to record their album at Capitol Records Studio, where Frank Sinatra, The Beatles, and others have recorded their music. Two of their songs from this album have been licensed for an upcoming movie produced by Kevin Spacey, so the last 17 months have certainly been interesting.

The Record Label, Maple Jam Records, is re-releasing their album that originally came out in April of 2005. Their debut album, *Small Town Computer Crash*, was ranked by *ink.19* website in the *Top 19 Best Independent Albums of 2005*, so the record label wanted to do a national release with a little tweaking. They replaced two songs from the album (took off "There She Was" and "Green Bird" and put on "Heartstorm Rescue"—inspired by Hurricane Katrina—and "Welcome to the Now, Evo Devo"—the song written for LSU's new nationwide promotional campaign) and did a "remix" of all the other songs. The jacket cover is completely different.

John Frank of *The MediaFix.Com* website recently wrote in his review of The TERMS: *The TERMS is definitely the best new band I have heard in a long time... While there is still a lot of time left in the year, I have no problem picking these guys as the best band of 2006.* WOW!

The parents of band members are kicking off their Parent Pre-Release CD Promotion this week. You may or may not know that The TERMS' picture and a short article made *Billboard Magazine* the week of March 11, 2006. Well, in order to make the Best-Selling Independent CD List in *Billboard*, the Vice-President of their Record Label, Starr, estimates they need 5,000 CD sales in the first week that the new CD is released. To accomplish that, we need your help. Anne and I have set a goal to sell 200 CDs. Starr, what a great name for the entertainment business, stated if the parents have good pre-release sales we will probably get a discount on the retail price.

E-MAIL CONNECTIONS

A reunion concert; wouldn't that be a blast? To see the guys on stage performing one more time? What a goal for Brandon to strive for. But we'll take one day at a time now. Let's get through this surgery on Monday.

Thanks for your great support and continue prayers. You are greatly appreciated.

The CD Promotion

E-mail has become a powerful tool today. Organizations manage by e-mail, families stay in touch by e-mail, friends and family send precious photos of their loved ones via e-mail, business is conducted over e-mail, and parents can promote the band that their sons are in with e-mail.

When talking with Scott one day as he was juggling college work, his part-time job, and the band commitments, he mentioned to me some of his duties with the band. It included practicing, composing new songs, playing gigs, and working MySpace.com to promote the band in order to spread the word about them with the larger goal of an ever-expanding fan base. That took up an inordinate amount of his time. I too, tried to do my part to expand their fan base and help with their success. One such example was the CD Promotion in the spring of 2006 when their CD would be tweaked and re-released.

Starr asked everyone for ideas on how to market their soon-to-be-released CD in order for the band to have enough sales to make it into *Billboard Magazine's* best-selling charts. Bruce Allen, Clyde's step-father, was very involved in fund-raising for the new Robinson Film Center in Shreveport. His idea was to hand out a CD to everyone who purchased a ticket for the fund-raiser that was to be held at the Greater Shreveport Chamber of Commerce. Great idea! My approach was more basic. I sent out letters and e-mails to friends and family asking them, "Would you like to buy a CD?" By this time my e-mail list had grown quite a bit.

My note to friends and family for this promotion read as follows:

And a Good Spring Day Greeting to You!

JACQUES LASSEIGNE

TERMS Group E-mail—June 16, 2007: Brandon Update:

Good Weekend Greetings to you, Dear Friends!

Brandon saw Dr. Nathan, his ENT, this past Wednesday. His surgery is set for Monday, June 18th. As many of you know, any surgery is serious business, and this one is no exception. Brandon and his parents have been so strong these last eight months. And what can I say about Brandon? He is ready for this surgery. But sometimes you have that nagging doubt in the back of your mind: "Is everything going to be okay?"

Dr. Nathan did a thorough job in explaining all the risks of this surgery, including the differing neurological opinions (two for and one against this surgery), the possible outcomes of the surgery, and, yes, the possibility of paralysis, to Brandon's parents. Jay and Angela are very appreciative of the "yes" opinion from Dr. Bernie McHugh, Jr. and Dr. David Cavanaugh, and of Dr. Cheri Nathan's courageous decision to move forward with this surgery.

You have been so supportive since the accident. Brandon and his family thank you from the bottom of their heart. They ask that you continue to do so, and if you can, please say a very special prayer for a very successful surgery on Monday.

One last comment about the get-together at Brandon's home a couple of Sunday's ago with all the band members. Brandon mentioned an idea that day that I have also thought about for quite awhile. He stated, "We need to perform a reunion show."

Brandon would need to continue to work on his bass guitar skills, but he has exhibited great drive in order to return to "normal." He has tackled his rehab homework and his physical rehab, including all those CRUNCHES he does! His motivation and drive since the accident has been phenomenal. If only more people had his drive; goodness, what could be accomplished in this world.

E-MAIL CONNECTIONS

July 23, 2007—From June F: "Good Morning and WOW! Those guys are all so inspiring—they don't let anything get in their way. Reminds me of an old '70s song, 'I've got the music in me.' My favorite line goes like this: 'If something gets in my way, I go round it!' Thanks for sharing!"

July 23, 2007—From Ramon B: "This is SUPER! What a difference a few months can make. Things were hopeful, but very frightening just a few short months ago. KEEP THE FAITH!"

August 8, 2007—From Ken E: "I did see the segment on TV; it was great! Brandon is a remarkable young man, and it is easy to see his determination when they talk to him. I can tell just from listening and observing him that his recovery is far from complete. His mother is a remarkable person. I see where Brandon gets his tenacity and positive attitude!"

August 8, 2007—From Terri B: "The TV segment was such a great piece. Brandon and Scott were so candid and encouraging. I am so amazed at Brandon's rehabilitation and progress. Having worked with many people with severe injuries, typically resulting in long-term or permanently disabling conditions, Brandon's story really is about the *Miracle Worker* presence in his life."

August 28, 2007—From Flo B: "Awesome news. I still continue to pray for Brandon and his family daily. Our God is an awesome God. He is not finished with this young man. I can't wait to see what His plans are for him. I thank you for the updates and look forward to them, so keep them coming."

What a vast support system. What wonderful family and friends that really care. What amazing prayer support all over the country. What amazing people. Yes, one can make a phone call to "reach out and touch someone," but e-mail can be an amazing and effective communication tool. It keeps many people connected on a regular basis. It sure did in this case.

June 17, 2007—From Terri B: "Your words of faith and encouragement over these eight months are truly 'life' to Brandon and words that I'm certain we all seek to be 'snared' or 'taken' in our prayers to the Father in the name of Jesus Christ for Brandon's complete and full restoration. If we didn't know Brandon (as I did not), then we have come to know him, his parents, The TERMS, and the host of people who stand in the gap for this young man. I believe in the purpose for Brandon's life, as apparently do you, and how he will certainly be able to tell all of us one day what this experience has meant in revealing God's love for him and for all who have shared in this trial of faith with him. At Centerpoint I see adversity every day, as do you and the others receiving this e-mail, and sometimes, just sometimes, I wonder if what we do makes a difference. Then I read your e-mails about Brandon's progress and am reminded that it's the enduring faith, the constant believing, the consistent effort that really makes the difference. We can't give up; we can't stop believing, even for a moment, because someone is depending on it that someone cares enough to stand in the gap when they cannot. I don't know if I will ever understand why certain circumstances, barriers, or delays must happen, except to give us more time, everyone or just one more person, more time to know God and to know that He is in control."

June 18, 2007—From Pat S: "Our thoughts and prayers are with Brandon and his family this morning and in the days ahead. And if they EVER do a reunion show, let me know because I WILL be there!"

June 18, 2007—From Flo B: "I have already said my prayer for Brandon. I pray for him and his family every day. Hope you have a nice Monday. Please let me know when you hear how the surgery went."

June 19, 2007—From June F: "AWESOME—WHAT A BLESSING!"

July 16, 2007—From Wendy T: "Misty, my daughter, just sent me a message that Brandon just called her. He said he was doing great. She said his speech was slower. He said he finally remembered her face and that he could not remember everything but that they were friends. I thought that was so sweet; wanted to share with you. Take care."

only knew how many people lift him up in prayer daily. Keep the good reports coming. Who knows if 'Cutie Pie' is not married and what may be in the cards for them. I had a friend whom I graduated with who is a rehab nurse. She fell in love with one of her patients and married him. They have been happily married for twenty-five years now! Have a great day. I do appreciate your updates. I look forward to reading them word for word."

April 16, 2007—From June F: "Wow! I certainly believe in angels among us and loved reading this update. Thanks for sharing, and have a blessed week!"

April 16, 2007—From Pat S: "Sounds like The TERMS are taking on the world—on their terms! Sure hope Clyde and Ben can produce some music—SOON! I think I'm addicted to their kind of music now! So long country-western!"

May 8, 2007—From Corinne P: "I am using Brandon's story with my son, as we learn to drive! I constantly remind him about how fast things can happen, and what a tremendous effect it can cause. Let Brandon know his story is traveling the continent!"

June 1, 2007—From Dane Andreeff: "My church and young-adult church group said many prayers for all the boys in the accident and their families, but extra special prayers for Brandon as we got to understand his condition and the extent of his injuries. I really believe in the power of prayer but even more so in a large group setting. We have church members asking Brandon's status as do Baton Rouge friends who saw them perform."

June 16, 2007—From Sherry & Carl P: "We appreciate your tremendous effort in keeping all of us informed. You can count on our prayers Monday and every day for Brandon and the group. Much love."

June 17, 2007—From Jane W: "Thanks for all the updates on Brandon—feels like we are there—which we are always through the spirit in prayer."

and making progress. And what a great son you have. You must be very proud."

February 26, 2007—From Wendy T: "This brought tears to my eyes. It is so great to hear that he is doing so much better and the milestones that he has achieved are remarkable! Thanks for the update. With continued prayers."

February 27, 2007—From Flo B: "As always I pray for Brandon and his family every day. He is truly a fighter. I look forward to your e-mails—keep them coming."

March 8, 2007—From Ivory Y: "Thanks for the pertinent information on Brandon and the former band and its members. One of my church members, the pastor's wife, met Brandon and his father at a basketball game two weeks ago. She told the dad that Brandon was on our prayer list and how it was a pleasure to meet him."

March 29, 2007—From Gwen F: I appreciate the e-mails regarding the progress of Brandon and the rest of the guys. Thanks for being genuine.

April 2, 2007—From Annette B: "Gosh! I hope they can do something to get the trachea tube removed. They are working miracles in all aspects of medicine. I know they will come up with some way to do the surgery that meets Brandon's needs. After all, he has beaten many, many odds so far, and I pray this one will also be added to his list. What his mother must be going through; a very strong woman she is. I'm sure to hear him play his guitar again must have been overwhelming. Thanks for the update, and you know our prayers will continue for Brandon and his family."

April 10, 2007—From Pat A: "I look forward to these updates. This one was especially moving and uplifting. Thanks for sending them."

April 10, 2007—From Flo B: "What a pleasant report. Brandon is a true trouper; he is not giving up. That strong will and his faith in God are unbelievable. He has a wonderful support group of friends and family. If he

E-MAIL CONNECTIONS

November 7, 2006—From June F: "Thanks for sending the address of Brandon's medical account and the update. With your permission, I would like to add Brandon's name to our confidential prayer list at St. Luke's in Baton Rouge. Please continue to keep us posted on Brandon's progress. Take care."

Ellen McGovern and my wife set up Brandon's medical account at Capital One Bank. The bank gave Ellen a copy of a letter it received from a donor and Ellen passed it on to Anne and me. *November 9, 2006—From Rob R*: "Dear Account Manager, On behalf of Brandon Young, the very talented bass player for The TERMS who was injured in an automobile accident several weeks ago, please accept this small donation to be credited to his account. Although I am old enough to have grown up with the Beatles and Rolling Stones' music, I have thoroughly enjoyed the music and the concerts of The TERMS. The father of The TERMS' drummer, Scott Lasseigne, is a co-worker and friend of mine. Jacques has kept me informed of Brandon's condition and the mounting medical expenses. I know that this small amount will not dent those medical expenses, but hopefully many small amounts will significantly defray those medical costs. I know that I speak for many fans of The TERMS when I say that we are praying for Brandon's speedy recovery and look forward to his return and his music with The TERMS!"

November 17, 2006—From Greg Ladanyi & Starr Andreeff when they received the e-mail update that Brandon was finally transferred to the Methodist Rehabilitation Center in Jackson, Mississippi: "Thank you, Lord!"

November 17, 2006—From Tammi A, responding to the same e-mail update: "I'm speechless! And teary-eyed. We wait for each bit of new news on him. You are keeping us in the know of each step in his slow, but steady recovery. Thank you so much."

December 18, 2006—From Nelda A, responding to an e-mail update and a picture of Brandon standing up with Scott at his side in the Methodist Rehabilitation Center: "I'm sitting here wiping tears from my face; those sweet pictures pushed me over the edge. I don't know Angela, but as a mother I can imagine how she is feeling; so grateful to have her son alive please the audience. I'd like to get this picture to his hospital room." Brandon was "rocking out" in that photo. Below the picture the caption read: "We Love You, Brandon! Get Well, Get Home, and Get Rockin' Again Soon!"

October 3, 2006—From Scott (his reply to my e-mail asking him how he was doing): "I'm doing well…I guess, I mean, I have my good times and my bad times, just like anyone would in this situation…I'm okay."

October 6, 2006—From Rob R: "Thanks for the updates. Make sure you continue to tell Brandon, Blake, Clyde, and their families that there are a whole bunch of people in Baton Rouge who have them, as well as the emotional well being of Scott and Ben, on their prayer list. Every piece of good news of improvement is a small step forward to what we hope will be complete and total recovery. You take care of them—and yourself!"

October 13, 2006—From Jack W: "Thanks for the updates. I forward them to my family; others on your e-mail list may do the same. So, bottom line is more people are interested in this than you will ever know."

October 15, 2006—From Doug B: "Thanks for the encouraging update! We were listening to the radio broadcast of last night's LSU-Kentucky football game. In the first quarter, Jim Hawthorne, Voice of the LSU Tigers Radio Network, made a brief mention of The TERMS recent accident during a break in the action. He indicated that two of the band members were now recovering at home, but one was still hospitalized in Monroe. He asked for all Tiger fans to remember their fellow LSU students as they recovered from this accident. Since LSU football games can be heard throughout much of the country via 50,000 watt WWL-AM in New Orleans, I'm sure that a lot of The TERMS' fans may have heard the news."

October 19, 2006—From Stephanie Netherton, writer for The Times *newspaper*: "Thank you for getting the information to us. The community has really attached to the news of Brandon Young's injury, and I know they would love to contribute to his medical-fund account. Please keep me posted on Brandon's recovery. My prayers are with you all."

Chapter Twelve
Our Electronic Connection in Today's World

The E-mail Connection

As word spread about the band's accident and as my e-mail updates were going out, people would call and e-mail asking me to please add them to the e-mail update list. The group e-mail list grew quite a bit during those early days after the wreck. Many people forwarded my e-mail updates to their family and friends, and they would forward them to their friends and family and so on. Family and friends' response was overwhelming. The caring, the concern, the prayers, and the support were there from day one. Many, many people sent back notes of encouragement, notes of prayer, and notes of support via e-mail. Below are a few of these e-mails:

October 1, 2006—From Martha C: "O dear God, Jacques. This is my prayer: Heavenly Father, we ask your intervention in our time of need. May every clinical care giver who touches this beautiful young man, Brandon, be compassionate, gentle, skilled, and knowledgeable. May every friend's prayer be heard. Be at his side. Be with his mother and father. Be with his friends and family members. Inspire the words shared among them so they reveal Your job in having created Brandon. Amen. P.S. My prayers are with all of you. And I praise God for choosing you and Anne to be with Brandon's parents at that terrible moment. He is truly wise."

October 3, 2006—From Tammi A: "Thank you for keeping us updated. I love this picture of Brandon (taken at The Bitter End in New York) that I've attached to this e-mail. He always put his heart into each song and played to

Angela, Brandon's mother, was upset at herself for forgetting about the blood clots he had experienced in Monroe. She said she should have told the hospital staff here so they would have used his other arm for the IV. She felt terrible about the whole situation, but many people told her to stop beating herself over this. She has been there every step of the way for Brandon. I cannot imagine being in her situation. That is what I call pressure.

The hematologist said the infection from the IV could have caused that clot, or the clot could have been left over from his time in ICU in the Monroe hospital.

A CT-scan was taken to make sure it was safe to give him a blood thinner. Good News—It showed that all of the bleeding in his brain was now gone! Finally, a clear CT-scan. What glorious news!

Speaking of glorious news, Brandon has his first "date" since the accident on Friday night. He went to dinner and a movie with one of his old friends from high school. She is a registered nurse at LSU Medical Center, so Angela knew he would be in good hands in case any glitch occurred, i.e., he began coughing, his trachea tube needed to be cleaned out, etc. Angela does get antsy on those few occasions when Brandon goes out with friends, but she is working on that. She can last a whole FIVE MINUTES with Brandon out of her sight before she gets worried! Who can blame her?

Surgery on his trachea is coming up soon. It is scheduled for June 18th. More on that later.

Thanks for all your support and prayers. May you and your family be blessed.

heard of this case, he quickly moved forward, realizing that his business would probably not receive any financial compensation, and gave a resounding, "Yes, we will accept this young man." This network of friends, a supportive family, the goodness of people, the giving nature of the business community, and, yes, faith in God speak volumes about this episode, this country, and its people. That is the America I know.

TERMS Group E-mail—June 9, 2007: Brandon Update:

Greetings Dear Family and Friends!

Sure hope your weekend was an enjoyable break from the work routine.

On May 22nd Dr. Alan Richards performed eye surgery on Brandon. It was an outpatient procedure where the doctor actually tightened the eye muscles of Brandon's left eye in order to bring it in line with his right eye. Dr. Richards stated that it sometimes takes a second surgery to get the eyes closely lined up. Surgery went well, and his eye is looking quite good. Sometimes it actually lines up pretty darn close with his right eye. Now, Brandon may need to eventually have surgery on his left eyelid, since it tends to droop a bit. One step at a time, but he sure is making his way back to pre-accident days.

With real life there always seems to be setbacks, or challenges, as Norman Vincent Peale might say. The young folks just asked, "Norman who?"

Anyway, Brandon received an infection from the IV used in his day surgery, and he also experienced a blood clot in that arm. He was home a day after surgery when he noticed red streaks going up his arm starting at his IV site. They dashed to the emergency room. He was admitted to the hospital and put on IV antibiotics and a blood thinner. That was a four-day hospital stay. Some of you remember the blood clots Brandon experienced while in the ICU Unit in the Monroe hospital. Back then he did not realize what was going on and the seriousness of the situation due to his heavy medication, but he knew what was going on this time. He was definitely concerned, to say the least.

alive and treating him for his many severe injuries, but it was time for him to make the move to a rehabilitation facility in order for his body to "wake up" and to begin the next phase in his recovery. As long as he was in his present situation his body would continue getting infection after infection, causing physical setbacks for Brandon and emotional setbacks for his family. Getting into a rehabilitation facility proved difficult due to Brandon's severe medical injuries and other complications. Brandon did not have health insurance at the time of the accident. That may have been a factor. Mark Adams, CEO of the Methodist Rehabilitation Center, knew that important detail up front. As Mark put it, "When Methodist made the decision to accept Brandon and begin his rehabilitation program, it was with the expectation there would be no funding for his care." It did not deter him. After he received a call from a fellow high-school classmate, he promptly made the decision that was outside of their usual policies for out-of-state patients, to commence the process of getting Brandon transferred to Methodist Rehabilitation Center as quickly as possible. He immediately contacted their outreach coordinator who informed Mark that one of their nurses was in Monroe, Louisiana, at that very moment. That nurse made a detour to the Monroe hospital to visit with Brandon's physician and with Angela regarding Brandon's medical condition and his stability for transfer. He was admitted to the Methodist Rehabilitation Center shortly thereafter.

Mark Adams stated, "Hospitals are incredibly expensive to operate, and, like any business, must find the financial means to cover the cost of providing services. Even a state's safety-net medical insurance program can be woefully inadequate to deal with the high cost of brain-injury rehabilitation. A network of good friends, a supportive family, and faith in God is the only reliable 'insurance safety net' when you are faced with handling a medical catastrophe." That last sentence speaks volumes. It is exactly what transpired in this episode. Some high-school classmates of Angela's contacted one another for help in trying to locate a rehab facility to take Brandon. They discovered another Southwood High School classmate who worked at a specialty hospital in Jackson, Mississippi, that deals with the recovery and rehabilitation of patients with severe brain injuries and spinal injuries. They contacted Mark, CEO of this facility for help. This high-school class of over 500 students was typical. You had a few friends and a few more acquaintances and a whole lot of people that you just did not know all that well. Mark and Angela knew each other back then, as he put it, "by name only." But when he during the game at Tiger Stadium was probably not an option, but maybe they could do something on the radio broadcast of that game. That is just what happened. The Sports Department did follow through with that commitment. Radio time is a precious commodity, especially with a big-time college football game such as an October game between SEC rivals, LSU and Kentucky. But Jim Hawthorne, the radio announcer, did take the time on the air to talk about the hurting band members and for fans to please remember them. People called me from a couple of states to inform me they had heard very nice comments concerning The TERMS' accident on that radio broadcast. A dear family member makes the extra effort to ask the college to remember the hurting band members during a major football game, and the school works it out. That is the America I know.

Ellen McGovern and my wife got together to set up the Brandon Young Donation Account at a local bank. That account could receive donations from people and from the many fund raisers that would help with Brandon's medical expenses. The generosity of people is simply amazing. Within just a few weeks that special medical account had several thousand dollars in it. Since Anne helped to set up the account she could have continued to check on the balance, but she decided that was not necessary. The account had strict parameters, the balance was growing nicely, and it was time to concentrate on fund raisers and the mental health of Brandon's parents. Ellen's son, whose name is also Brandon, set up a website to inform people of Brandon's situation, the status of the band members and a place for donations to be made. Donations came in immediately and from all over. People were handing me cash and checks that did not personally know Brandon, but felt a strong connection to him since they had been reading about the band for a while now. Other people just donated funds, some extremely generous, out of love for their fellow human being. One co-worker shoved a folded bill in my hand as he was going home one afternoon. I was talking with another co-worker at the time so I did not look at the bill. A few minutes later I retrieved the bill from my pants pocket to place it in the envelope I was using to collect donations and noticed that it was a $100 bill. Another co-worker who had never even heard The TERMS' music gave me a $100 bill the next afternoon. People like them continued that trend. As the saying goes, "They did not just talk the talk, but they walked the walk." That is the America I know.

St. Francis Medical Center staff performed superbly in keeping Brandon mother on the elevator going up to his room. Soon after we entered his room, three friends and fans came to say hi and presented Clyde with a huge get-well card on poster board signed by many people. Two more people entered the room. One was Clyde's brother, Billy, and the other was Greg Chiartano, The TERMS' original bass player. They were cutting up big time, much to Clyde's amusement. Friends being there with you in your time of need. That is the America I know.

Ben and Scott were still in school that semester; in fact, the week after the accident was mid-term exams. Ben and Scott's professors gave them the option of taking their mid-term exams that week as scheduled, or they could postpone them for a week or two. That was a very nice gesture. Ben did delay his mid-term exams, but I encouraged Scott to go ahead and take his exams. Sometimes a father gives good advice. That was not one of those times. Scott did fine on his exams, but he could have done better. He told me later that it was extremely difficult for him to concentrate while trying to study and taking those tests, since his mind kept going back to Brandon lying in that hospital bed with all those tubes and wires connected to him. In all this swirl of activity I failed to realize the depth of his anxiety and depression. Ben was going through the same emotions. These five young men had grown very close over the last couple of years, had been through a lot, and now, their world had been turned upside down. Ben and Scott would travel back to Monroe weekend after weekend after the accident to visit with Blake and Brandon and their families and to Shreveport to visit with Clyde. Their bond was stronger than ever. That is the America I know.

Anne's sister, Liz, was also devastated by the accident and wanted to do something to spread the word. She did something I would never do. She picked up the phone and called the LSU Sports Department. She talked with two gentlemen, including the Athletic Director. She asked them, "Have you heard of The TERMS?"

They replied, "Yes."

She than asked, "Are you aware of their accident?"

Once again the reply was "Yes."

Liz's request was for an announcement to be made during the upcoming Saturday football game between LSU and Kentucky concerning The TERMS' accident and to ask those 90,000 fans to please remember them. Their response was sincere and heart-felt. Making such an announcement

E-MAIL CONNECTIONS

Monroe, Louisiana, was the city where the accident took place. It was also the site of an extremely successful fund raiser. Blake Oliver is from Monroe. He worked with Brady Ragland from the Sixth Street Bar and set up a fund raiser for Brandon's medical expenses. Blake worked tirelessly on this event along with members of his family. He presold many tickets. The night of the fund raiser featured Ben Labat, Alan West Brockman and his band, Brockman y Los Tres Gringos, and another band giving their heart and soul for a fallen fellow musician and a fellow human being. Brady gave Blake 100% of the door proceeds. He asked for nothing; he even threw in a couple of hundred dollars from the tip jar. When it was all said and done, Blake was able to present to Brandon's mother almost $4,000 from that sterling event. Friend helping friend, neighbor helping neighbor, people taking the initiative to make positive things happen, going above and beyond just to do the right thing. That is the America I know.

The local media, both print and television, were very supportive of the band members and all the fund-raising efforts. Their sensitive and professional coverage were quite welcome to everyone involved. The media today can be quite cruel and exceedingly intrusive, but this was not the case. Early on, Brandon's mother, Angela, decided that she just could not deal with all the media requests for information so she asked Scott to be the spokesperson for the family. *The TIMES*, local Shreveport newspaper, KTBS-Channel 3 TV, the local ABC affiliate and KSLA-Channel 12 TV, the local CBS affiliate, had great coverage of all the happenings. KTBS-Channel 3 continued to have follow-up reports on the band and updates on Brandon's condition. They have been very supportive, from reporter Jim Roberts to anchors Ed Walsh, Sonja Bailes, Gerry May, and Sherri Talley. *The TIMES* reporter, Stephanie Netherton, was also involved in a wonderful and quite thorough follow-up story on Brandon. Many times the media focuses on bad news. But in this case one could not ask for better coverage concerning good news. That is the America I know.

These young people cared for one another. Blake was released from St. Francis Hospital and was ordered to stay at home to recover, but he did make it back to the hospital to visit with Brandon and his family on a regular basis, even though he was disobeying doctor's orders. Clyde was transferred from St. Francis Hospital in Monroe to Christus Schumpert Highland Hospital in Shreveport. One afternoon Anne and I went to pay him a visit and met his

Anna Ruth, Blake's grandmother, served as a dear friend and confidant to Angela during that difficult six-week stay in the Monroe hospital. Angela has stated that she would never have made it through that difficult ordeal without Anna Ruth. She was there with Angela during those dark times and discouraging moments. They were not related and had never met before the accident, but developed a deep kinship among all the turmoil. She was there because, "We are all one family; it was the right thing to do." One person was there for another person in their time of need, giving her all without asking for anything in return. That is the America I know.

Fund-raising events and programs were quickly put together. Brandon's sisters met with El Chico's management and organized a fund-raising event for Brandon. For the restaurant to donate 10% of the evening's take for a cause, at least one hundred people would have to participate in the fund-raiser. The restaurant manager stopped taking count only thirty minutes into the event. He knew he would have well over one hundred people coming in for Brandon's fund-raiser, and he did. Dear, loving family members working with the business community to raise money for a good cause in a very short time-frame. That is the America I know.

Bruce Allen, Clyde's step-father, is one of the biggest supporters of The TERMS. On the side of his white van he has a black silhouette of the band members. Yes, a huge supporter of these young men as well as a very good promoter. He is also a big supporter of the Robinson Film Theatre project. The Robinson Film Center's website states its mission as, *Providing a venue for the best in international, independent, and classic cinema while serving as a resource for filmmaking and film education.* For one of the fund-raisers for that business enterprise, Bruce purchased many TERMS' CDs to give out as a complimentary gift to the many donors supporting that fund-raiser. The festivities were held at the Greater Shreveport Chamber of Commerce building in downtown Shreveport with The TERMS performing. He had almost two hundred CDs left after that benefit so he offered those CDs to us to sell to raise funds for Brandon's Medical Account. We sold every single one of those CDs in a very short time. Bruce also provided the lights and built a 16' X 12' stage for The TERMS' 2005 New Year's Eve "Party of the Century" at McArthur's in downtown Shreveport. His work behind the scenes made that evening a smashing success. Time after time after time, Bruce stepped up to the plate to generously help out. That is the America I know.

Chapter Eleven
The America I Know

The America I Know

In the weeks after the accident it was a whirlwind of activity. Many e-mails and phone calls went out, fund-raisers were being planned, friends and family traveled the roads to Monroe to visit the hurting band members, and many prayers were being said all across the nation. It was a time of hope, of angst, of assurance, of fear, of anticipation, of worry, and of renewed faith in your fellow man.

Angela stayed by Brandon's side in the hospital every second that she could. She lived for the few minutes that she was allowed to visit with him in the Intensive Care Unit in the Monroe hospital. After a while the nurses allowed her to stay for longer visits. They were very attentive to the family's emotional needs. Angela's employer graciously and generously told her to stay with her son because that was where she needed to be at this time. He also said not to worry about her job; it will be there whenever she could return to work. In the meantime, he continued to pay her. That is the America I know.

Anne and I tried to visit with Brandon's family at least once a week while Brandon was still in the Monroe hospital. We would just be there to listen or to give Angela and Jay the wonderful words of encouragement and prayer that people from all over the country were sending back my way via e-mail. The visits were full of smiles, tears, and every emotion in between. After a few nights sleeping in the hospital, Angela and Jay had to move to the Ronald McDonald House. The staff was absolutely fabulous. What a wonderful idea that has blossomed all over the country to serve a real need for families in this type situation. That is the America I know.

Clyde: his upper right leg (on the outside) is still numb from the accident, but his movement in that leg is pretty good. He is recording a lot of music in his studio, and some of his songs are on iTUNES.

Ben: is writing a lot of music and working in the evenings as a bartender in New York. His girlfriend, Khanh, was making this trip with him. She is a lawyer and has an MBA. She works with Viacom in New York.

Scott: is still in the manager trainee program with Enterprise Car Rental Co. He is doing real well with them; in fact, the big boss is moving Scott to the Bert Kouns store tomorrow. And Scott should be a father by the weekend. Yes, the baby is coming early. His wife has been in the hospital over a week now and is receiving superb medical care.

Brandon: I guess he knew the importance of today since this morning he made a decision NOT to use his cane anymore. For his morning walk with his mother he accomplished that without the use of his cane. He made sure to tell all his band members of his decision. What a sight to behold. What a conversation to witness. What a memorable occasion.

After our visit, the band was leaving for one of their favorite eating places in Shreveport, Tacomania, when Brandon began walking down the steps. He did NOT use the ramp that was constructed for him, but the steps. He took off leading the pack by walking down those steps! I was walking behind Brandon holding an umbrella so he would not get too wet with the mild rain that was coming down. It was a joyful scene seeing them riding off together again.

In my next update I'll give you the latest on his recent eye surgery, but just wanted you to know what a wonderful day today was. True, Brandon still does not remember much about The TERMS, but today they were a family again.

Bless you.

E-MAIL CONNECTIONS

TERMS Group E-mail—June 3, 2007: Brandon Update:

What a Glorious Day!

Greetings dear Family & Friends,

I knew *The TIMES*, the local Shreveport newspaper, was coming out with an article on Brandon, but did not know which Sunday it would appear. Well, today was that day. The writer, Stephanie Netherton, did an excellent job, and we were all amazed at how much 'ink' they gave Brandon. It was a HUGE write-up! And the pictures in the paper showed Brandon doing his walking therapy in the swimming pool, it showed him standing up playing his guitar, and it showed a hand-made get-well card made by Scott's wife, Sara. I have attached the article in a MS Word attachment along with the website link to the article. The on-line article does not have the photos with it, but you can read the whole article that appeared today in *The TIMES*.

That started the day out on a wonderful note. Later we drove to Brandon's home to greet each of The TERMS' band members who were arriving for a glorious reunion visit! This was the first time since the accident that all the band members would be together again. Ben Labat, lead singer for The TERMS, had flown to his home in South Louisiana in order to pack up some items (actually a LOT of items), pick up his vehicle, and drive back to New York—but with a slight detour to Shreveport. All of the guys worked their schedule to be here today around 1 P.M. They all looked absolutely GREAT! It was interesting to see them with SHORT hair cuts! They all seemed so grown up. That's what this kind of event, the accident, can do for young men.

Blake: passed his Commercial Insurance License test recently and is selling commercial insurance out of Austin, Texas. He looks great. His cracked vertebra in his neck has healed well, although he has to watch when he turns his head to the right too quickly—ouch. The pain in his left arm (his thumb was almost severed in the accident), for the most part, has subsided.

anointing as part of a religious, ceremonial, or healing ritual." I had never participated in receiving the sacrament of unction until that morning.

Anne and I have commitments to the weekly church service at St. Mark's. Anne has been in the church choir since high school, and I help out as the acolyte master, so our presence at the main service on Sunday morning is a given. That Sunday was no different. We slept for a couple of hours then left for church. Upon arriving there, two of the priests met me in the hall to ask how everyone in the band was doing. These priests were two among many on the group e-mail lists that had been sent the news of the accident. Their genuine concern was deeply appreciated. They had added Brandon, Blake, and Clyde to the list of people who would be given a special prayer today.

After communion that morning, I did something that I have never done. I went to receive unction. Of course, I was going on behalf of Brandon. Anne and I went together. We knelt at the altar rail in the chapel. Father Kirkland "Skully" Knight performed the unction ritual that morning. He laid his hands on Anne's head first and prayed the special prayer for that ritual. Then it was my turn. I told Skully what Anne had stated, "This is for Brandon." When Skully placed his hands on the top of my head and began praying for Brandon's healing, the top of my head became very, very warm; bordering on hot. I was thinking, "What in the world is going on here?" Afterwards, Anne went back to her place in the choir stall, and I went back to my designated place in the hallway. I wondered to myself, *What just happened?*

I did not tell anyone about this for the next three weeks. I did receive unction for Brandon on two more occasions, but did not experience the acute heat that I did that first time. After the third week I told Anne what had occurred that morning of October 1st. She responded that maybe with our emotions so raw and the events so real to us the morning after the accident, maybe we were open to the healing power of God. A week later I finally told Skully about this experience. He succinctly responded to me this way. "Two things I'm pretty sure of. (1) There IS healing power, and (2) It's not MY healing power."

Did healing take place that Sunday morning with Brandon through that ritual of unction? Maybe yes and maybe no; I do not know. But I'm very grateful that Brandon lived through that first night, and he lived through that second night, and he kept conquering one physical challenge after another. All I know is what I experienced that Sunday morning. I'll leave the interpretation to others.

Vekovius will perform another surgery to lift the eyelid so it will not droop. Since I had not seen Brandon in about a month, it was amazing to me how much his eyelid was open and how good it looked.

Concerning surgery to deal with his "stenosis," as you may remember, one neurosurgeon stated the surgery to correct that is too risky, while another neurosurgeon said it would be no more risky than if you or I had that surgery. To play it safe, they will get a third opinion. A good friend of ours, who is also a doctor, told Anne and me early on that if he needed a neurosurgeon he would highly recommend Dr. David Cavanaugh. Well, that is the doctor they will see for a third opinion in this matter. In case the recommendation is good, Dr. Cherie-Ann Nathan, their ENT, has scheduled Brandon's surgery for June 18th. Your support, with words, deeds and prayers has been phenomenal. Please continue your prayers. It is truly working wonders.

Angela continues to be amazed by the support of Brandon's friends. As she says, "I am so thankful to his friends. I am discovering that support is so very important to someone that has had an injury like Brandon. His friends continue to surround him and care for him. The recovery time is so long; it would be easy for them to just forget and go on with their lives, but they have not. I want to thank them all from the bottom of my heart because that has been so instrumental in Brandon's recovery."

Ya'll are just great. What else can I say?

Thanks.

Sunday, October 1, 2006—Holy Unction

People have told me over the years that one of the reasons they returned to the Episcopal Church is the sacraments. Among those sacraments are Baptism, Eucharist, Confirmation, and Unction. At the church Anne and I attend, St. Mark's Cathedral, Dean M.L. Agnew had instituted the sacrament of Holy Unction after communion at the 9:45 A.M. Service. Many people went to receive unction at that time, either for themselves or on behalf of someone else. Unction, as defined by the on-line dictionary by Farlex, is "the act of

TERMS Group E-mail—May 7, 2007: Brandon Update:

Dear Friends and Family,

A Good Spring Day to You!

Anne and I visited with Brandon and his parents, Jay and Angela, after church on Sunday. We parked on the street in front of their house. Within seconds, the family was pulling into their driveway. They were returning from the grocery store. Brandon stated from his car window, "I have a surprise for you." He then got out of the vehicle and proceeded to walk away from the car and up the ramp into his house with the aid of his new cane. No more walker for him! The cane has four prongs on the bottom. What a sight to behold. He walked really well for getting the cane only a couple of days before (May 4th).

He is so determined to get better and to make progress. It shows in his "homework" that he is given by the therapist, in his quest to get off the walker and onto a cane, and in other physical exercises. He asked Angela to buy him a ten-pound weight for his arms, and he also does a TREMENDOUS number of "crunches" each day. Some days he does over 700 crunches: 400 in the morning and 300 in the afternoon. I've done that many crunches before. Well, in a year. Okay, two years. He is determined to move forward. What an indomitable will on display. What an inspiration.

He looked great. His left eyelid is almost all the way open, and he is talking very well. Yes, he still has the trachea tube, but that does not stop him. All of his sense of humor is back—big time. That not only means his personality is coming back, but his cognitive-thinking processes are coming back strong. That has to be working in order for him to make the kinds of funny comments/jokes he makes.

His eye doctor is Dr. Bryan Vekovius. He will be making measurements of Brandon's eyes this week. It has to be stable before he can perform the operation to "straighten" the eye. After the eye is straightened, Dr.

sprained wrist. I did not say much the entire time she spoke, as I really was not concerned with anything except for what was going on with Brandon, Clyde, and Blake.

"Her son then walked out of the emergency room doors and approached her. He had a deep hesitation as he recognized me and I him. He was the driver of the red car that had collided with Blake's 4Runner. He was at fault in the accident, and he only had a scratch while my friends were in serious condition in ICU. I politely, but rather sternly, asked the young man, 'What Happened? Why didn't you stop?' I then lit another cigarette and let the rage in my eyes penetrate deep into his skull.

"He said he looked down for a second and did not see any stop sign. I then asked both the mother and her son, 'Get away from me.' My teeth were beginning to grind, and my eyelids were twitching. I asked them again, 'Get away from me.' They then turned and walked away without a word. If I could replay that episode I would like to believe that I would have acted differently, but I did not."

Who would have acted differently in that situation in the heat of the moment with emotions so fresh, so raw and so real?

Later that night we visited with the rest of Brandon's family. We gave Angela a big hug. She was taking a short breather from the intensity of the emergency room environment. I had already decided to send out an e-mail to my TERMS' group e-mail list to inform them of this sad news and to ask for their prayers. Anne told Angela what I was going to do, and she heartily agreed to that action. She was in such pain, but she told us thanks for the wonderful gesture. She added, "That would really be nice, and all prayers would be greatly appreciated."

Anne and I also visited with Ben. We offered him our home to sleep, but he was going to stay at the hospital a bit longer, then sleep at Blake's home in Monroe that night. After hugging him and telling him that we loved him, Scott, Sara (his girlfriend), Anne, and I left to return to Shreveport. Around 2 A.M. Sunday morning I got on the computer to send out an e-mail to The TERMS' group e-mail list that I had accumulated over the past couple of years informing them of the awful news and to ask them for their prayers. The response was overwhelming.

Anne and I entered the emergency waiting room and visited with a couple who were one of the first, if not the first, to call 911 that afternoon. He was working in his yard when the crash occurred. He yelled to his wife to call 911 and ran to the scene of the accident to see what help he could provide. They were there to lend any support they could. We also met Blake's grandmother that evening, Anna Ruth. She would sustain Angela during the next six weeks of their stay in that Monroe hospital. Scott finally took a break from being with Brandon and Blake's family and entered the general waiting room where we were. Our hug that evening was a special hug. Anne didn't want to let go of Scott. As she hugged him and as the tears flowed down her cheeks she asked him, "Do you wear your seatbelt? Do you wear your seatbelt? PROMISE ME that you will always wear your seatbelt!"

Scott then gave us an update on Blake, Clyde, and Brandon. Clyde was located at another hospital in Monroe called St. Francis North Hospital. His pelvis was fractured, and he might have internal injuries, but his condition was stable. Blake had a fractured vertebra in his neck, but there was no paralysis. Brandon's condition was quite severe. It was an hour-by-hour situation. The doctor was not sugar-coating his prognosis. Brandon's father, Jay, confirmed later that evening what Scott had told us. Jay stated that the doctor looked them in the eye to tell them of the seriousness of Brandon's condition. If Brandon lives through the night, that would be the first test. If he lives a couple of more days then the swelling in his brain will subside, and tests could be run to see the extent of his injuries. Each day that Brandon lives would be a victory, but the doctor did make it clear that if he did live, he would have a long road to recovery. Brandon would not wake up in a week or two and jump out of his hospital bed exclaiming, "Time to go home! Where is my bass guitar?"

What a wide range of emotions that evening for everyone. Things were happening fast, but that was followed with a period of just waiting; thinking, praying, and waiting.

Ben has never told anyone about this next episode, until now. "I must have smoked a pack of cigarettes that night outside the emergency room. At one point, a couple of hours after we arrived there, a woman began talking to me about how 'accidents happen' and 'God has his plan' and 'everything happens for a reason.' She explained that her son was in a car accident that evening and was being treated by hospital emergency-room staff. He had suffered a emergency flashers on. We could only imagine what was going on in their minds on that long drive to the Monroe hospital that dark evening. Our trip to Monroe was mostly a quiet drive in the dark. Our thoughts ranged from, "Will Brandon be alive when we get to the hospital?" to "Will he be permanently disabled?" "What words of comfort can we tell his family?" "Are there any words that we can say that will provide comfort to his parents?" "How are Clyde and Blake doing?" "How are their parents handling this situation?" prayers to God, and, of course, guilt. Guilt that our son was okay. He was not physically injured that awful night in the crash. Feeling guilty that some of my emotions are of relief that he was in the other vehicle that evening and of thanksgiving that he is okay and that in a few minutes we can hug him and tell him that we love him—and he can respond back to us without the aid of heavy medication or not being in a hospital bed or not having to come out of surgery. Then you come to the conclusion that you are there for everyone else. You may just have to listen, you may just have to hold someone's hand, you may just have to give a hug. Just be there. We parked in the hospital's parking garage, took a deep breath, and walked to the emergency room waiting room.

Angela and Jay and their two daughters worked their way to the emergency room area. Angela said later she felt "like I was in a haze. I just wanted to see Brandon and hold him—to make it right, just like any mother would do." The neurologist, Dr. McHugh, entered that area and announced that he wanted only family there, since he needed to talk with Brandon's family about his condition. Angela responded to him that Ben and Scott were indeed family and they would stay—and stay they did. Angela recalls, "The thing I will never forget is Dr. McHugh. He looked me right in the eye and kept telling me over and over that it is very, very serious. I knew then that Brandon might die. I remember people talking to me, but I don't remember what they said. I was in another world at that time. I just wanted to see Brandon and hold him and tell him that everything will be okay."

Later Angela told me of her first encounter that evening at the hospital with Blake. She could not recall the exact conversation, but she vividly remembers that she desperately wanted to talk with one of the band members who had been in the accident and was awake and could talk with her. She could not talk with Clyde yet, since he was at the other hospital (St. Francis North Hospital). She recalls, "I can't remember what I said to Blake that evening; I just know it made me feel a little better seeing and talking with him."

don't know if Brandon would have survived," Brooks said. "I'm no angel, but we're all sort of part-time angels. You don't know how what you say or do will affect somebody. In this case, Brandon is alive. It's very humbling because I'm no angel. I'm not perfect in any way."

But in his truck he was listening to a song about part-time angels. "The song says all of us can be angels because we never know what will happen. Everyone is capable of being a part-time angel."

Brandon and Brooks were able to meet months later in Monroe, an experience they both describe as an honor. "He kept thanking me, and I just don't feel worthy of all that thanks. I'm an average Joe who happened to have training in CPR and applied it before, and no one survived. I'm extremely happy he did," said Brooks.

Brandon's survival has profoundly impacted Brooks' life, too. Brooks found the experience restored his hope. "To see one person survive had a very positive affect on me. I feel better about myself now," Brooks said. "This changed my perspective."

Three ambulances took Brandon, Blake, and Clyde to their hospital destination. Ben recalls, "Scott and I were left standing in the street with 'What the f#$@ just happened?' looks on our faces. A police officer then instructed us which hospital to go to, and we jumped back into the nineteen-foot box truck and took off."

Blake and Brandon were taken to St. Francis Medical Center while Clyde was rushed to St. Francis North Hospital. Blake remembers being rushed to different areas of the hospital where X-rays, CT-scans, and MRIs were taken. Those tests confirmed a cracked vertebra in his neck, but it was a "good break," meaning no paralysis, and it would heal with time. Blake recalls, "After I was finally done with all these tests Brandon's mom came in my area to check on me. She told me that Brandon probably would not make it. He only had a five-percent chance of living through the night. Seeing my family and friends crying over Brandon, Clyde, and me was absolutely horrible. Words could never describe the pain I felt emotionally and physically that evening. I pray that is the worst I will ever feel."

Jay, Angela, and their two daughters left for St. Francis Medical Center in Monroe, Louisiana, around 7 P.M. that Saturday evening. Anne and I left soon afterwards, but somehow we got ahead of Brandon's parents. As we were traveling east on I-20 to Monroe, Jay and Angela passed us up with their or not being very attentive to the flow of traffic or weather conditions, or we are trying to multi-task as we are driving, i.e., talking on the cell phone, putting on makeup, playing with the CD player, eating, or we drive way too fast in foggy conditions or in a driving rain, or we think that we should have the right of way over every other driver on the road. By being inattentive or by not devoting our full attention to our driving, disastrous consequences can result from our poor judgment.

The "accident" occurred. My faith tells me that God did not cause that accident, but he does have an arsenal at his disposal when bad things occur. An argument can be made that there are guardian angels here on Earth doing God's work. Angela sure does believe that Gary Brooks is one.

Gary Brooks loves ice cream. His weekly routine involved him traveling down the road from his home in Monroe, Louisiana, to buy his weekly sweet treat. Saturday, September 30, 2006, was no different. He got in his truck and drove a block or two, but for some reason he decided that he did not need any ice cream that day. He turned his truck around and went back home. On this short trip he was listening to a music CD about angels. He went back inside his home and began working on his computer. A few moments later he heard the horrific sound of the wreck. He paused a few moments before deciding that he may be able to help and walked out of his house.

Stephanie Netherton, a writer for *The TIMES*, wrote about this on June 3, 2007. *Gary Brooks, "When I first looked out the window and then went outside they were pulling one person out through the window. Another person was screaming on the ground. The SUV was being turned upright, and I saw a face covered in debris in the back window."*

Brandon was unconscious for roughly four minutes before Brooks began administering CPR. As a former police officer, Brooks taught the technique to others and had given CPR many times before, but no one ever survived.

"*Brandon was not breathing and everyone was concentrating on Clyde because the car actually rolled onto Clyde. They were trying to get the car off him, and Gary Brooks noticed Brandon in the back and pulled him out and started CPR immediately. That's what saved him,*" stated Angela Young. *After nearly seven minutes of CPR, Brandon coughed a little bit and was transported to St. Francis Medical Center.*

"*If I'd gone to get ice cream, the wreck would have occurred, and I* people. A doctor came upon the scene and commenced CPR on him. Soon afterwards, Gary Brooks, a CPR instructor appeared and took over. In a few minutes he had resuscitated Brandon. Angela, Brandon's mother, credits Gary Brooks with saving Brandon's life. She considers him Brandon's guardian angel. Who can argue with that?

Scott will never forget the look on Brandon's face as he was pulled from the vehicle. It is etched forever in his memory. Brandon's face was expressionless; there was no life in his countenance; Brandon was gone. His face was also quite bloody, since one of his ears was almost torn off in the impact of the wreck. Scott remembers trying to help the other volunteers on the scene as they began CPR on Brandon by trying to open his mouth. Brandon's teeth were strongly clenched together. Scott took the bill of his baseball cap and tried to push it between Brandon's upper and lower teeth in order to pry his mouth open, but did not have much success. He backed off when Dr. Charles Joyce and Gary Brooks arrived to take over CPR functions. It was in that state of shock, disbelief and helplessness that he made the call to Anne and me, imploring us to contact Brandon's parents immediately.

Finally, after several minutes of CPR by Gary Brooks, Brandon finally coughed and the crowd breathed a sigh of relief, but he was not out of the woods yet. Brandon was also choking on the food he had vomited, so Ben, who had previously been certified in CPR, reminded the men working on Brandon to turn him on his side. Ben then took off his T-shirt to begin digging food out of Brandon's mouth and throat. From his previous training in CPR he knew the importance of getting the airway clear, whether it involves a collapsed trachea or choking on vomited food. Shortly after Brandon was revived by Gary Brooks the paramedics arrived and after a quick assessment, began his tracheotomy.

Ben later recalls, "I distinctly remember the T-shirt I had on that evening. At the time it was my favorite T-shirt. It was the one I wore at the taping of the Megan Mullally TV Show. It had a little fly imprinted on the shoulder. I don't know why I remember that, but I do."

Some people will say that it was "God's will" that Brandon was in that accident. Sorry, but I do not agree with that belief. I do believe that God gives us free will. We are free to do good or to do bad or to do nothing; it is our choice. Same philosophy I have of car accidents. There are very few true vehicle "accidents." Most wrecks occur due to human error. We were driving too fast the car. I'm not sure how much help I was, but my adrenaline was very high. Soon Clyde was pulled from underneath the vehicle." Clyde's pelvis was cracked in four places, and he was in horrendous pain. At the time it was unknown if he also had other internal injuries. Shortly after Clyde was pulled from his precarious position, more people from the neighborhood arrived to help.

Ben jumped out of the box van to join other people who had gathered at the accident scene to pull Blake out of the vehicle through the driver's door. Blake remembers someone instructing him to turn off the vehicle. Once that was done he looked for Brandon. "I could see him in the back hunched over, and I yelled for him. Brandon gave no response, but at the time I didn't think he was that bad. About that time one of the bystanders told me they would get him, but it was my turn to be rescued from the vehicle." Blake had a huge gash on his right hand around his thumb area. His thumb was almost severed. Once Blake was pulled free from the vehicle he sat down and a feeling of numbness descended upon him. Blake recalls, "As I leaned down my entire upper body went numb. I could not move." That was not a good sign. People at the scene instructed him to try to keep very still. Later he learned that he had broken one of the vertebrae in his neck, but he would not be paralyzed.

Blake remembers, "As I was sitting down trying to be still, I noticed my thumb was barely hanging on my hand. Blood was everywhere. After what seemed like an eternity Scott ran up to me crying that Brandon was not breathing. I could still hear Clyde screaming in the middle of the street. The rest is a blur until the EMS person put me on a stretcher and taped me down. I was in the ambulance when I was finally given some information about Brandon. They informed me that he was now breathing, but it looked bad."

Other people from the residential neighborhood arrived to help right the 4Runner. Ben and Scott were calling Brandon's name, but he did not respond. Brandon was in the back seat, motionless. One of his arms was quite bloody. On impact, Brandon was thrown to the other side of the 4Runner. When the 4Runner collided with the telephone pole, it is speculated that Brandon's head came into contact with that pole. Ben recalls, "Brandon was unconscious and half hanging out of the back window. He could not be helped in that position. It was unanimously decided that we bring the 4Runner back in its upright position so Brandon could be removed and receive CPR." He was pulled from the vehicle and was placed gently on the ground by Ben, Scott, and 3 other at the time, the accident had just occurred. Ben recalls, "We noticed the power lines began to shake violently. Either Scott or I made a joke that those squirrels must have been fighting or something to cause those lines to sway so fiercely. We laughed about it." The traffic light turned green, and Ben proceeded to make a left turn with the nineteen-foot box truck that carried all of their equipment. The street curved gently to the right. In a few moments they would come across the horrible accident scene. Ben and Scott remember seeing something up ahead in the middle of the road.

Both commented: "It looks like a car on its side…oh no, it looks like Blake's 4Runner….damn, it is Blake's 4Runner." Ben stopped the truck about a block away, and he and Scott sprinted to the accident scene.

Blake was driving through a residential neighborhood with Clyde in the front passenger seat and Brandon in the back seat directly behind Clyde. They were only driving two miles to their destination that evening and were quickly approaching the intersection at Hudson Lane. Unfortunately, they were not wearing their seatbelts on that short drive to Sixth Street Bar. A red car with an eighteen-year-old driver and his male passenger were also driving in that neighborhood that late Saturday afternoon. That driver's cell phone rang, and he leaned down to pick it up. At that point he failed to notice the stop sign, hence, he failed to stop; that is, until he broadsided Blake's Toyota 4Runner on the driver's side. Blake recalls seeing a car quickly approaching them out of his peripheral vision, more like a red blur, but it was too late. On impact, Clyde was immediately ejected from his front passenger seat, the 4Runner then turned around and slammed against the telephone pole; the vehicle then fell over and landed on its side. Unfortunately, it also landed on Clyde. What saved Clyde was a portion of the 4Runner landed on the curb. The support that cement curb provided was just what was needed to prevent Clyde from being crushed to death.

Blake remembers a red flash, then spinning and jerking around. When he came to he was standing up in the 4Runner. His feet were planted where the passenger side window was located and he was looking right through the sunroof. After realizing that he had lived through this violent collision he looked down to the sound of horrifying screams. Blake recalls, "My buddy Clyde was lying perpendicular to me underneath the car. I remember the two young guys from the car that hit us trying to lift the vehicle off of him. After several failed attempts, I suggested one pull Clyde while the other guy and I would try to lift which is just across the river from Shreveport. As Angela was calling family, Anne was calling the local Bossier City police to ask them to go to the local theatre at the Louisiana Boardwalk to try to reach Jay due to this emergency. It was a long sixty minutes from the time Anne broke the news to Angela that Jay finally made it back home. More family members had made it back to Angela and Jay's home in that first hour. Before any family member had returned to be with Angela she did talk with Scott for the first time that evening. He tried to reassure her when she asked how Brandon was doing. He said, "Brandon has been revived," hoping this would give his mother some relief from her worries, but it only reinforced what Anne had said, "Brandon is the most seriously injured."

The band had driven up to Monroe on a beautiful, sunny Saturday. As the band often did when they performed in the Monroe area, they stopped at Blake's father's home. He had plenty of room for the guys to rest and sleep for the evening. Besides providing the band members with a friendly "hotel" to stay for the night after their performance at the Sixth Street Bar in Monroe, he also cooked up quite a meal for them that afternoon. Can you spell "steak"? Hmmm, good. Mac Oliver treated these young men to a hearty and scrumptious meal that afternoon.

The meal was eaten, and it was time to travel to the place of their gig that evening, set up the equipment, and perform "microphone checks." It was Ben's turn to drive their nineteen-foot box truck, and he walked towards that truck. Blake, Clyde, Brandon, and Scott walked towards Blake's Toyota 4Runner. As the group walked towards their respective vehicles, Ben shot back at the other four, "Isn't anyone going to ride with me?"

After a couple of seconds of silence, Scott replied, "Yeah, I'll go with you."

Ben later recalled that Brandon had driven up in the nineteen-foot box truck from Baton Rouge earlier that day and exclaimed, "Four hours in that truck with no air conditioning was enough!"

It was only two miles from Blake's home to the Sixth Street Bar. Blake's silver-colored 4Runner took off first with the white, nineteen-foot box truck trailing behind. Shortly after leaving Blake's driveway Ben caught the traffic light. The 4Runner went on ahead. The street curved ahead, so the 4Runner was quickly out of sight. A few moments later, the traffic light began to sway as well as the adjacent telephone and cable wires and utility lines. Ben and Scott both noticed that and thought that was highly unusual. Unknown to them

In the five minutes it took Anne and me to return home, Anne and Scott must have called each other four times. In the last conversation, Scott kept insisting that we had to contact Brandon's parents and tell them what has happened; the quicker the better.

We could not find Brandon's parents' phone number in the telephone book. Anne did talk with Clyde's mother, and she was in the condition that any mother would be in this instance—she was in a state of shock, not able to function. Anne just kept reminding her to get some things packed for a stay at the hospital and made sure that her dear, sweet husband, Bruce, Clyde's stepfather, was going to drive them to the Monroe hospital, which was an hour and forty-five minutes away. Clyde's father and stepmother were out of town; in fact, they were out of state. They were attending an LSU football game in Alabama, many hours away. They would soon receive one of those dreaded phone calls that afternoon also, a phone call that a parent hopes never to receive.

Scott and Anne talked a few more times as we frantically looked for Brandon's parents' phone number. Luckily we did not find it and had to go, in person, to break the awful news to Brandon's parents. Scott gave us directions to Brandon's house the best that he could remember. We found it without any trouble. We walked up to the door and rang the doorbell. The door opened, and there stood Angela, Brandon's mother. When she saw us, a big smile appeared on her face, and she greeted us with a "Well, hi!"

The thoughts are numerous that run through your mind at a time like this. Your mind is racing. How do you break the bad news? You know that whatever you say, her smile will come off her face immediately, and her life will change forever. Anne stood closer to Angela and said, "The band's been in an accident and Brandon is the most seriously injured." You could literally see the blood drain from Angela's face. Your mental faculties literally shut down when met with such awful news. Anne encouraged her to gather up some clothes and other essentials, like a toothbrush, to make the trip to the hospital. Angela went from room to room, trying to get things together, but was not making any progress, but who would in a time like this?

Cell phones are commonplace today. Everyone has one, or so it seems, but sometimes, that instant connection is still not there. Angela called her husband, Jay, and her daughters, but did not get anyone initially, although she did leave quite a few messages. Jay and his sister were scheduled to attend a movie that evening at a new mall complex called the Louisiana Boardwalk in Bossier City,

Chapter Ten
That Fateful Day

September 30, 2006

Saturday, September 30, 2006, was like most fall Saturdays for me. It started with a good ten-mile run with my Saturday Morning Run Group. Running with this group in the early morning air, through the streets of Shreveport, was standard fare for me. After returning home to clean up and fuel up, it was time to hit the recycle center then travel to the office to work for a couple of hours. Finally it was time to return home and get in an afternoon nap. The one difference in the normal routine that day was our trip to the voting booth; yes, it was Election Day in Louisiana. It would turn out to be a historic day in the mayor's race in Shreveport, Louisiana.

It was a gorgeous-weather day in North Louisiana. The sun was out, and the sky was blue. Anne and I had just voted, and now it was time to get a bite to eat. It was 6:00 P.M. We were driving away from University Elementary School where we had just voted, traveling north on Youree Drive when Anne's cell phone rang. I was driving when that call came in, and that was a very good thing. When another person near you receives a phone call that has bad news you know it almost immediately. This was one of those times.

Anne was trying desperately to understand the person on the other end. The atmosphere in our vehicle immediately turned somber. I heard Anne reply: "Are you okay? Scott, what did you say? Are you okay? What happened?" Scott was crying hysterically on the other end of the phone, "Brandon is not breathing! Brandon is not breathing! We were in an accident—not Ben and me, but Brandon, Blake and Clyde. You've got to call Brandon's parents!" Anne tried her best to calm Scott and to get as much information as she could.

is a very special person. She attended to Angela during those six long weeks at the Monroe hospital. As Angela puts it, "She literally saved me time and time again during our stay in Monroe. She holds a very special place in my heart."

Thank you for your continued prayers and support. Brandon is working very hard to work his way back. You would be proud.

would be for anyone else to have that surgery. That important piece of information will be provided to Dr. Cherie-Ann Nathan, Brandon's ENT in Shreveport. Brandon desperately wants that trachea tube OUT!

Brandon continues to improve his walking ability. He now goes to water therapy once a week. He is lowered into a swimming pool that has a treadmill in it. The water helps Brandon keep his balance. When Anne was visiting with the family Monday afternoon Brandon was asked what young lady he had met during those therapy session. He replied, "Pie." Brandon's family asked him why he called her "Pie." He responded, "Because she is a cutie pie!" Yes, the old Brandon is definitely coming back!

During the visit to the Monroe Hospital last week, the nurses were just amazed and excited to see how well Brandon was doing. In fact, in the SICU unit they had the picture of Brandon standing up next to Scott in his room in the Jackson, Mississippi, rehab facility. Many of you saw this photograph in one of my past e-mails. That one is now hanging up on the wall in the St. Francis Hospital's SICU unit!

Brandon's family also found out that at St. Francis Hospital in Monroe, Louisiana, they have basically designated the SICU room where he was staying as "Brandon's Room." Those excellent staff members keep Brandon alive and helped him deal with one medical challenge after another. They prepared him well for the challenging rehabilitation that he would encounter next. What an excellent gift they gave Brandon.

Random memories keep popping in. While in Monroe, Blake's father, Mac Oliver, came to visit with them. After talking with Mac, Brandon starting describing Mac's home and how the band members would stay at his house when they played in the Monroe area. That was a great conversation.

They also were able to visit with Blake's grandmother, Anna Ruth. She looked like they were enjoying playing music again; they were enjoying this time they had on stage; they were relishing their interaction in front of a crowd, and it showed. A fresh start, a new beginning, a new chapter for the band was unfolding and we were a witness to it. You could feel their connection.

    Brandon's parents, Jay and Angela, were also in Ruston that evening for the band's performance. Little did we know of the special performance that Brandon was going to perform that evening. The band's first set was complete. Ben announced from his microphone that they were going to take a short break. But instead of stopping, Clyde kept strumming his guitar, Blake kept hitting his bongos, and Scott kept beating his drums. Ben then said, "And then again, I guess not." As those words left his microphone, he switched positions on stage with Brandon. Ben began strumming his guitar and Brandon began singing a rap song by Afroman called "Palm Dale" that he had been practicing since his high school days. It was great fun. The audience loved it, Brandon's parents loved it—they had heard him perform that song just a month earlier at Flannigan's in Shreveport, but the second time was even better—it was a special moment that will forever be frozen in time in our memory. What a performance; the last performance of Brandon on stage that his parents witnessed, that we witnessed, that his band members and friends witnessed. Sixteen days later the accident occurred. That wiped out Brandon's memory of that special time. He cannot remember that performance, but he can live it vicariously through our memories that we continue to share with him.

    TERMS Group E-mail—April 11, 2007: Brandon Update:

Dear Family and Friends,

Sure hope you enjoyed a nice Easter Holiday Weekend!

Time for a second opinion. The Youngs took a trip to Monroe last week to visit with many fine people, including Dr. Bernie McHugh, Jr., neurosurgeon at the Monroe St. Francis Hospital. He had taken great care of Brandon while he was there for six weeks last year. In his opinion, after reviewing the MRIs and flexion/extension X-rays, Brandon's neck is stable; it does not move with flexion/extension—that this surgery would require—and it would be no more of a risk than it

This show was broken up into two performances. One for people of all ages from 7 P.M. to 9 P.M., then adults over twenty-one years of age, from 10 P.M. My friend, Rob, did not notice anything unusual about their performance, but he left early that evening. There was discord between the band members on stage which climaxed with the playing of The Rolling Stones' song *Sympathy for the Devil*. That song had been performed many times as the band's finale. During the song that evening, Ben did not sing any words to the song. He moved about the stage, but sang not one note. Scott was furious. Once the song was finished, he packed up what needed to be packed up and quickly left. He did not say anything to Ben. He later told me, "If I would have confronted Ben that night I probably would have punched him out."

The next week, Ben and Scott had a long talk. It was a good talk. Scott told Ben that if he pulled that stunt again, he would quit the band immediately. They had a good reconciliation meeting that evening. Band members who were that close were just like family. You have your arguments and disagreements, but if you have respect for one another and have a healthy communication process you can work through the difficult times.

It seemed that after that evening of the stressful performance at The Caterie on September 8, 2006, the band seemed to get their rhythm back with each other. Their camaraderie was back. They had gone through some rough times the past few months, but things were looking up. They were back in sync with each other. That was clearly evident during their performance at Rabb's Steakhouse in Ruston, Louisiana, on September 14, 2006.

Anne and I ventured to Ruston that weeknight to listen to the band perform. I am so glad we made that decision. Before the band played, Anne and I were sitting at an outside table in front of the stage area. Ben came to visit with us. His presence at our table spoke volumes. It said, "I'm sorry about what I did at The Caterie. That won't happen again." We made small talk, and it seemed that he was getting ready to verbally apologize to us for The Caterie episode, but another band member came to sit down at that very moment. More small talk ensued until it was time for their performance. One comment Ben had that evening with us was: "I'm drinking water tonight." We both knew what he was referring to. Ben did not need to apologize to us that evening. He is like a son to us; in our eyes he can do no wrong. We were just excited to see him and the band members turn the corner on a rough few weeks and get back on track again.

What a joy it was watching the band perform that evening in Ruston. They audience reception, of lukewarm audience reception, cheap hotels, a memorable stay at the Philadelphia Four Seasons Hotel, and many more memories filled that action-packed time frame, including their nineteen-foot box truck breaking down a mere one hundred and fifty miles from home. Their truck had to be towed back to their home base of Baton Rouge, Louisiana. The nineteen-foot box truck seemed to be in sync with the band members. They were all very tired. That trip taxed the truck's capability, taxed the band's scheduling skills, taxed the band's performing abilities, and taxed the band members' physical endurance.

The band wanted to "chill out" for a while, but that was just not in their schedule. They had gigs set up from Tennessee to Alabama to Texas to California to Louisiana. People handle stress in different ways. One band member consumed a lot of adult beverages back in his hometown and, unfortunately, missed a couple of shows. The record label was, understandably, upset, and wanted to fire that band member immediately, but the rest of the band stuck together and pleaded his case. They were going to stick together. The record label reluctantly agreed to keep him in the group.

Scott confided to his mother that his plans were to return to Shreveport in January, get a job, and apply for graduate school to pursue his Masters in Business Administration. He was not contemplating returning to Shreveport to be closer to his Mom and Dad, but because of a special young lady. He had found someone who had stolen his heart, although he would not leave the band before finding a good replacement. I reasoned that there was too much togetherness on this trip, and that wore on Scott. He was always one that needed his own space, and that just was not possible during this five-and-a-half-week tour. I was hoping that he would change his mind as the fall semester wore on and, especially, once they returned to California to perform again on the Megan Mullally Television Show.

A couple of other band members turned to adult beverages also in order to deal with the turbulence of their fast-paced and long summer tour. On September 8, 2006, it was Ben's turn. As with most shows, each band member would get on their MySpace.com website and promote their upcoming gigs in order to insure good fan support. Scott spent a lot of time promoting this particular gig at The Caterie in Baton Rouge. I also promoted that performance and was able to entice an attorney friend from Baton Rouge, Rob Roux, to that performance.

was a CD of some of The TERMS' songs that only had the bass parts on it. Brandon was ECSTATIC! He exclaimed, "Do you know how much easier it will be for me to learn the songs now?"

Last Monday he began practicing, and before long, he was playing a song as it should be played. Angela just listened with tears streaming down her face. When I picture Brandon in his hospital bed in Monroe with his fist tightly clenched and his arms drawn up to his chest, and now, just six months removed from that devastating accident, he is playing his bass guitar again, it is truly a miracle. With his family's dedicated support, with his indomitable will to get better, and with your tremendous prayer support he is already at this unbelievable stage. This past Tuesday he practiced and learned another TERMS' song! Brandon REALLY LOVES music. One of the shirts he would sometimes wear when the band performed had these words written on it: "No Job, No Money, No Car, But I'm in a Band!"

Speaking of making progress, last week Brandon took 227 steps WITHOUT the aid of a walker! Yes, the therapist is walking beside him, but Brandon is walking on his own. That equals about 450 FEET! Soon he will be challenging me during my long runs on Saturday morning.

THANK YOU SO MUCH for your great prayers and support. It means so much to Brandon and his family. Concerning the other band members, Clyde is back in Shreveport working, Blake is in Austin, Texas (I hope to have an update on him soon), Ben is in New York working a job and working on his solo music career, and Scott just finished his third month with Enterprise Car Rental Agency.

May you and your family have a GREAT WEEK!

Early Fall Semester of 2006— Unwinding from the Summer Tour

The long summer tour up and down the East Coast finally came to an end. Five and a half weeks of performing, of long road trips in between gigs, of great

JACQUES LASSEIGNE

TERMS Group E-mail—April 1, 2007: Brandon Update:

Greetings Dear Family and Friends!

Sure hope you enjoyed this BEAUTIFUL WEATHER we experienced in Shreveport this weekend. I celebrated this gorgeous cool and sunny weather by taking a glorious nap this afternoon. My dog is influencing me way too much in that department.

The Roller Coaster ride continues.

Brandon went for a follow-up visit with Dr. Cherie-Ann Nathan this past week to check on how successful his surgery was. She scoped his trachea. The good news is the granulation is gone, but the stenosis is still there. Stenosis is an abnormal narrowing in a blood vessel or other tubular organ or structure. To correct the stenosis Brandon needs another surgery. That surgery requires the full extension of his neck. His neurosurgeon, Dr. Patwardhan, was contacted for the okay on that procedure and surgery. He would not give clearance for that surgery. He stated it would be too risky. He further explained that Brandon's C6 vertebra did not heal correctly after the accident. Without this surgery Brandon will have to have the trachea tube for the rest of his life. This setback is hitting Brandon and his parents pretty hard.

There are tremendous medical advances today, and Brandon's mother is thinking "surely something can be done." They return to Dr. Nathan in early May and may seek a second opinion. Angela is always fearful of a lung infection or pneumonia with a trachea tube. Before Brandon's appointment with Dr. Nathan he had been coughing a lot and was running a fever.

On the upside is music. Yes, there is live music being heard in the Young household these days. Recently, Brandon requested that his mother drive him around in his vehicle. He had not been in his car since the accident. Well, lo and behold, a true treasure was found in his car. There song's lyrics and music were being hatched. Good vibes were bouncing around the studio amongst band members as their creativity flowed:

Enthusiastic ruby in the rough,
Playing it smart is never enough,
Fast forward at a breakneck speed,
On a road less traveled wherever it leads,
This is just the beginning.
The merging urge energized,
Twist of fate splinter in time.
Imagine now the biggest bang yet,
Full throttle to the cutting edge,
This is just the beginning.
Welcome to the Now, Evo Devo,
More here than meets the eye!
Welcome to the Now, Evo Devo,
Curiosity Running Wild!
Retrorockets, vital signs,
New frontiers boggle the mind,
Dare to be different, stand on the brink,
The final ingredient, the missing link,
Brains conquer beauty, horizons expand
Today's the day do it while you can.
Power to the dreamer, Evolution in the air,
Push it to the limit, Push it full speed ahead,
Blow it sky high, Blast the master plan,
Make the great escape, Electric easy-chair.
Power to the dreamers, Revolution in the air,
Push it to the limit, Push it full speed ahead,
The verge of a breakthrough, Synergistic rush,
The whole world's watching, The world is not enough.

songs until the five members of The TERMS will be back on the stage. So if that's what it has to be, then that's what it has to be."

Many people criticize. It is easy to do. It is much more difficult to create something. Looking back I wished I would have "Googled" criticism. These are some thoughts from people over the years on critics and criticism from the website *The Quotations Page*:

Far better it is to dare mighty things, to win glorious triumphs even though checkered by failure, than to rank with those poor spirits who neither enjoy nor suffer much because they live in the gray twilight that knows neither victory nor defeat. —Theodore Roosevelt

To avoid criticism do nothing, say nothing, be nothing. —Elbert Hubbard

Do what you feel in your heart to be right—for you'll be criticized anyway. You'll be damned if you do, and damned if you don't. —Eleanor Roosevelt

Any fool can criticize, condemn, and complain—and most fools do. —Dale Carnegie

Criticism comes easier than craftsmanship. —Zeuxis

Now in reality, the world has paid too great a compliment to critics, and have imagined them to be men of much greater profundity than they really are. —Henry Fielding

Yes, the band members had been through an intense couple of years, had encountered many different scenarios in the music industry, had forged ahead in the tough music business, but they were still very young. Quotes from famous people who had encountered much criticism in their own lives may have helped with the band's education in the area of criticism. Next time...

Here are the words from the song "Welcome to the Now, Evo Devo." As you read the words, imagine an upbeat, fast-paced, rocking anthem accompanying those words. Feel the creative energy that was released as the *home earlier this month may have noticed a change when advertisements for the University aired on television. Absent were references to the "Welcome to the Now" campaign, recordings from rock band The TERMS, and mentions of "Evo Devo."*

Robin Kistler, director of marketing at the Office of Public Affairs, said, "The Office of Public Affairs determined at the beginning of the campaign that 'Welcome to the Now' would exist approximately one year. The campaign reached the one-year mark in December, so we began a phase-out process at that time.

"Welcome to the Now allowed us to associate LSU with a fresh and modern look to a national audience."

Kistler said the Office of Public Affairs was particularly happy with the involvement of The TERMS, the local rock band that recorded the campaign's theme song.

"They are gifted musicians and song lyricists," she said. "We greatly appreciate the talent and hard work they put behind the song."

Ben Labat, The TERMS' lead singer, said, "We wanted to really bring people into Louisiana, bring people down to Baton Rouge from wherever, and let people know that LSU is alive and kicking. When you create something you have to be able to accept the criticism." Labat said he wishes he did a better job of defending the song and the good cause it stood for when the controversy over the band started.

"When people started to criticize it, I started to dislike it, and that was a weakness in my character," he said. "We wrote this song for a great cause for a great purpose, and it's really pushing something positive, and I should have stuck by it a little more."

According to Kistler, the Office of Public Affairs is open to future collaborations with The TERMS to once again help promote the University. It is still unclear whether there will be a future for The TERMS after an automobile accident left three band members seriously injured last year.

"The future is very uncertain," Labat said.

From an earlier interview with Travis Andrews in *The Daily Reveille*, dated November 30, 2006, *For all the questions and uncertainties, one thing remains clear. The TERMS are a family, and Labat said it will not continue without every member. "I don't want to play any more TERMS*

JACQUES LASSEIGNE

I thought it was a great commercial and so did the Southern Public Relations Federation during their annual conference in July of 2006. From *LSU Today, LSU's Biweekly Newsletter for Faculty and Staff*, article by Kristine Calongne, dated August 11, 2006, *The Southern Public Relations Federation (SPRF) is an organization of public relations, marketing, and communication professionals from Louisiana, Mississippi, Alabama, and Florida. Members come from the private sector, government agencies, and nonprofit organizations.*

The LSU Office of Public Affairs edged out top public relations firms, major universities, and large ad agencies, from around the South to win the coveted "Best of Show" and other awards from the SPRF's annual conference in July.

In addition, LSU Public Affairs received a Certificate of Merit for the "Welcome to the Now" 30-second television public service announcement, which was the TV component to LSU's "Welcome to the Now" image and recruiting campaign. Not bad; not bad at all.

In trying to help Scott and the band keep things in perspective during this firestorm of criticism about them and the "Welcome to the Now" campaign, I sent them a couple of e-mails of support. One stated that no matter what criticism they are receiving in this endeavor, there are very few bands that have a song being featured on a 30-second commercial that is airing on nationwide television. With the LSU football team having a banner year, they were featured on many Saturdays in the fall of 2006 on nationwide television stations. They ended up the season being ranked #3 in the nation. That was a lot of exposure for the fighting LSU Tigers. That was also a lot of exposure for that 30-second "Welcome to the Now" commercial; and a lot of exposure for a Baton Rouge band called The TERMS.

One weekend after the accident, Ben and Blake came by the house to meet with Scott. They were going to visit with Brandon that weekend. Ben stated that he had recently completed an interview with the LSU news journal, *The Daily Reveille*. He told them he was proud of the work with that marketing campaign and was proud of the song the band had composed and performed. What a change in attitude. Yes, all these young men had matured a lot since that awful night of September 30, 2006, and that statement from Ben was just one indication of that maturation process.

From *The Daily Reveille*, an article titled "End of the Now," by Michael Mims, dated January 6, 2007: *Tiger fans watching the Sugar Bowl from award-winner, wrote "Welcome to the Now, Evo Devo." The title of the song is just a title—it is the lyrics that are important. The music adds energy to the spots and incorporates LSU tradition by featuring Tiger Band and the LSU choir.*

Visual and text in the TV spots, video, print ads, and on the Web and billboards, speak to the excitement and enthusiasm associated with LSU right NOW-academic excellence; outstanding faculty, staff and students; research opportunities; international partnerships; and experiences. All are highlighted. The campaign also showed that LSU was undamaged by last year's storms and increased the University's visibility prior to the launch of Forever LSU.

As we segue into the campaign's next phase, "LSU NOW," I invite students, faculty, and staff, to join Public Affairs in helping to promote LSU. With your positive involvement, we can come together to make great things happen and let the world know about LSU-NOW"...Holy Houk Cullen, APR, Interim Assistant Vice Chancellor, Public Affairs.

College football games are normally very exciting affairs. There is an energy and enthusiasm that is contagious. Many adults tell me that is one of the main reasons they thoroughly enjoy watching college football games.

Many of us have also seen the promotional 30-second television commercial for the two universities who are battling on the college football field. It is typically a quiet and reserved commercial with people smiling as they sit in a classroom or walk on a beautifully landscaped campus. One word comes to mind concerning those promotional television spots—BORING! That is NOT what the LSU Public Affairs Office produced in their "Welcome to the Now" television spot. It displayed high-energy, fast-paced movement, and notable segments of the LSU university community.

My first encounter with that commercial was on a beautiful and sunny Saturday afternoon. I was enjoying a wonderful nap that afternoon when I was awakened by the thunderous singing of "Welcome to the Now, Evo Devo." My dear wife saw the commercial and immediately upped the volume on our television set to around 150 decibels. I jolted out from the sofa in our bedroom to the living room and caught the rest of the commercial. What a snazzy advertisement. It blew away the other university's promotional commercial. Most people watched those fall football games with intensity; my wife and I watched those commercials with intensity!

According to the Web site built around this media campaign, www.lsu.edu/now, "EVO DEVO," or Evolutionary Development, is a field of science combining the approaches of evolutionary biology and developmental biology.

Well, I still don't know what that means. So I read on.

"Evo Devo scientists research stages of an organism's development from egg to mature adult to gain insight into the flexibility of the developmental process and how it is altered over time. Many say the fusion of the two approaches will result in groundbreaking discoveries."

The furor over this media campaign, at times, was overwhelming for the band. They began to hate the song they wrote, along with their involvement in this campaign. I sent Scott an e-mail concerning a quote from Theodore Roosevelt concerning the topic of criticism. Theodore Roosevelt once said, "It behooves every man to remember that the work of the critic is of altogether secondary importance, and that in the end, progress is accomplished by the man who does things." That helped him a bit in this time of turmoil.

On September 28, 2006, this letter to the editor was printed in *The Daily Reveille*: *This letter is in response to a recent column regarding LSU's national image and recruiting campaign.*

As a proud alumna who is passionate about all things LSU, and as the marketing director who worked closely with the creative team on this project, I am thrilled that students are talking about the campaign and want to play a part in enhancing LSU's image.

The creative team's task was to design a bold, progressive campaign, different from what other universities are doing. We wanted something that would make our primary target audience—prospective students—take notice of LSU.

We set out to create a campaign that celebrates the unique culture of LSU, which cannot be measured by US News & World Report rankings, and emphasizes those qualities that can be measured, In short, we wanted a campaign that says look at LSU—NOW. We are a changed university, aggressively seeking to become a nationally recognized flagship institution.

The TV spot is but one of the image campaign's components. Music is an effective way to grab attention in TV spots, and we approached The TERMS, a local band composed of LSU students, to write an original song to serve as the music bed. The TERMS, whose producer is a Grammy upcoming fundraising tour, or as it seems to our cynical eyes, beg-a-thon. We recognize as we do with almost everything we criticize, the noble intent behind the search for money. Everyone who attends this University wants the best for this place of learning. We want state-of-the-art equipment, renowned professors and the best rankings money can buy. Unfortunately, none of that will be brought even remotely closer to fruition by the traveling circus of 30 that will begin in New York City on June 19th. [The TERMS will perform at that function]

The goal of this tour is to drum up funding from potential donors by showing presentations on the proposed future of the University as well as recruiting future students. Laudable goals, though one hopes that they will forbear from showing The TERMS' "Welcome to the Now" video, or for that matter almost any material from the current marketing campaign.

We do not honestly believe that it is worth it to send an entourage to three different cities to ask for money from those who already have connections to this University. Instead what we think that the University needs is simple, honest to God hard work. Not gimmicks such as the rancid "Evo Devo" nonsense.

As Sonny and Cher would say, "And the beat goes on." And as some LSU students would say, "And the criticism goes on." From another article in *The Daily Reveille* titled, "LSU's Media Campaign Lacks Focus," dated September 18, 2006: *As a self-professed media junkie, I always wondered why LSU didn't have a quality television spot to run during nationally broadcasted sporting events. So in many ways, I'm pleased that we've launched a new television spot in congruence with the "Welcome to the Now" media campaign. We've added our name to the list of major universities using the media as a recruiting tool.*

...my problem with our University's media campaign is I don't know how it is supposed to persuade high school students to come to LSU. The media campaign, with the television spot as its centerpiece, features a local band, The TERMS, singing the lyrics "Welcome to the Now, Evo Devo," implying that the University is both in "the Now" and "Evo Devo."

I'm 22 years old and will become an alumnus of this university in December if I pass all my classes this semester. So if I don't know what "Evo Devo" means or how LSU is in "the Now," how can we expect prospective students to understand these phrases?

the Now" is a slogan accompanying a larger push to increase national recognition.

Ruffner said the image campaign has three goals: increasing recognition of teaching, research and service missions; increasing recruiting of "high caliber" students and faculty; and encouraging donors to give money to the upcoming capital campaign. He explained the campaign was more complicated and involved than just "Welcome to the Now" and "Evo Devo" T-shirts. "'Welcome to the Now' is simply a rallying point—a slogan—to get people behind the campaign," Ruffner said.

Ruffner said the advertisements say "Welcome to the Now" in the bottom corner, but the dominant message is about programs at the University or opportunities for potential students. "It's putting hard facts in front of people across the country."

Ruffner also defended local rock group The TERMS and the "Evo Devo" song written about the University, which many students have mocked and criticized. Ruffner called The TERMS a campus "success story" and said students should be proud of their peers who are thriving in the music industry instead of insulting the group.

Ruffner said being the only university with a band and song is a "pretty cool" distinction.

But the "essence" of the increased publicity and presence in the media, Ruffner said, can be found in "LSU in the Eye of the Storm," the book the University printed chronicling its response to hurricanes Katrina and Rita.

Kristine Calongue, director of media relations for the Office of Public Affairs, said there has been an increase in media requests to interview University professors, which she said can be attributed to the University's increase in popularity after the hurricanes.

Ruffner said by increasing exposure and explaining the Flagship Agenda through the image campaign, the effort will "prepare and invigorate" donors to give money. "We can't raise money until we articulate what we stand for. Part of getting the funds is raising your visibility and prestige," said Ruffner.

Criticism continued as we see in *The Daily Reveille* in an article entitled "Our View: University fundraising effort is ill-advised," dated June 15, 2006: *Before we weigh in with our criticism, let us allow a word for the*

Ouch. It is bad enough having the stress of college courses, the stress of a full-time schedule for a touring band, the stress of criticism from fellow LSU students about your upbeat, rocking new song written to promote LSU, but to have the Chancellor downgrade your artistic effort on LSU's behalf, that was quite disheartening.

225 Magazine is a Baton Rouge, Louisiana, entertainment magazine. The last page of their magazine is a tongue-in-cheek "recap" of local news. Their "humor page" is called The Cayenne Report. On one of their Spring 2006 issues, the last page had the group photo of The TERMS from their CD. Clyde Hargrove, their lead guitarist, was missing from that photo. In his place was a reclining tiger. The caption read something like this: *The TERMS complied with the LSU Chancellor's request to replace their guitarist with Mike the Tiger, to give a greater tie-in to the "Welcome to the Now" campaign. The Chancellor then said that Mike should fit in fine. He is really sweet. You should hear him play, "Smoke on the Water."*

It was a surreal time for the band members, not to mention the Public Affairs Office at LSU.

It was also time for the Public Affairs Office to respond to this wave of criticism. On *The Daily Reveille*, March 29, 2006, article by Ginger Gibson, titled "Selling LSU": *The Flagship Agenda faces several obstacles before the University can achieve its goal of becoming a top-tier University. One hurdle is dollar signs. Image is another. But University officials say its image is not the root of the problem; funding is. And the University can't bring in more money without improving its image.*

The University's image and its fundraising are intertwined—the more money the University raises, the better its image and the better the University's image, the more money it can raise.

"Everything we do relative to the capital campaign is to advance the Flagship Agenda," said Michael Ruffner, vice chancellor for the Office of Communications and University Relations. This semester the University embarked on a national image campaign, which focuses on the current "success" of the Flagship Agenda.

In February the University launched the "Welcome to the NOW" campaign as part of this image campaign. And in June the University will embark on an unprecedented push for private funding with the new image campaign paving the way. Ruffner said the "Now" campaign should not be confused with the image campaign because "Welcome to

Change is good. But I cannot be the only person that sees all the faults of this new project. In my mass communication class even my professors had to laugh at some of the outlandish ways LSU is trying to promote its new image.

Whether changing for better or worse, LSU has one thing right—a change is needed. But can we start from the inside and work out instead of from the outside working in? If flashy new web designs and a new image can bring students to LSU, what will we do to retain the students? It sure won't be brightly colored T-shirts and bands. Or, at least, I hope not.

It is understandable that some students will not agree with every campaign or idea that their university comes up with, but in March of 2006, some disparaging comments were reported from none other than LSU's Chancellor.

From *The Daily Reveille*, March 15, 2006, in an article titled "Chat with the Chan over Coffee":

Students met with Chancellor Sean O'Keefe at the first Chat with the Chancellor off campus Tuesday at CC's Coffee and discussed campus concerns over lattes and frappes.

SG (Student Government) sponsored the event where students discussed concerns about student-professor relationships, the "Welcome to the Now campaign," class sizes, and the condition of buildings on campus. About 10 students attended the laid-back conversational meeting.

Amber Fontenot, finance freshman, said she went to Chat with the Chancellor because she wanted to meet with the Chancellor and to know "what is up" with the "Welcome to the Now" campaign and mentioned that she has joked about the "then" versus the "now."

O'Keefe chuckled at the mention of the marketing campaign the University launched last month. O'Keefe said the marketing department "test drove" the idea of the campaign and was excited about the concept before it launched. "But they didn't test drive it far enough," O'Keefe said. O'Keefe explained the campaign created debate on campus about how the University should be promoted.

Fontenot then asked O'Keefe what his favorite joke is. O'Keefe asked Fontenot what hers was while he thought about it. Fontenot started her joke with "this is kind of stupid."

O'Keefe responded, "Kind of like Evo Devo."

"sold out," (3) Some students may have thought "Why were The TERMS chosen? Couldn't another local band have been chosen for this honor?," and (4) Maybe some people were just plain jealous.

As time when on, the band began losing some of their fan base due to this controversy. It was so bad that one day Scott was asked by one of his college professors to stay after class. He asked Scott, "What in the world is going on with all this?" That was a fifteen minute heart-to-heart conversation.

Some of the printed comments from *The Daily Reveille*:

February 10, 2006: One student wrote: *First of all this new branding idea comes to us compliments of Michael Ruffner, the vice chancellor for the Office of Communications, the very same office that brought us "Eye of the Storm: LSU in the Eye of the Storm," a creative do-it-yourself guide for universities caught in the middle of a disaster. It's pretty much crap and utterly useless, but it has a creative name—don't you think?*

Hey, there's a better slogan, "Welcome to the Four Years from Now." And what about this, "Evo Devo," song by The TERMS. For those of you who don't know, Evo Devo is short for Evolutionary Development. How that fits into "Welcome to the Now" is beyond me.

Perhaps, other than, look at us now, we don't pick fleas out of our loved ones' hair anymore. Oh, we're so far past bone tools. Oh my God, that was so last season. How about this one—"LSU: The Missing Link." I think it's killer.

February 22, 2006: Another student commented: *I don't know what sounds worse: the soundtrack to the "Welcome to the Now" campaign or hearing that Vice President Dick Cheney is scheduled to speak at spring commencement. I cannot be the only person that thinks at least one of these new developments is ridiculous.*

The University is trying to attract a new age of students with an advertising mechanism that is supposed to be new, hip, and young. I feel old just talking about it.

The home page was probably everyone's first taste of the "Welcome to the Now" campaign. Following that were "Evo Devo" shirts that I see many of us sporting in purple, blue, green, and whatever other color we could get our hands on when they were being passed out in the Union. I know I have one or two. On the home page under the chancellor's welcome, it reads, "Who are the TERMS?" My question is, "Who really cares?"

JACQUES LASSEIGNE

On January 31, 2006, the campaign was launched. These are some excerpts by Justin Fritscher from *The Daily Reveille:* The University's Office of Public Affairs launched its new image campaign January 30th with a two-day celebration in the Union's Cotillion Ballroom. Public Affairs spearheaded the campaign that includes print and television advertisements and billboards, all meant to convey a new and updated image for the University. The campaign's theme is "Welcome to the Now."

Kristine Calongne, director of media relations for Public Affairs, said the campaign will show all of the new events and activities going on at the University and how LSU is dealing with athletics, academics and research. Although Hurricane Katrina put the University in the national spotlight, Calongne said the campaign will show some of the opportunities the University offers.

Michael Ruffner, vice chancellor for Communications and Public Relations, stressed in a news release the importance of an effective visual image. "A strong visual identity program combined with effective communications outreach garners attention and recognition," Ruffner's release said. "Heightened visibility improves both awareness and knowledge, all resulting in favorable increases across the board for LSU."

The Office of Public Affairs also teamed up with a local Baton Rouge band, The TERMS. "I hope the band makes students feel the energy of what is happening at LSU now," Calogne said. Calogne said Public Affairs approached the band and asked for their help, and the band created a song that became the campaign's central slogan. The TERMS will be shooting their music video for the song between noon and 3 p.m. Thursday in the Union Theater. The band is looking for students to take part in the music video and will allow the first 200 students to participate.

I remember my time in college (back in the Stone Ages). It seems that some of the more radical, anti-establishment voices could be heard in the local university newspaper. Back then we only had a newspaper, since Al Gore had not invented the Internet yet. Voices were soon heard expressing discontent with the new "theme" of this campaign as well as The TERMS' involvement in it and their newly-created song. On one of my visits with Scott, he mentioned to me this increasing roar of discontent. My first thoughts to him were: (1) Maybe some students thought the band had joined with the "establishment" (LSU administration), (2) Maybe some students thought the band must have

Chapter Nine
Mom Said You Would Have Days Like This

Welcome to the Now—Evo Devo

Colleges and universities are a big business today. Public universities receive adequate funding from their respective state legislatures, but to really move forward and to excel they have to raise private funds. Capital-fund campaigns are commonplace in academia today. Louisiana State University in Baton Rouge, Louisiana, is no exception. They launched such a campaign in 2006 to include an image-and-recruiting campaign. The campaign was labeled, "Welcome to the Now." What made this campaign different was the involvement of a local, talented band called The TERMS.

The TERMS were quite honored to have LSU ask them to get involved in this campaign and to write a song that would air on national television. The song was written, titled, and recorded. At that time, the LSU Public Affairs Office made the decision to name their image campaign after the song, "Welcome to the Now." There were "Welcome to the Now" banners all over the LSU campus, on the LSU website, and in printed material. There was an interview with the band about this song and this campaign featured on the LSU website. The final song product was a collaboration between The TERMS, the LSU Band and Choir, and Greg Ladanyi's music-producing expertise. That was an exciting time for The TERMS, at least in the beginning of this process. Soon after this campaign commenced, criticism began. That was followed with more criticism. At one point, the band hated the song they had composed for this campaign due to all the acrimony associated with it. An outstanding song, a good, decent hard-working band, and a new national image campaign were being pummeled by a few people who were able to get space in the local LSU newspaper, *The Daily Reveille*. It took on a life of its own.

Band Reunion: June 3, 2007; It was the first time that all the band members were together since the accident. Left to Right: Ben Labat, Blake Oliver, Clyde Hargrove, Scott Lasseigne, Brandon Young.

Brandon performs a concert for his therapists at Willis Knighton Hospital in Shreveport, Louisiana, on July 31, 2007.

The right side of Blake's Toyota 4Runner where it came into contact with the telephone pole—and where Brandon was sitting at the time of the accident.

LSU Tiger Stadium in Baton Rouge, Louisiana. Left to Right: Scott Lasseigne, Greg Ladanyi, Clyde Hargrove, Blake Oliver, Brandon Young, Ben Labat.

Four Seasons Hotel in Philadelphia, Pennsylvania. Left to Right: Blake Oliver, Brandon Young, Scott Lasseigne.

Brandon at Methodist Rehabilitation Center in Jackson, Mississippi. From Left to Right: Brandon Young, Scott Lasseigne.

The TERMS performing at Flannigan's in Shreveport, Louisiana. From Left to Right: Blake Oliver, Clyde Hargrove, Scott Lasseigne, Ben Labat, Brandon Young.

The TERMS relaxing before their performance at Einstein's in El Dorado, Arkansas. From Left to Right: Ben Labat, Scott Lasseigne, Blake Oliver, Walter Schmidt, Clyde Hargrove, Brandon Young. Their fan being held up is Amanda Clampit.

Cutting Room performance of June 23, 2006. From Left to Right: Clyde Hargrove, Scott Lasseigne, Ben Labat, Brandon Young.

Band was returning to Baton Rouge from a North Louisiana gig—stopped at a restaurant along the way. From Left to Right, Front Row (semi-kneeling): Walter Schmidt, Wylie Chris Whitesides, Clyde Hargrove; Back Row: Ben Labat, Scott Lasseigne, Greg Chiartano, Blake Oliver.

Jacket Cover for The TERMS' first CD, *Small Town Computer Crash*. Left to Right: Blake Oliver, Greg Chiartano, Ben Labat, Scott Lasseigne, Clyde Hargrove.